Thomas Rudolph, Markus Schweizer

Successful Business Model Transformations in Disruptive Times

Thomas Rudolph, Markus Schweizer

Successful Business Model Transformations in Disruptive Times

A conceptual framework for established corporations

DE GRUYTER

ISBN 978-3-11-077208-1
e-ISBN (PDF) 978-3-11-077211-1
e-ISBN (EPUB) 978-3-11-077216-6

Library of Congress Control Number: 2024934760

Bibliographic information published by the Deutsche Nationalbibliothek
The Deutsche Nationalbibliothek lists this publication in the Deutsche Nationalbibliografie;
detailed bibliographic data are available on the internet at http://dnb.dnb.de.

© 2024 Walter de Gruyter GmbH, Berlin/Boston
Cover image: FangXiaNuo/E+/Getty Images.
Typesetting: Integra Software Services Pvt. Ltd.
Printing and binding: CPI books GmbH, Leck

www.degruyter.com

Foreword

The word 'transformation' now occupies a prominent place in the vocabulary of countless businesses. Beyond digitalization, the COVID-19 pandemic and the war in Ukraine have also created significant friction and heralded major shifts in consumer behavior. A surge in consumer frugality in 2023 has thrown down the gauntlet for many companies. They must now take a hard look at their established processes—across procurement, logistics, and sales—and radically overhaul them to stay afloat in these disruptive times. In today's fast-paced world, where digital advances and a shifting competitive landscape are the new normal, constant change is the only constant.

Past publications on disruption have celebrated the courage, foresight, and ingenious tactics of a rising generation of founders. In a dizzying dance of progress, established businesses are losing their footing as a new world order asserts itself, as documented in various academic contributions. Companies with household names are now facing a harsh reality: they're being accused of failing to see the early warning signs of their own demise, and even when they did, that their response was woefully inadequate. The advice in the academic literature rarely ventures beyond this critique.

When faced with disruptive challenges, established companies often find themselves without expert guidance on how to overcome the threat. Our book addresses this gap. Drawing on extensive research, workshops, and executive discussions, we've developed a transformative management approach that empowers established companies to disrupt themselves from within. This approach has to be fundamentally different from the method used by the aggressors. Instilling the 'agile spirit of a start-up' within a large, established organization burdened by inertia is no easy feat. However, established companies are often bogged down by cumbersome processes, making it painfully slow to drive innovation through isolated start-up labs and then scale it up to the core business. Therefore, the crucial focus becomes achieving successful transformation within the existing core business itself. To truly thrive in today's disruptive landscape, established players must embrace the imperative of continuous self-disruption. This book is your guide to making it happen.

The **first chapter** establishes the critical importance of disruptive transformations, unpacks the concept of disruption, and illuminates the challenges it presents for management.

The **second chapter** deepens your understanding of disruptive transformations in businesses and equips you with the initial management tools to navigate them. We identify the key driving forces of disruption, expose the most common management pitfalls, reveal how to recognize the critical moment for proactive action, and unveil the playbook of aggressors as they seek to dethrone established players.

Chapter three unveils our High 5 Management Approach for navigating successful business model transformation. We begin by drawing insights from research on business models, delving into their core function, defining characteristics, and ulti-

https://doi.org/10.1515/9783110772111-202

mately extracting five essential key drivers. Building upon these fundamental pillars, we then unveil a hands-on management approach. For each of the five critical key drivers, we provide you with concrete management tasks to consider and implement for a smooth and successful transformation journey. In conclusion, this section emphasizes the critical need for close alignment and synergy between the identified key drivers and their corresponding tasks. In this third edition, we have enhanced our High 5 Approach by incorporating a rigorous project evaluation for the core transformation initiatives. This comprehensive approach is designed to mitigate the risk of failure associated with business transformation.

The fourth chapter illustrates the application of our High 5 Approach. We use numerous case studies to describe successful and unsuccessful transformation processes in companies. The cases come from a variety of industries and underscore the need for a strategy and resource-driven approach.

The **fifth chapter** focuses on leading transformation processes. Guiding principles for orchestrating successful self-disruption are presented to mitigate the risk of failure. The discussion addresses common pitfalls and offers initial suggestions for cultivating the mental prerequisites for successful change within the workforce.

This book is written for the management of established companies, the backbone of the business world, representing approximately 95% of all companies. It provides your managers with a roadmap for successful transformation, grounded in theory and brimming with practical insights. More than twenty in-depth case studies from diverse industries illustrate our High 5 Approach, empowering you to navigate the transformation of your business model.

Without the dedicated support of our team of assistants, the case studies would not have reached their current level of excellence. Our sincere thanks go to Christopher Schraml for his invaluable contributions to the publication of this new edition.

St. Gallen and Hannover in March 2024
Thomas Rudolph
Markus Schweizer

Contents

1 The Challenges of Leadership in Times of Disruption

1.1 An Omnipresent Phenomenon With Existential Consequences

Disruptive change is not a new phenomenon; it has driven economic development for centuries. The curiosity of human beings has repeatedly spawned revolutionary technologies and services that have fundamentally changed the way we live, produce and consume. As Klaus Schwab, founder of the World Economic Forum (WEF), reminds us, we have already seen four different industrial revolutions [1].

The first revolution, from 1760 to 1840, was defined by mechanical production—ushered in by the invention of the steam engine and the construction of railroads. The second revolution, driven by the harnessing of electricity and the breakthrough invention of the assembly line, took place in the late 19th and early 20th centuries. Finally, the third (digital) revolution began in the 1960s with the development of semiconductors, computers, and the Internet. We are at the dawn of the Fourth Industrial Revolution, driven by the mobile Internet, artificial intelligence, and machine learning. As a result of this revolution, science, journalism, and publishing are facing significant changes. ChatGPT, a conversational AI system based on artificial intelligence and machine learning, is already capable of generating text that is almost indistinguishable from human-written text. ChatGPT is currently being used by students to write term papers and has the potential to significantly reduce the need for journalists, authors and other experts. For example, Microsoft has announced that it will offer a paid version of ChatGPT through Teams, which will generate meeting summaries and recommend tasks to participants. The disruptive potential of ChatGPT is huge.

Each of these revolutions triggered fundamental social and economic transformations. This resulting change fundamentally alters an existing order and replaces the established way of functioning with a radically new form. Steering through these disruptive transformation phases demands a sharpened and judicious understanding of management. With this book, we aim to achieve two goals: first, to illuminate the characteristics of disruptive processes, and second, to promote an understanding of how to successfully navigate such disruption through engaging case studies and a clear methodology.

This book focuses on helping established companies meet the challenges of disruption. While most companies recognize the presence of disruptive forces, many struggle to manage the necessary transformation process. Even Clayton Christensen [2], the father of disruption theory, admits that very few incumbents successfully meet the challenge of a disruption.

Note: The corresponding references can be found at the end of the chapter.

https://doi.org/10.1515/9783110772111-001

An example from the banking sector illustrates how new technological capabilities are developing disruptive forces that will completely change the way businesses operate. These forces are being driven by computerized investment programs, also known as robo-advisors. New entrants are using these programs to challenge the dominance of large, established banks. Will robo-advisors eventually replace traditional asset managers? Will incumbents adapt the technology and use it to create new business models? Or will the two coexist as competitors? The answer from many incumbents is captured in the following statement: "Wealthy or sophisticated investors will always demand personalized advice." This defensiveness, or insistence on the status quo of a previously successful business model, is a common pattern. Christensen identifies a tendency for incumbents to cede markets freely to their aggressors [3]. They may choose to focus on more profitable market segments, believing that the aggressors do not pose a serious threat because of their initially small size or limited customer base. This was seen with the rise of Amazon in the bookselling industry and is also happening in the music and pharmaceutical industries. In the health care sector, protectionist policies are (still) throwing a lifeline to incumbent providers worried about job losses. This may succeed in delaying disruption but not indefinitely.

New market entrants do not appear out of thin air, and markets do not change overnight. But established players regularly underestimate new entrants and give them free rein to build and optimize their business models. For example, Betterment, the largest independent robo-advisor founded fifteen years ago, now manages over $30 billion US [4]. Within just one and a half years, the start-up's assets under management have quintupled, and the overall market is also experiencing similar spurts in growth: while robo-advisors were managing $300 billion US at the end of 2017, this figure had already risen to $820 billion US by 2019, and is expected to reach $1.66 trillion US by 2022 [5]. This initially restrained and then explosive growth is a typical phenomenon. In the worst-case scenario, existing markets or products and services are partially or completely cut out.

In times of disruption, established companies often lack the management methods necessary to navigate these relentless disruptions and realign their businesses in a timely manner. When it comes to managing disruptive change, tried and true management methods from the past are of limited help.

1.2 Disruption: A Process that Engenders a New World Order

Disruption has degenerated into a buzzword. Every little change these days is branded as 'disruptive,' whether it's the introduction of a click-and-collect point in a bricks-and-mortar store or the installation of a camera in the fitting room to instantly share your new denim jacket with your Instagram followers. Silicon Valley has become a pilgrimage destination for many executives who believe they have captured the essence of disruption after a whirlwind tour of the Californian valley.

For us, disruption is not a singular event, but rather an ongoing process. It starts with a disruptive idea that, over time, has the potential to completely or significantly transform an existing market (cf. Figure 1.1). This transformation occurs by displacing established business models with new and innovative technologies, products, or services. Or to put it more simply in the words of Jeff Bezos, founder of Amazon: "Anything that customers prefer to what they were used to is disruptive."

The Austrian economist Joseph Schumpeter (1883–1950) coined the term 'creative destruction' in the last century to describe this phenomenon. By 'creative destruction' he meant the dismantling of old structures through the novel recombination of factors of production, which then successfully establish themselves as new products or services.

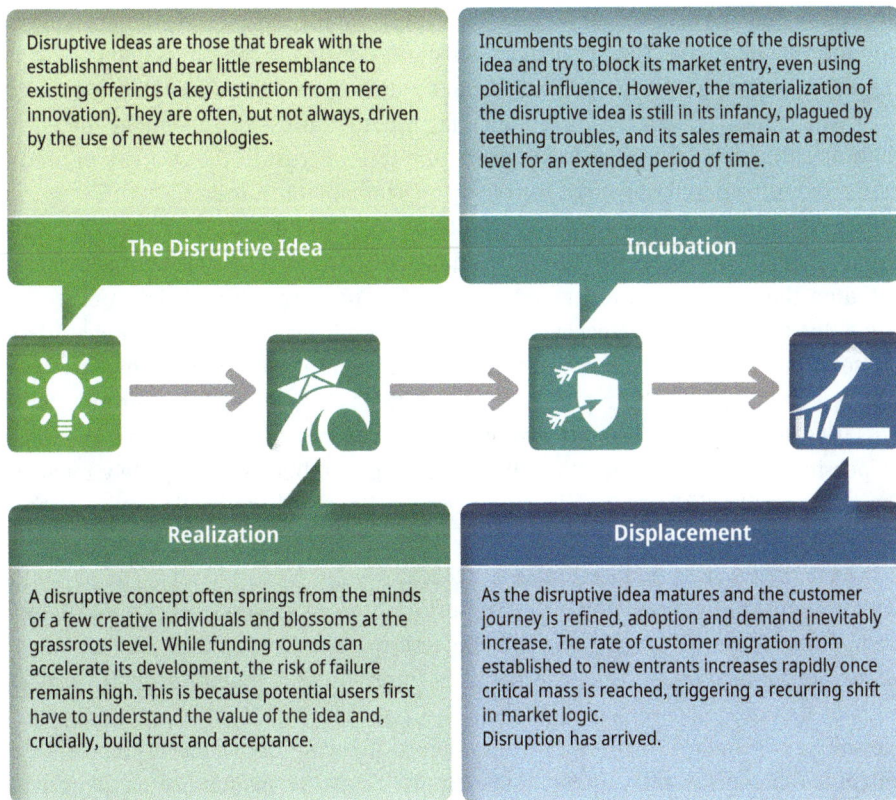

Disruptive ideas are those that break with the establishment and bear little resemblance to existing offerings (a key distinction from mere innovation). They are often, but not always, driven by the use of new technologies.

The Disruptive Idea

Incumbents begin to take notice of the disruptive idea and try to block its market entry, even using political influence. However, the materialization of the disruptive idea is still in its infancy, plagued by teething troubles, and its sales remain at a modest level for an extended period of time.

Incubation

Realization

A disruptive concept often springs from the minds of a few creative individuals and blossoms at the grassroots level. While funding rounds can accelerate its development, the risk of failure remains high. This is because potential users first have to understand the value of the idea and, crucially, build trust and acceptance.

Displacement

As the disruptive idea matures and the customer journey is refined, adoption and demand inevitably increase. The rate of customer migration from established to new entrants increases rapidly once critical mass is reached, triggering a recurring shift in market logic.
Disruption has arrived.

Figure 1.1: Disruption as a process.

Disruptive ideas often build on effects already known from the Industrial Revolution. They are therefore not necessarily linked to digital capabilities. Digitalization is *simply* a catalyst or driving force of disruption, just as electricity was at the end of the 19th century. That is why we do not talk about digital disruption. Disruption comes from an innovative idea that challenges the status quo. Technology can significantly accelerate disruption, provided it is coupled with clear customer value. For example, asking how new digital capabilities can be used to create a better refrigerator without having a clear understanding of changing customer needs is unlikely to lead to disruption. Consumers increasingly expect their refrigerators to do more, such as intelligently reordering food according to their calendar. If these needs prevail, refrigerators will have to be completely redesigned. Apple achieved such a customer-centric approach many years ago with the iPhone. With the iPhone, Apple did not revolutionize the phone, but the way we organize our daily lives. The technology was there, but the impetus came from tailoring the new technology to the needs of the customer.

Many disruptive ideas **die on the vine** because corporate incentive systems often act as a brake on change. Managers are held accountable for missteps, and a failed experiment can have career-ending consequences. On the other hand, there is no penalty for playing it safe. The predictable outcome? Clinging to the status quo or tinkering about with what already exists. But that's only half the story. Disruptive ideas also stall when they lack trust or acceptance from potential users. Remember the early days of online shopping? For many years, the lack of trust in the security of credit cards for online purchases was a seemingly insurmountable hurdle.

In November 2022, OpenAI released ChatGPT to the public. Fortune Magazine called ChatGPT a 'meteor' that could fundamentally change the business world and threaten the existence of technology giants [6]. This form of artificial intelligence could, for example, make Google searches obsolete for many queries. However, Google sees little threat to itself from ChatGPT. That's typical. Incumbents often see new competitors as potential threats, but underestimate their impact on their own business. Google is trying to keep its highly profitable search engine revenue for as long as possible. Google describes ChatGPT's path to profitability as completely unclear. Even though ChatGPT's success is still uncertain, Google's behavior is similar to that of apologists from past eras.

Incumbents often underestimate the threat of aggressors and let them get away with it, significantly increasing the disruptors' chances of success. Incumbents' skepticism of new ideas gives aggressors the time and space to develop their business models without interference. They can focus on improving the quality of their services without fighting price wars, making their business models profitable, and finding stable sources of funding for growth. After a while, the wind can *suddenly* change. New entrants can quickly gain market share. By the time this 'moment of truth' arrives and incumbents realize what is happening, it is often too late to respond effectively. They may try to copy the aggressors' services, but they often do so poorly or they may try to buy them out, sometimes at exorbitant prices.

While Apple, for example, took a quantum leap with the iPhone and ushered in the **displacement** of Internet-enabled mobile phones in the market, Nokia, the long-time leader in mobile phones, resisted the smartphone for many years. Stubbornly sticking to its turf, Nokia continued to produce and optimize keypad phones, failing to anticipate the paradigm shift. Even years after the iPhone's launch, Nokia's management remained convinced that its supposedly higher-quality devices would ultimately win over users [7]. A fatal miscalculation.

Disruption describes a process that begins with an innovative idea and ultimately leads to a fundamental shift in market logic, causing incumbents to lose significant dominance or even exit the market altogether.

In reality, drawing a sharp distinction between disruption and innovation can be challenging, as a disruption can only be definitively identified at the final stage of the process. Before that, it's mostly speculation as to whether the disruptive idea will truly revolutionize the market. Figure 1.2 provides indicators that help distinguish between the two.

Unlike innovation, disruption fundamentally changes the landscape. It displaces established business models and renders obsolete the skills and competencies built up within organizations. While innovation typically builds on and evolves existing structures (cf. Figure 1.2), disruption creates entirely new markets and requires customers to adapt to unfamiliar services and products. 'Early adopters' embrace these new offerings and pave the way for mainstream adoption. However, bridging the gap often requires considerable perseverance. This is where venture capital often plays a critical role, providing essential resources to overcome the initial uncertainties. In contrast, established companies mostly tend to use familiar analogies when innovating. This allows customers to seamlessly transition to new models. For example, moving from the iPhone 7 to the iPhone 10 was intuitive, while moving from a Nokia E90 to the original iPhone 2G was a much steeper learning curve.

Bringing a disruptive idea to life often involves high risk and a significant element of chance. Typically, these ideas germinate in small, agile organizational units. Moreover, yesterday's disruptors can quickly become tomorrow's targets. Take Apple, for example. After the phenomenal success of the iPhone, Apple is unlikely to disrupt this product category again with a fundamentally different technology. The risk of cannibalizing existing sales and devices is simply too high. As a result, Apple has adopted a strategy of successful model iterations that incorporate numerous innovations. The next disruptive force in smartphones is likely to come from another company.

It would be remiss of us not to acknowledge that disruption also poses a significant challenge to society as a whole. Oxford economists Carl Benedikt Frey and Michael Osborne conducted a groundbreaking study that calculated the probability of automation for hundreds of occupations. According to their research, 50% of all jobs in North America and about 42% of all jobs in Germany are at risk of being automated within the next twenty years. This digitalization of our economy, driven by connected machines, artificial intelligence, and collaborative robots, is not only revolutionizing our service offering, but fundamentally reshaping the very fabric of our work world [8].

	Disruption	Innovation
Existing business models	Are displaced	Undergo further development
Existing competencies	Lose importance	Are expanded
Market	Not yet available—first need to be developed	Already available—existing channels can be used
Customers	Younger customers initially with high learning requirements.	Existing customers. Simple process of readjustment.
Market players	Start-ups (often backed by venture capital firms)	Established companies
Organization	Often in small, independent incubators	As process or lab in established companies

Examples

	Disruption	Innovation
Products	iPhone 1	iPhone 7, Tesla
Channels	Music streaming	Dash Button from Amazon
Products + Channels	Robo advisors	Online language courses

Figure 1.2: Distinction between disruption and innovation.

1.3 Profound Implications for Management Practices

The interconnectedness of our computers, the rise of virtual reality, and the expanding capabilities of artificial intelligence, among other factors, will lead to a significant increase in disruptions in the coming years. Compared to past disruptions, the effects of the Fourth Industrial Revolution, particularly digitalization, are characterized by an accelerated pace of change. This rapid evolution has the potential to fuel a surge in disruptive ideas.

Experts predict that the banking industry, for example, will undergo fundamental change in the coming years. The established earnings model of traditional banks is being challenged on multiple fronts: in wealth management, sophisticated robo-advisor algorithms are gaining ground; in financing, emerging crowdsourcing platforms are gaining traction; and in payments, a looming threat from China is on the horizon. Alipay, a subsidiary of Alibaba, has already captured a commanding 54.5% market share of mobile electronic payment services in China [9]. In the first half of 2017 alone, China saw a staggering eight trillion mobile payment transactions. By comparison, PayPal only managed half a trillion transactions for the entire year. Given these developments, it's no surprise that Ant Group, the parent company of Alipay, is projected to have a market valuation of between $70 billion and $150 billion US by 2022 [10]. Figure 1.3 describes disruptions in the banking sector.

A disruptive inflection point is also emerging in the field of (continuing) education. Language instruction in its traditional form is about to lose relevance. Experts recognize that real-time translation technology is producing better and better results. In addition, applications in virtual reality and the Metaverse now offer low-cost and high-impact language training options. This suggests that language instruction, interpreting services, and/or translation agencies may be rapidly losing their viability in their current forms.

These two scenarios, one more tangible than the other, pose new challenges for the management of these industries. How can a language school prepare for the coming disruption? Most of today's state-of-the-art management methods are tailored to the management of dynamic markets and assume that structural and procedural changes can be planned to a high degree. Temporary phases of change with clearly defined change objectives are usually followed by a period of acculturation to ensure the stability of the concepts developed and implemented and to avoid overwhelming the organization.

However, these rules for successful management are only partially suitable for coping with disruptive change [11]. In fact, change can no longer be planned in clearly definable cycles; instead, continuous agility is required. This essential agility comes with the risk of change fatigue and a longing for stability. The exclamation, "Not another transformation program, we haven't even had a chance to get used to the new processes we've just implemented," is a common refrain from senior executives. This means that the demands on management increase significantly in times of disruption.

The disruptive process is characterized by discontinuity, uncertainty, lack of transparency, and risk. Therefore, the action of conducting a strategy development exercise once a year and implementing the resulting concepts more or less successfully throughout the year will no longer suffice. The innovation cycle will change from a predictable linear development to an erratic path of change. An agile organization turns into the new challenge and the new competency. In agile organizations, the corporate culture, organizational structures, processes, management systems, and tools must be designed to be flexible and adaptable to change. Uniformity, repetition and transparency of market developments, customer and competitive behavior can no longer be referenced.

After market disruption, incumbents often lament that they missed the early signs of change, clung to past successes, or failed to grasp the significance of new technologies. But such self-flagellation rarely captures the full picture. More often than not, the real problem lies not in misjudging the disruptive process itself, but in the paralyzing uncertainty about how to respond to this new phenomenon. In such moments, it is easier to retreat into the comfort of established strengths than to face the risk of confronting disruption head-on.

	Earlier	Today
Innovation Cycles	Future ↑ — Evolutionary innovations — Past → Innovative activity	Future ↑ — Transformative/ Disruptive innovations — Past → Innovative activity
Competition	e.g. Volksbanken Raiffeisenbanken, UniCredit Bank, savings banks (Sparkasse), Deutsche Bank, Postbank, Commerzbank, DZ BANK	e.g. Revolut, N26, Stripe, Betterment, Sumup, Binance, Coinbase, Blockchain.com
Description	Need for cost savings and low competitive pressure to innovate Predominantly evolutionary innovations designed to evolve existing products (e.g., automotive industry: new model generation)	Significant increase in competition and, in particular, pressure to innovate due to the activities of start-ups Innovation cycles become shorter Transformative and disruptive innovation as a major threat to banking business (e.g. pharmaceutical research: only a small proportion of innovations are successful, but they bring about major changes).

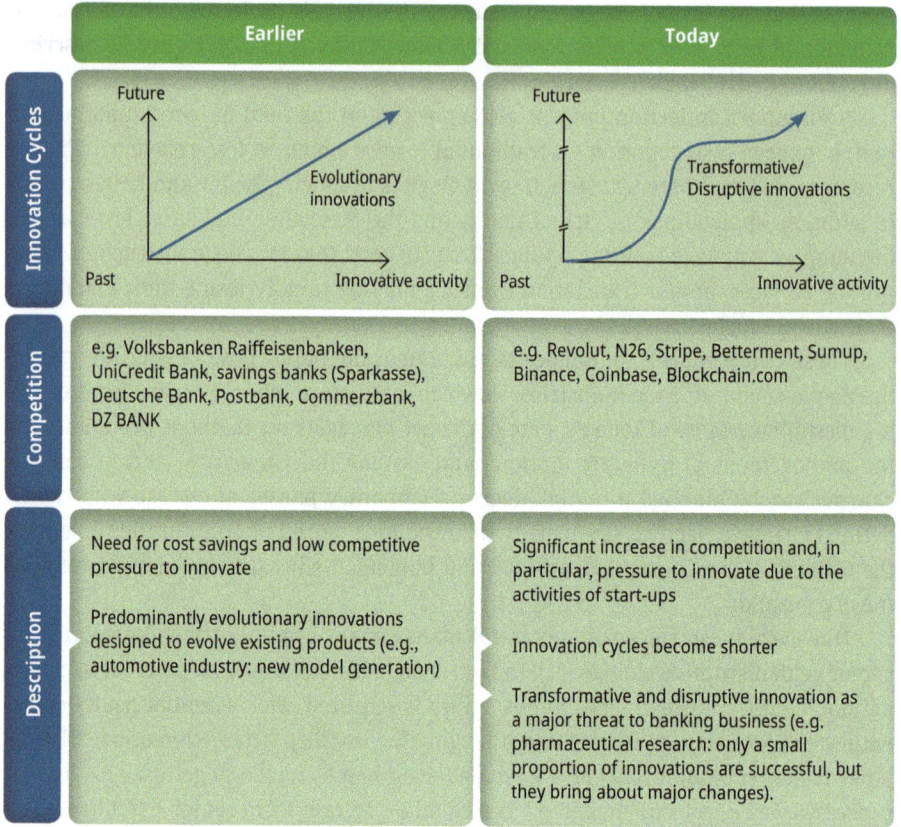

Figure 1.3: Disruption in the banking sector (source: own illustration based on Wings, H./Klein J. [2015], Next Generation Banking, Steinbeis Edition; The Fintech 250 Report by CB Insights [2022]).

Our intention here is not to defend the management of failed companies, but rather to highlight the declining effectiveness of certain widely accepted management tools. These include an emphasis on short-term performance and historically entrenched incentive systems that reward growth in company sales rather than customer value creation. As the recent problems in the banking sector show, this one-sided focus can be detrimental.

In this book, we take a holistic approach that provides *disoriented* leaders with innovative guiding principles, thought models, and operational tools for success in the face of disruption.

References

[1]   See Schwab, K. (2016), The Fourth Industrial Revolution, World Economic Forum, Cologny, Switzerland.

[2]   See Christensen, C. M./Overdorf, M. (2000), Meeting the Challenge of Disruptive Change, in: Harvard Business Review, Vol 78 (2), March-April, 2000, p. 67 ff.

[3]   See ibid. pp. 66–77.

[4]   See Betterment website, last referenced on 2023-01-05, retrieved from: https://www.betterment.com/.

[5]   Statista (2022), robo-advisors, Statista.com, 2023-01-06, retrieved from: https://www.statista.com/outlook/dmo/fintech/digital-investment/robo-advisors/worldwide

[6]   See Fortune, Feb/Mar2023, Vol. 187 Issue 1, p. 6.

[7]   See Isaac, M. (2012), Nokia's CEO explains plan for smartphone dominance, retrieved from: https://www.wired.com/2012/01/nokia-ceo-stephen-elop-qa/.

[8]   See Frey, C. B./Osborne, M.A., The future of employment: how susceptible are jobs to computerisation?, in: Technological Forecasting and Social Change Vol 114 (2017), pp. 254–280.

[9]   EnterpriseAppsToday (2022), Alipay Statistics 2022 – Market Share, Facts and Marketing Trends, 2022-11-10, retrieved from: https://www.enterpriseappstoday.com/stats/alipay-statistics.html#:~:text=It%20has%20around%2054.5%25%20of,a%20total%20of%2027%20currencies.

[10] Bloomberg (2022), Fidelity, BlackRock Cut Fintech Giant Ant's Valuation Lower, 2022-08-16, retrieved from: https://www.bloomberg.com/news/articles/2022-08-16/fidelity-blackrock-cut-fintech-giant-ant-s-valuation-further.

[11] See Christensen, C. (2013), The innovator's dilemma: when new technologies cause great firms to fail, Harvard Business Review Press.

2 Preparing for Potential Disruption

In this chapter, we want to address the key issues faced by apologists in established companies in disruptive markets. Drawing on insights from academic literature and our own extensive research, we help managers deepen their understanding of these challenges and provide practical guidance for successfully navigating behavioral change during periods of disruption (cf. Figure 2.1).

To gain a fundamental understanding of disruption, we must first ask: **What are the key forces driving it?** Rather than exhaustively list every possible factor, Chapter 2.1 focuses on the key driving forces that management should watch closely. By identifying these driving forces, we can conduct targeted market research.

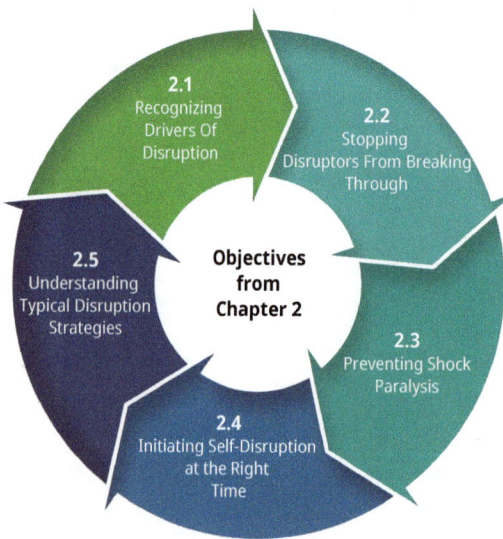

Figure 2.1: Objectives of Chapter 2.

Chapter 2.2 explains **why disruptors succeed in the marketplace**. In Chapter 2.3, we describe common management mistakes that incumbents make during the transformation process. To successfully drive change in your own organization, you must avoid the shock paralysis that often occurs in these situations. In Chapter 2.4, we present an innovative **approach to successfully fending off disruptors.** This approach helps companies systematically prepare in advance for potential aggressors. In Chapter 2.5, we look at the behavior of aggressors. Two **promising strategic paths** can be derived from the findings of disruption research. Understanding these pathways will

---

Note: The corresponding references can be found at the end of the chapter.

https://doi.org/10.1515/9783110772111-002

help you identify dangerous aggressors and target your competitive analysis more effectively.

The final section delves into typical challenges and guiding principles for **management** that arise during periods of major corporate transformation and pose significant difficulties.

2.1 Recognizing Drivers of Disruption

Leaders need to have the foresight to identify transformative processes early and accurately gauge their speed. This critical skill depends on understanding the key driving forces of such disruptive change—the very triggers and catalysts that set these changes in motion. In selecting these key driving forces of disruptive change, we conducted an extensive review of academic literature that encompassed both macro- and micro-environmental factors [1].

The **macro-environment** can be divided into four key areas: political-legal, technological, socio-cultural, and economic [2]. For example, disruption can be triggered by legislative changes, such as the abolition of fixed book prices or pandemic-related bans on in-store shopping. But it can also be driven by broader societal changes, such as a surge in demand for sustainably produced food (sociocultural dimension), strong economic downturns (economic dimension), or sudden climate events (physical dimension). The technological dimension is particularly important given the pervasive impact of digitalization. **New technologies** emerge in the literature as the first key driving force of disruptive change [3]. They are a major force driving digital change. Notably, the Internet and related technological advances, such as virtual reality, artificial intelligence, robotics, and, most importantly, the increasing interconnectivity of Internet-enabled devices, are driving widespread product and process innovation.

A company's **micro environment** consists of customers, competitors, suppliers, and other market partners. When one of these players undergoes a major change in market behavior, it can trigger disruptive processes in an industry. In our Driving Forces Model, we will take a closer look at the change in **customer behavior** as the second key driving force. This is because it is usually the behavioral change in society that leads to a disruptive effect. The speed of behavioral change fundamentally shapes the disruption process. In many industries, changes in customer behavior are accelerating the disruption process. For example, we now buy shoes and clothes online, book travel on our mobile phones, keep fit with smartwatches like the iWatch and other fitness trackers, and seek health advice not only from doctors but increasingly from the Internet. But customer behavior can also slow down a disruptive process. This is the case when a new technology or service is not (yet) widely accepted. For example, the automatic grocery ordering feature with refrigerators, where personal calendars need to be shared, has not been widely adopted.

With respect to potential competitors, we focus on a third driving force that is particularly important in the context of disruptive change: the innovative **earnings models** of potential disruptors. Earnings models explain how companies generate revenue and how that revenue generates profit. Disruptors often pursue an innovative revenue logic. Airbnb, which now arranges more nights than any other hotel provider, generates its profits from commissions for arranging private accommodations. The old earnings model in the hotel industry was very different: revenue from room nights was offset by the cost of buildings, maintenance, staff, etc. Airbnb's completely different earnings logic made the incumbent hotel operators miss the threat it posed. This has since changed. Where Airbnb arranges private overnight stays, hotel prices quickly fall by 10 to 15% because an additional offer is created. Amazon was also slow to be recognized as a competitor because selling goods through an online marketplace and charging a commission was unusual in retail [4]. In Chapter 3.3, we explain Amazon's earnings model.

Against this backdrop, our model hinges on three key driving forces (cf. Figure 2.2) that are responsible for propelling many disruptive changes.

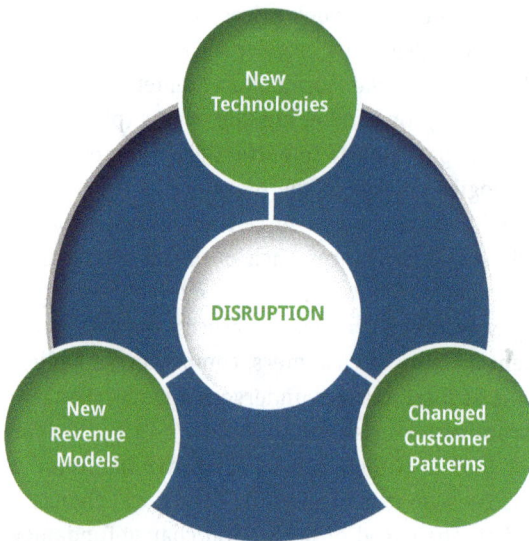

Figure 2.2: Key driving forces of disruptive change.

Table 2.1 below illustrates the influence and characteristics of the three key driving forces across five selected industries.

Disruptive change occurs in an industry when significant changes are expected or occur in all three dimensions of our Driving Forces Model.

In the music industry, this happened with the iPod. The iPod forever changed the way we listen to music. Apple's success was driven by three factors: extraordinary tech-

Table 2.1: Key driving forces of disruptive change across five selected industries.

Industry	New Technologies	Customer Behavior	New Earnings Models and Income Sources
Banks	– Algorithm-driven investment computers: Automated investment according to personal risk appetite by robo-advisors (e.g. scalable) – Crowd investing: Facilitates real estate investing for small investors (e.g. Exporo). – Artificial intelligence (algorithmic trading, e.g. Vontobel Plug'n'Trade)	– Customers are no longer interested in immersing themselves deeply in their investments or constantly monitoring them – Customer expectations for personalized, digital and mobile financial advice are rising – Institutional clients are automating their financial activities (banks are increasingly becoming IT service providers)	– Vontobel's service for institutions [5]: Offer of a comprehensive and customizable trading platform to simplify institutional trading. – Betterment: Online financial advice to help clients manage their money through cash management, guided investments and retirement planning. Customers only need to answer a few questions about their aims when opening an account, and algorithm-driven robo-advisors do the rest.
Healthcare Market	– Leveraging real-time data streams (e.g. through the monitoring of eating and exercise behavior using fitness trackers) to predict illness (e.g. heart disease) – Automatic and early identification of health problems (critical care in an emergency)	– Increasing focus on health – Focus on diet and exercise – Demand for health knowledge	– Ada Health: Questionnaire-based diagnosis app without direct interaction with a doctor Free for patients, revenue generated through collaborationwith health insurers that benefit from lower costs due to fewer visits to the doctor. – OnlineDoctor: Diagnosis of skin diseases by uploading photos to the app [6]. Doctors receive inquiries through the OnlineDoctor teledermatology tool and can bill for them; OnlineDoctor earns money from each inquiry. The result: faster and cheaper for the patient, easier for the doctor since not tied to office or consulting hours.

Table 2.1 (continued)

Industry	New Technologies	Customer Behavior	New Earnings Models and Income Sources
Insurance	– Mobile end devices (faster processes expected, also for insurance companies) – Big Data empowers organizations to gain deeper insights into customer behavior (see also see Health Market) – Individual eating and exercise habits are becoming increasingly measurable due to the growing digitalization of everyday life.	– Flexibility: Customers no longer want permanent insurance, but only when it matters most – Choosing the right insurance policy is very complicated, so it is important to make this process understandable and simple for customers.	– Insurance on demand: Cuvva offers short-term insurance through an app, for example to borrow a friend's car for a short period of time. – The Oscar app gives a dollar a day in the form of an Amazon voucher if the policyholder wears an activity tracker (smartwatch) every day and meets their exercise goals; technology incentives lead to lower costs due to healthier policyholders (www.hioscar.com). – The CLARK app allows users to manage all of their insurance policies in one app, reviews and evaluates existing policies, and shows how customers can save on their insurance or improve their insurance benefits.

Table 2.1 (continued)

Industry	New Technologies	Customer Behavior	New Earnings Models and Income Sources
Retail	– Just Walk Out Technology (e.g., Amazon Go employs a combination of cutting-edge technologies, including computer vision, deep learning algorithms, and sensor fusion, to revolutionize the retail experience by automating the entire purchase cycle, from selecting items to paying for them.) – Facial recognition (Identifying the facial expressions and mood of individual customers with regard to the product range and specific product categories in stores) – Digital marketplaces (e.g. Amazon, Zalando; leveraging supply and demand)	– Consumers are increasingly turning to digital shopping – Consumers are connected and share information about products – Consumers are buying directly from manufacturers – Consumers are automating their shopping and orders	– Advertima's 3D computer vision platform lets retailers use digital signage devices (e.g., screens) to capture in-store customer characteristics and patterns in real time and display personalized advertising. – (Semi-)automated shopping with higher revenues through increased consumer repeat purchase rates. (Subscription models like HelloFresh or Alexa Voice Shopping; Alexa is a cloud-based voice service that allows consumers to add products to a wish list, reorder items, check order status, and more—all by voice).
Automotive	– Self-driving cars (e.g. Google Waymo, Tesla) – Connected cars (cars that can connect to other services and devices over the Internet, such as notebooks and smartphones, but also other connected car technology, your own home, office, or parts of the infrastructure such as traffic lights or emergency call centers)	– Craving for variety – Greater diversity of occasions where mobility is key (family outings, camping, solo business trips) – Drive for sustainability; higher capacity utilization through ride-sharing – Owning a car is no longer a priority	– Car flat rates (also known as car subscriptions) allow consumers to drive a modern car of their choice for a fixed monthly price with everything included. Consumers only have to pay for fuel (e.g. SIXT+ Auto Abo, FINN, meinauto.de). Fleet management and collaboration on mobility solutions of the future (syndicate partnering with Google on fully automated transportation solutions) and ride-sharing solutions (e.g. Moia by VW: self-driving electric buses).

nological innovation that made the iPod easy to use and portable; meeting the needs of customers who wanted to listen to music on the go; and creating an alternative earnings model. When the iPod was first introduced in 2001, it was not a major innovation, because Apple had not invented the portable music player. Other companies such as Compaq, Creative, and Sony had already introduced portable music players capable of storing and reproducing digital songs. But the iPod's breakthrough came with the third generation in 2003. The Clickwheel made the device easier to use (technology), Windows users could now transfer music to the iPod via iTunes (customer behavior), and in 2003 Apple opened the iTunes Store, which created a profitable earnings model. From then on, Apple also made money from music downloads. Incumbent competitors were caught off guard by the iPod's success, because all three driving forces of disruption occurred almost simultaneously. But in 2006, Spotify managed to make music subscriptions popular. It was not until 2015 that Apple responded with its own streaming service, Apple Music. This triggered a rather late self-disruption that led to a decline in revenue for the established iTunes earnings model.

Major changes are also evident in the automotive industry. A **technological revolution** is underway with the networking of vehicles combined with electric motors and autonomous driving technology. The **mobility behavior** of younger consumers demands new mobility concepts, which are now being offered in large numbers and are challenging existing **earnings models** such as new car sales. In contrast to many other industries, established car manufacturers are actively trying to drive forward the disruption of their industry. VW is already in the midst of transforming itself and Mercedes has made a name for itself with the 'Case' program. The 'C' stands for Connected Cars, the 'a' for Autonomous Driving, the 's' for Shared Mobility, and the 'e' for Electrification—Daimler aims to be a leader in all four areas. BMW is showcasing new digital and mobility services, including DriveNow car sharing, ParkNow parking and ChargeNow electric vehicle charging. In particular, incumbent car companies and their associated dealer networks are being challenged by the new mobility services because they challenge existing **earnings models**. If BMW can deliver on its promise of 'driving pleasure' with a subscription model that allows customers to choose freely from the vehicle fleet, it would be a revolutionary step. The sales-oriented distribution system would be disrupted. Therefore, new earnings models are particularly important.

Lessons

Our Driving Forces Model for disruptive change:
-   Identifies three dimensions that heavily influence potential disruptions,
-   Provides a valuable analysis tool to track and more accurately predict disruptive changes,
-   Can be turned it into an early warning system by allowing companies to set monitoring metrics for each dimension and define thresholds for critical developments.

2.2 Stopping the Aggressors' Breakthrough

In retrospect, it is easy to wonder why so many companies have been caught off guard by disruption over the past few decades. Entire industries have experienced landslide-like upheavals: computing (from mainframes to PCs to smartphones), tele-communications (from landlines to mobile), photography (from film to digital), stock trading (from trading floors to online), music (from vinyl to CDs to downloads and streaming), retail (from bricks-and-mortar to online, omnichannel, and marketplaces), and automotive (from the internal combustion engine to electric mobility and car sharing models). The list goes on and on.

In workshops, we have often asked why disruptors succeed. A number of factors have been mentioned that certainly play a role. The most frequently mentioned factors for successful disruptors in our workshops were:
- Technological superiority of innovation,
- Charismatic personality of the CEO and founder,
- Sufficient human and financial resources in the company,
- Sudden change in purchasing behavior,
- A clear quality advantage for customers,
- Offering aimed at a niche market,
- Lack of willingness or the ability of competitors to follow suit.

However, a central explanation that has been identified in numerous empirical studies as a key driving force of disruption is often missing [7]. Superior quality, unlimited resources, and a charismatic CEO are necessary conditions, but they are not sufficient. According to Clayton Christensen's research, disruptors' chances of success increase significantly only when incumbents initially classify aggressors as harmless and let them get away with it [8].

Established companies often report an element of surprise: "We were aware of the changes in the market—as we have been aware of many times before—but we never expected this impact." When the disruption began, many thought the aggressor would never succeed. Their business model would have been too opaque and unprofitable for too long, and our own customers would have shown little interest in their offering. But suddenly the wind changed, and the aggressors quickly gained market share.

When incumbents take their perceived aggressors seriously from the outset, disruption tends not to occur. When incumbents recognize the disruptive potential of aggressors early on, they quickly try to copy them or, failing that, they buy out their aggressors and incorporate them into their own companies [9].

According to Christensen's arguments, the incumbents' skepticism about the new idea gives the aggressors time to make their business model profitable, improve the quality of their services without entering into price wars and find stable funding for growth. 'Flying under the radar' of incumbents hinders costly attacks by defenders, allowing the aggressor to make the big breakthrough over time [10].

There are many reasons why disruptors prevail. The strengths that new competitors have and the emergence of new technologies certainly make it easier for aggressors to succeed. But the main reason—and this cannot be emphasized enough—is the hesitation and passivity of incumbents and therefore the behavior of the incumbents themselves. This is also the conclusion of a 2017 study by the World Economic Forum, which found that companies are failing to make the necessary changes primarily because they underestimate disruptive aggressors [11].

Lessons

The findings from disruption research

- Warn against treating the success of aggressors as something that cannot be influenced,
- Call on incumbents to adapt their behavior in the market early on and actively pursue new lines of businesses, even at the expense of existing ones,
- Advocate for more courage and entrepreneurial agility and
- Call for the adoption of new management behaviors that follow the laws of disruptive markets.

2.3 Avoiding Shock Paralysis

In this chapter, we tackle the key question of why established incumbents often fail to respond early to disruptive challenges. After all, disruption pioneers like IKEA, dm, and MediaMarkt were hardly operating in the shadows. From day one, their overflowing parking lots, bustling crowds, and full shopping carts were impossible to ignore. This was something that incumbents could neither overlook nor deny. Yet most struggled to formulate an effective response. What explains this inertia?

How did Nokia, Sony, Acer, Bloomingdales, and countless other companies fall from market dominance? After all, they were once industry leaders, armed with brimming war chests and highly skilled managers. The problem probably wasn't a lack of awareness of impending tectonic shifts. Early warning was a priority for all. They diligently explored new business ideas and actively invested in start-ups. Yet they still found themselves in precarious positions. The culprit? They lacked the agility to adapt quickly enough.

This phenomenon is often attributed to the principle of inertia. Like any object in motion, large organizations resist change. The larger they are, the more force is needed to change their course. Companies have tried to fight back, but their efforts have been half-hearted and ultimately ineffective. Innovations designed to weather the storm came too late or never materialized at all. But the inertia analogy doesn't quite capture the essence of the problem. A more appropriate term, in our view, is 'shock paralysis'. Here's why: The inaction that results from inertia is often rooted in a state of shock.

Companies are so overwhelmed by the reality of major industry shifts that they become figuratively paralyzed.

There are a number of explanations for this 'shock paralysis'. A look at biology provides interesting clues. When faced with imminent danger, the body's release of adrenaline increases the amount of oxygen available to the muscles for the fight or flight reaction. At the same time, activity in some organs (such as the stomach or intestines) and parts of the brain are inhibited. However, in a particularly hopeless situation, where neither fight nor flight seems to offer a solution, the body goes into a kind of shock paralysis; the body's reserves are not used and the path back to a normal state is also blocked [12]. We have developed our model of shock paralysis based on this phenomenon, which explains why many established companies are unable to find an appropriate response to the aggressor and therefore fall into shock paralysis. Figure 2.3 explains the key barriers to innovation that paralyze established companies.

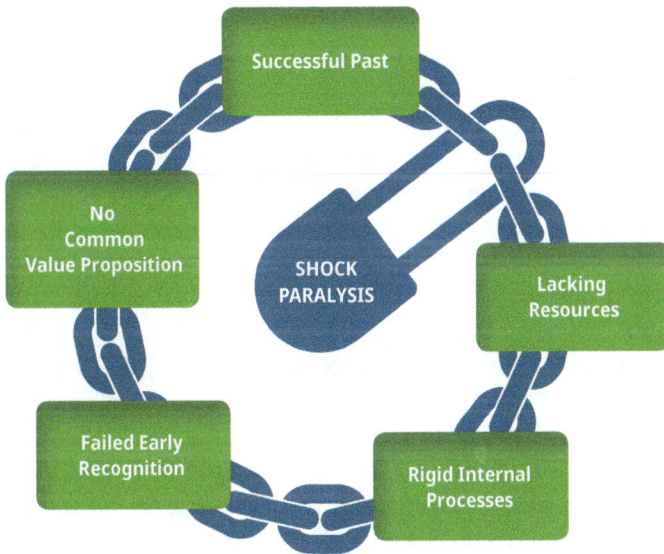

Figure 2.3: Shock Paralysis Model.

Failure to recognize disruptive change early can foster inertia. As long as companies remain unaware of disruptive forces, they're tempted to maintain the status quo and attribute declining returns to external factors such as a sluggish economy. We often see companies that fail to establish a proper early warning system. The three key driving forces of disruptive change outlined in Chapter 2.1 are often monitored superficially, without a systematic approach. Many companies limit themselves to measuring customer satisfaction, lulled into a false sense of security by the results. However, surveys that measure satisfaction only reflect the patterns of existing customers. Dissatisfied customers often go unheard because they have already abandoned the company.

Many companies are unwilling to systematically analyze why customers switch brands, understand the reasons for customer churn, identify the strengths of emerging competitors, or track their own innovative strength using the right methods. In some cases, they even resort to eliminating unfavorable market research altogether. Customer surveys, for example, are conducted only every two years in the mistaken belief that not much will change within a year anyway. Survey agencies themselves often downplay shortcomings, and companies are quick to drop any service provider that delivers uncomfortable truths.

But the search for new earnings models also paints a bleak picture. Which company systematically searches for new sources of income? Who regularly identifies the Achilles' heel in their own business model and brings in experts to dissect it? And when it comes to technological change, widespread half-knowledge pervades many companies. How many companies have their own dedicated labs that use new technologies to develop and test potential new business segments? We're not talking about labs used for mere marketing ploys ("By the way, we're digital now!"), but real sources and incubators of innovative solutions that ultimately translate into real-world applications. Unfortunately, such forward-thinking labs remain the exception, not the rule.

If you have no idea where the problem lies, you cannot even start to fix it. We recommend a more proactive and systematic analysis of the risks of disruptive change, especially in adjacent (technology-related) industries.

A **successful past** can make you complacent. As the saying goes, "What made us strong yesterday will make us even stronger tomorrow". This attitude makes managers often cling to proven concepts and try to defend them as long as possible. But the longer you wait to act, the greater the risk that a disruptive innovation will come along and disrupt your business. Incumbents can improve their existing business models in increments, but this is highly unlikely to create disruptive innovations. This is hardly surprising. The old recipe for success should be made to work for as long as possible, and if it evolves, it should do so in small steps to leverage past investments for as long as possible. Established vendors look for innovations that preserve the old recipe for success for as long as possible. Disruptive innovation is at odds with this approach and has historically been the domain of new entrants. Incumbents are afraid of cannibalizing their own business model.

Established companies are often tempted to focus on reviving their cash cows. They are driven by the belief that even reduced profits are better than the large initial losses that can be associated with developing new business fields. However, this approach can cause companies to miss out on early entry into disruptive markets. Many innovations fail very quickly, so the idea of a cash cow should not be dismissed out of hand. Rather, we urge a more nuanced approach. When disruptive changes are imminent, (see our model for key driving forces in Chapter 2.1), managers should consciously initiate self-disruption, rather than focusing solely on reviving their existing business fields.

In organizations, the finance department is responsible for sustaining past successes. It decides when to invest in new markets. The discounted cash flow method (DCF method) is typically used for this. In addition to projected revenues, it takes into account all project costs and calculates the potential return on investment. When a company invests in new business fields, the return on investment (ROI) calculated using the DCF method is often very low. This is due to low initial sales combined with high investments. Compared to established business fields, innovation projects perform much worse using this method. For this reason, the finance department is critical of innovation projects. They prefer secure revenues from existing business fields. But are these revenues really secure? What appears to be secure under apparently stable conditions can quickly become highly uncertain in times of disruption. In established businesses, returns that were previously thought to be stable can decline precipitously. This vulnerability stems from market share gains by aggressors, leading to fierce price wars and eroding profitability. Finance departments need to actively address this potential erosion by adding a risk premium to their calculations for established business fields. Failure to do so risks entrenching the status quo and preventing a timely change of course [13].

Scarcity of **resources** impedes necessary change. Without capable employees, state-of-the-art production technologies, a suitable infrastructure for exceptional product and service creation, and the necessary financial resources, a transformation is unlikely to be successful. A lack of intangible resources, such as high-quality master data, well-established brands, and well-developed relationships with suppliers and distribution partners, can significantly impede the necessary or desired transformation [14]. The resource of IT is becoming the dominant bottleneck for many companies, as the need for change has long exceeded the staffing capabilities of many IT departments.

The design of **internal processes** can help or hinder the development of innovative and marketable products and services. These processes include product development, logistics and production, and, for example, selling. Disruption demands that these processes be accelerated. What was once formally regulated must now be accomplished more quickly and, in some cases, informally. Intangible processes can often be inhibiting factors: For example, how are budgets coordinated and approved? How do companies learn from market research? And how do companies prioritize key projects and ensure a focused use of resources? These processes are often designed to preserve existing systems, which can prevent the disruption of conventional ways of thinking and acting.

A lack of a clear value proposition can also impede progress. A clearly defined value proposition serves as a guiding principle for management. For Amazon, this means striving to be the most customer-centric company on the planet ("to be earth's most customer-centric company") [15] and avoiding projects that do not align with this value proposition. The clarity of the value proposition provides two key benefits: Firstly, employees can concentrate on projects that reinforce the company's existing competitive advantage and secondly, the shared value proposition helps to prevent the company from getting bogged down in too many projects.

Companies naturally challenge established value propositions in the wake of disruptive change. Adapting one's value proposition is, of course, sometimes unavoidable. However, this period of uncertainty can be dangerous if the management believes the old value proposition is outdated but fails to define a new one. If the phase without a value proposition lasts too long, the crystallizing effect of shared values is missing and shock paralysis sets in. Centrifugal forces quickly arise that impede jointly supported change processes. We recognize the lack of a value proposition, or one that is vaguely formulated, as one of the main reasons why companies fall into a state of shock paralysis. We therefore recommend paying more attention to this success factor.

Shock paralysis is not caused by a single factor; rather, it results from the interplay of several factors in our shock paralysis model (see Figure 2.3). Thus, while the provision of adequate resources is a critical element in coping with the impending transformation, it is by no means the sole determinant.

Lessons

Our Shock Paralysis Model
– Identifies specific triggers for lethargic and hesitant management behavior
– Warns of concrete obstacles to greater agility in turbulent times,
– explains that the simultaneous occurrence of these obstacles can lead to stasis, paralysis, or rigidity.

2.4 Knowing When to Initiate Self-Disruption

We believe that established companies have the opportunity to transform themselves in disruptive processes. While this may not be possible for all companies, the majority can initiate successful self-disruption in their core business by acting proactively, courageously, and above all, appropriately. Self-disruption is a transformation initiated by one's own efforts. It must start with the core business, because the separation of old and new can plunge an organization into a deep crisis. Previously profitable business fields may become increasingly unprofitable, while new ones may not become profitable until much later than planned. This can lead to insurmountable conflicts between old and new business units that can tear the company apart. Therefore, self-disruption must start with the core business. It must be led into the new world with a sense of proportion, which means responding appropriately to market changes. Not too fast, not too slow, but at the right speed to achieve the desired success.

Too much change too fast can be excessive, while doing nothing can leave you in the wake of disruptors. Nearly all managers subscribe to the principle of doing the right thing at the right pace, although the balance between revolution and evolution is not easy to find and varies from industry to industry and company to company.

We are seeing radical changes in the music, computer, and media industries, for example. However, not all industries have changed at the same pace. The postal service, railroads, and construction are in the second category. Fifteen years ago, there were predictions that the postal service would experience a dramatic decline in mail volume with the advent of email. However, few experts realized that this would be offset by the growth of online shopping, which requires the delivery of packages. In the construction industry, the efficiency and cost benefits of digital blueprints have been clear for some time. However, there has been little change in the behavior of construction engineers. And despite the enormous growth in air and road traffic, with faster and more efficient means of transportation, rail has still maintained its market position after almost 200 years. In some countries or market segments, it has even expanded. This could change with new technologies such as drones, 3D printing, and electric vehicles—but it doesn't have to.

New technologies disrupt entire industries only when consumers recognize the benefits of the new offering and adapt their buying and consumption patterns. If they do not, the status quo remains. One example is the Philips do-it-yourself hair clipper. The clipper promised a professional and affordable haircut. The unique 180-degree rotating head made it easy to reach even the most difficult areas. This meant that everyone could evenly and precisely cut their hair themselves. So why did the breakthrough in this innovation fail and not put barbers out of work? This was due to a number of factors, including the limited functionality of the appliance, and in particular the need for grooming advice and pampering. People also lacked the necessary self-confidence. Some people doubted their ability to use the appliance correctly. If Philips had wanted to meet these additional needs, it would have had to invest in barber shops and training and build a whole new skill set. This would have required significant investment and the price advantage would have been lost. Therefore, there was no disruption and the profession of barber is not in danger of extinction.

MAPS – An Effective Approach to Self-Disruption Management

Whether a company builds computers or houses, whether its employees make movies or cut hair, management faces the challenge of accurately assessing the speed of change and developing appropriate and therefore effective policies and projects. The art of management is to neither overreact nor underreact to disruptive change. This is where the MAPS concept comes in. It enables a market-oriented approach that realistically captures buying and competitive behavior to assess the speed of potential change. It is designed to empower managers and help them drive successful self-disruption. The four-stage model is consistently aligned with the market and its changes. It encourages management to,

1. Understand customers' **m**otives for choosing companies and products,
2. Assess the **a**ttractiveness of potential aggressors,

3. Estimate the potential for existing customers to migrate, and
4. Develop an appropriate defense strategy.

We illustrate this process with two examples. In both, we conduct an analysis of customer motives by focusing on three strategically important customer segments: First, a company's fans, second, customers who switch, and third, so-called churners. Motive analysis is particularly important for switchers and churners because these groups can initiate potential disruption by threatening to leave. The following fictional examples illustrate the core concept of MAPS and describe how our approach is used in practice.

MAPS Taking the Automotive Industry as an Example

M – Motives
One of the **fans** is Hubert Gomez. He is 60 years old and lives in the country. His car is very important to him. Hubert likes to drive to work every day. On weekends, he likes to take a trip with his wife, by car of course. He sees self-driving cars as a loss of freedom. With the exception of cabs, Hubert avoids public transportation altogether.

Peter Miller, a **switcher**, is 45 years old. He uses public transportation during the week. That way, he doesn't have to sit in traffic on his 40-minute commute. On the weekends, he enjoys going on trips with his family of three. He doesn't want to give up his car (yet).

Greta Herwig is one of the **churners**. The 36-year-old lawyer lives in a big city with her partner. Both believe in the future of swapping and sharing and see it as more than just a trend. Greta regularly swaps clothes with friends and occasionally borrows their cars. She also uses a car-sharing service every few weeks. She sold her car three years ago.

All three of these prototypical customers have a basic need for mobility. However, this basic need takes different forms depending on the situation.

A – Attractiveness of the Aggressors
For switchers like Peter, car sharing and mobility providers are of interest. Rising parking fees and better public transport slowly but surely make owning a car questionable, even on weekends. Churners like Greta appreciate the growth in alternative mobility services. The simplicity of changing vehicles whenever needed and the large number of electric vehicles make the offer even more attractive. This customer segment cannot imagine going back to owing their own car. Only Hubert sees no alternative in the new services.

P – Potential for Customer Churn

"For each of the three customer segments, the percentage change over the next three years is extrapolated based on market analysis. The market researchers conclude that the group of fans could lose about 5% of the total number of potential customers over the next three years. The main reason for this is the aging of this customer segment. The switchers group could gain 3% market share and the churners group could gain 2% market share. By calculating the market share, the company can also estimate the potential change in purchasing power between the three groups. The 5% decline in the fan segment over the next three years indicates a disruptive change that requires the development of effective countermeasures through the selection of appropriate transformation projects.

S – Strategy for Defense

The defensive strategy of the established car manufacturers is mainly focused on the group of churners. With new services, they could provide weekend offers to compensate for declining sales. These include temporary rental offers (for holiday trips or weekends, coupled with freedom of choice between different vehicle types). The role of car rental companies, mobility providers and car-to-go services should be explored. What all these approaches have in common is that they try to be innovative in the niche, but hardly touch the core business. This is unlikely to be enough—car manufacturers are unlikely to be able to avoid disrupting their legacy business.

MAPS Taking the Threat Posed by Online Universities as an Example

Online learning and Massive Open Online Courses (MOOCs) are seen as having great potential to transform traditional university education in the long term. This raises the question: should students continue their studies at a traditional university, or would a digital university offer a more compelling alternative? Moreover, the growing popularity of taking standard undergraduate courses online and having them count toward a master's degree at a prestigious university poses significant challenges for many universities, because the Bachelor's degree would lose much of its importance. The need for lecturers, lecture halls and course formats would become superfluous. To illustrate this point, let's examine the MAPS approach to business studies.

M – Motives

Anette is one of the **fans of traditional universities.** She believes in the old model of a on-campus universities. A well-ranked university guarantees quality and good connections in the business world. Her father benefited enormously from his fraternity. The only thing that has gained in importance is studying abroad, which a prestigious university could help her with.

Ute is **ready to change**. She is less interested in the elitism of a top university. Her parents are both employees with just a high school diploma. She can imagine studying for a bachelor's degree online. That way, she wouldn't have to move, she'd save money, she'd be able to continue working, and she'd benefit from the best courses in the world. For her master's degree, she would then go abroad to a lesser-known university to enjoy student life.

As an **churner**, Carl has turned his back on the traditional model altogether. He got his college degree through the second chance route, so he believes in online universities. This way, he can advance his career while earning an affordable bachelor's degree from a third-tier online university. This will give him the chance to get an MBA later at a better university, which his employer will pay for. His bachelor's degree will be enough for admission to the MBA. It doesn't matter where it was earned.

A – Attractiveness of the Aggressors

Ute is considering universities that offer so-called micro-degrees. These are non-traditional degree programs that consist of a certain number of online courses in a specific subject area. Digital universities such as Kiron in Berlin could specialize in specific subjects such as accounting, marketing, or the networked economy. In the same way, several specialized digital universities might offer a bachelor's or master's degree in business administration. It is also possible that competitors to traditional universities will offer their courses internationally using the Amazon marketplace principle. This would be an English-language approach that could resell the services of renowned providers. One provider from the USA is Minerva University, based in San Francisco. Students at Minerva do not study in one place, but at different locations around the world, moving every few months or so. Their course materials are available exclusively online, and they meet for seminars via videoconferencing. They can also contact their professors online. Karl finds this model very appealing. Not only can he study during his planned one-year sabbatical, but he can also improve his language skills.

P – Potential for Customer Churn

According to a survey by several experts, the potential of would-be student switchers who do not want to study at a traditional university will be around 10% by 2023. This is mainly due to the high dropout rate of 50% in the field of business administration at renowned universities in the DACH region. In addition, many first-year students complain about the focus on rote learning. Established universities are being called upon to take countermeasures, even though the digital offering is still in its infancy and seeking recognition. It is likely that the quality of the new competitors will improve rapidly and that the recognition of their degrees will increase.

S – Strategy for Defense

Traditional models can no longer be the sole focus of the defense strategies of established universities. Instead, they must embrace the benefits of e-learning, MOOCs, and other innovations and integrate them into their teaching operations and conduct a critical evaluation of long-standing practices, such as the broad range of Bachelor's programs and the need for many large new lecture halls.

2.5 Understanding the Attack Strategies of Disruptors

According to the findings of distribution research, the first important prerequisite for the success of disruptors is the initial skepticism of incumbents toward aggressors (see Chapter 2.2). They cannot imagine that the new business idea will work. However, aggressors need to take advantage of this opportunity to achieve their hoped for breakthrough. To do so, they must choose an appropriate strategic path to conquer the market. Porter's well-known but still relevant approach distinguishes between cost leadership, differentiation and niche as generic competitive strategies [16]. According to the first empirical results of disruption research in the 1990s, cost leadership or differentiation can promote breakthroughs in new markets (see Figure 2.4).

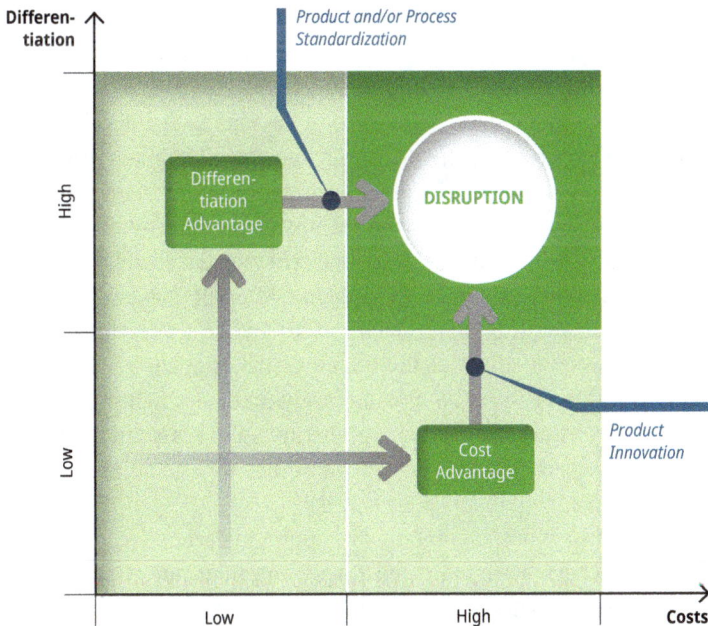

Figure 2.4: Strategic Management in Companies (source: own illustration based on Hungenberg [2004]).

Strategy Path 1: Cost Leadership in the Entry-Level Price Segment

With a strategy of cost leadership, aggressors can conquer the market from the bottom **as price breakers**.

Swedish furniture retailer IKEA has always seen itself as a price leader. When it expanded abroad, competitors were very skeptical about whether the self-assembly concept could succeed in Switzerland, its first market outside Scandinavia. Skepticism was particularly high in Switzerland, where service is very important. IKEA's first successes were in the lower income brackets, which the established players could easily handle. They voluntarily gave up the low-margin entry-level segment and concentrated on the mid- and upper-price segments. IKEA then gradually improved its quality and reached the middle class, becoming the market leader in Switzerland after about 30 years. In 2019, IKEA had a 30% share of the Swiss furniture market [17]. Compared to industries that are currently being affected by digitalization, this process took longer than expected in the Swiss furniture industry.

It also took several years for low-cost airline Ryanair to gain a dominant position in the airline industry. The airline's bare-bones service quality initially appeased many established C level executives. They reasoned that Ryanair's flights from *Frankfurt-Hahn* in the Hunsrück region (more than an hour from Frankfurt by car) couldn't possibly be profitable at just €12.99. "Who cares if budget-conscious travelers fly with them?" they thought. "It keeps them away from the main Frankfurt airport, freeing up space for higher revenue passengers who contribute to airport revenues through duty-free purchases, even as flight numbers continue to rise."

What initially seemed like a good idea turned out to be a major Achilles' heel for the established airlines. The low-cost carrier continually improved their services without raising prices. Gradually, even higher-income customers and business travelers began to use low-cost flights. The market was turned upside down, leaving less and less of the pie for the incumbents. It remains to be seen whether the establishment of their own low-cost airlines can really help the incumbents. After all, Ryanair now also flies from Frankfurt am Main, and the difference in prices and cost structures is still significant. Then there is the toxic effect of the ongoing strikes at the incumbents. While understandable from the perspective of cabin crew members fighting for fair wages, strikes at established airlines are a major competitive disadvantage: Strikes at established airlines fill the low-cost carrier's planes and if they do a good job, customers are unlikely to return to the incumbents after a strike.

The German grocery industry has also seen a disruption in recent decades. For a long time, the Albrecht brothers were ridiculed for selling food out of cardboard boxes in spartan stores in poor neighborhoods. Who would go there and buy so-called own brand labels that no one knows? After a few years, there was still a consensus in the industry that **Aldi** posed no threat. In terms of trading up, the established players increasingly focused on the middle class. Their stores and product ranges were much more upscale than Aldi's. But fewer and fewer customers saw it that way. Aldi's manageable but good assortment made shopping faster and, above all, much cheaper. Weekly non-food promotions kept the stores busy, and the market share gains increased the discounter's purchasing power, which was reflected in even greater price differences. The result was the same as with IKEA and Ryanair: The middle class started to shop at Aldi more and more, and soon the upper class started to shop there as well, as the quality of the product ranges continued to improve. With a market share of more than 10%, the company has long since arrived in the middle of German society.

As we can see from these examples, it is not so easy to respond successfully to disruption. The established companies in the market have not been idle. As a rule, the management companies defending against disruption did not make any significant mistakes. The disruptors, Aldi and Ryanair, were underestimated as described above. At first, the incumbents tried to compete with them, but then they were no longer able to do so. Edeka and Rewe have built up a discount format similar to Aldi's, but even after many years of optimization they are not making much money with it either. Lufthansa, British Airways/Iberia, Air France/KLM, etc. have also tried to establish a low-cost airline. Also, with very limited success. The incumbents are probably failing due to the transformation required in the existing business model. Although these companies have created new businesses, it is extremely difficult to reorient the originally highly profitable and still very important core business in terms of revenues. Customer habits are another reason. Former customers who switched to the disruptor because of the price rarely return. They will only do so if the price drops significantly again while the quality remains reasonable. But only new disruptors can do that. Former market giants generally fail to do so.

Strategy Path 2: Creating Better Products and Services for a New Market

In line with Christensen's theory of disruptive innovation, as adapted in 2015, Apple achieved the feat of launching a disruptive innovation in an entirely new market twice in a decade.

The iPhone was perceived by many experts as an expensive phone with lots of extra features. But the iPhone's apps, design, and ease of use quickly made it much more than just a phone to consumers. The iPhone's sensational sales figures initially had a devastating effect on competitors in the mobile phone market. Just four years after the launch of the iPhone, Nokia had to relinquish its role as market leader [18]. The completely new product category of the smartphone also hit other markets hard: Dictaphones, alarm clocks, watches, cameras and laptops all suffered significant losses with the advent of the smartphone.

The breakthrough of the iPad and subsequent tablets at the expense of the PC was equally swift. Despite the huge initial skepticism that questioned the appeal of a device to customers with fewer capabilities than a PC [19], the reluctance of incumbents to innovate against the completely innovative iPad fueled Apple's success. Not only did the tablet quickly become the market leader, but it also replaced the laptop as the primary portable computer [20]. Few experts could initially define the market targeted by the iPad.

According to our findings, there are two strategic paths that inspire disruption: the first, focusing on the entry-level market segment and the second, developing products and services for a new market.

That said, though, in business practice, it is not decisive whether a new development is defined as disruptive or not. At the very least, it would be dangerous for companies to take innovations seriously only if they are offered at a lower price or address a new market. On that basis, the auto industry should not dismiss Tesla as completely benign. Tesla is expensive and is not trying to launch a completely different product, even if the new Model 3 does seem to be very attractively priced. Suddenly, a misjudged company could become a force for great change after all.

Three key takeaways for established companies in this section:

1. Pay attention to innovations that offer substantially lower costs than is usual in your industry. These innovations can disrupt your industry.
2. Calibrate your early warning systems to identify disruptive innovations from other industries. With the rapid advance of digitalization, new competitors from other industries could become a threat. Google has disrupted the map business, Uber has disrupted the taxi business, Apple and Google are introducing the concept of autonomous driving, and Airbnb has disrupted the hotel industry.
3. Don't rely on your ability to recognize all threats in time (see points 1 and 2). There will be aggressors who do not pursue traditional strategies. At that moment, you need to be able to quickly transform your existing business model.

This book provides advice on how to do this.

References

[1] Müller-Stewens, G.provides an overview of trend models and their approaches. (2007), Früherkennungssysteme (Early Warning Systems). In: Köhler, R. & Küpper, H. (ed.): "Handwörterbuch der Betriebswirtschaft" (Handbook of Business Administration), Stuttgart Schäffer-Poeschel, pp. 558–570.

[2] See Ulrich, H. (1987), "Unternehmenspolitik" (Corporate Policy), 2nd Ed., Bern/Stuttgart, p. 64 ff.

[3] See Gilbert, C. (2003), The disruption opportunity, MIT Sloan Management Review, Vol. 44 (4), pp. 27–33, and Christensen, C. (2013), The innovator's dilemma, op. cit.

[4] See Amazon.com Inc. (2018), 2017 annual report of Amazon.com Inc., retrieved from: http://phx.cor porate-ir.net/phoenix.zhtml?c=97664&p=irol-reportsannual/info/reports/2018-report.pdf.

[5] See Vontobel, "Zugang zur gesamten Bandbreite unserer innovativen Plattformen" (Access to the Full Range of Our Innovative Platforms), retrieved from: https://www.vontobel.com/de-ch/plat forms/ (in German only).

[6] See "Online Doctor, Ihr OnlineDoctor für Hautprobleme" (Online Doctor, your OnlineDoctor for Skin Problems) – OnlineDoctor, retrieved from: https://www.onlinedoctor.ch/ (in German only).

[7]   See Christensen, C. (1997), The Innovator's Dilemma: When New Technologies Cause Great Firms to Fail, Boston, in: Harvard Business School Press.

[8]   See Christensen, C./Overdorf, M. (2000), Meeting the Challenge of Disruptive Change, in: HBR, March-April, 2000, p. 67 ff.

[9]   See Christensen, C. (1997), The Innovator's Dilemma: When New Technologies Cause Great Firms to Fail, Boston, in: Harvard Business School Press.

[10]   Christensen, C./Raynor M./McDonald, R. (2015), What is disruptive innovation?, in: Harvard Business Review, Vol 93 (12), pp. 44–53.

[11]   See Fortune.com, 2017-05-01.

[12]   See Kozlowska, K./Walker, P./McLean, L. (2015), Fear and the Defense Cascade: Clinical Implications and Management, in: Harvard Review of Psychiatry, Vol. 23 (4), pp. 263–287

[13]   See Christensen, C./Kaufman, S./Shih, W. (2010), Innovation killers: how financial tools destroy your capacity to do new things, in: HBR, No. 1 2008, p. 98 ff.

[14]   See Christensen, C./Overdorf, M. (2000), Meeting the Challenge of Disruptive Change, in: HBR, March-April, 2000, p. 67 ff.

[15]   Lecture by Hauke Jansen (Amazon Europe), on March 16, 2018 at the University of St. Gallen/ Switzerland.

[16]   See Porter, M. (1980), Competitive Strategy: Techniques for Analyzing Industries and Competitors, Free Press: New York.

[17]   Statista (2022), Market shares of the largest furniture retailers in Switzerland 2019, 2022-08-11, retrieved from: https://de.statista.com/statistik/daten/studie/277871/umfrage/marktanteile-der-groessten-moebelhaendler-in-der-schweiz/ (in German only).

[18]   See Monaghan, A. (2013). Nokia: the rise and fall of a mobile phone giant, retrieved from: https:// www.theguardian.com/technology/2013/sep/03/nokia-rise-fall-mobile-phone-giant.

[19]   Alexiou, J. (2011), One Year Later, Here Are 8 Naysayers Who Thought The iPad Would Fail, Business Insider, retrieved from: http://www.businessinsider.com/here-are-tk-dummkopfs-that-thought-the-ipad-would-fail-2011-1.

[20]   IDC (2018), Despite Steady Commercial Uptake, Personal Computing Device Market Expected to Decline at a -1.8% CAGR through 2022, According to IDC, IDC: The premier global market intelligence company, retrieved from: https://www.idc.com/getdoc.jsp?containerId=prUS43596418.

3 The High 5 Approach to Transforming Business Models

This chapter provides the theoretical foundation for our High 5 Approach to Business Model Transformation. To this end, we explain the difference between a business model transformation, a business model change, a strategy change, and a strategy adjustment in Chapter 3. In Chapter 0, we explore the history, definition, and constitutive characteristics of business models in management literature. Chapter 0identifies five key drivers that need to be considered in the course of a business model transformation. The coordinated interplay of these key drivers forms the foundation for our High 5 Approach to Business Model Transformation. Chapter 0 advocates a moderate alignment of the areas of action based on system-theoretical considerations. Finally, Chapter 0 offers suggestions on how to configure the areas of action in practice. Figure 3.1 summarizes the objectives of Chapter 3.

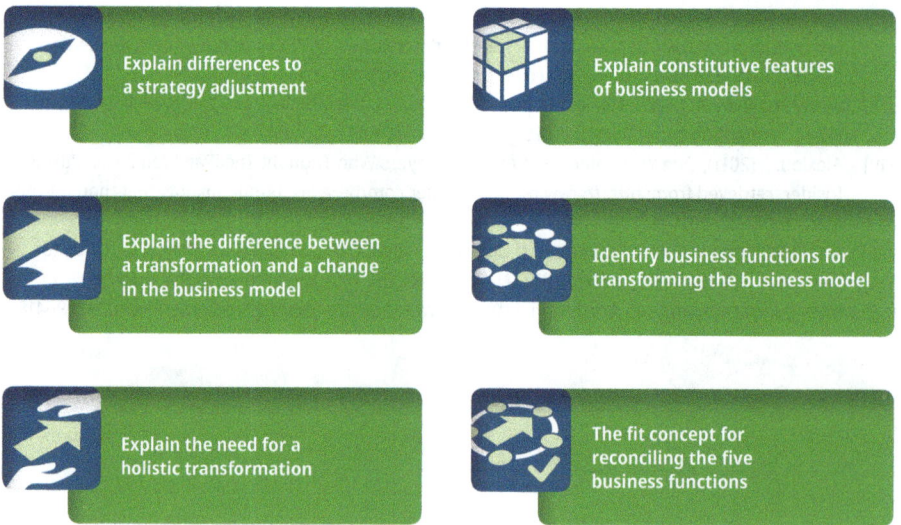

Explain differences to a strategy adjustment	Explain constitutive features of business models
Explain the difference between a transformation and a change in the business model	Identify business functions for transforming the business model
Explain the need for a holistic transformation	The fit concept for reconciling the five business functions

Figure 3.1: Objectives of the third chapter at a glance.

Note: The corresponding references can be found at the end of the chapter.

https://doi.org/10.1515/9783110772111-003

3.1 Fundamentals and Characteristics of Successful Business Models

Before we present our planning approach, it is important to understand the specifics of business model transformation and the characteristics of successful business models.

Foundations

In the 1960s and 1970s, management literature recommended that companies adapt their strategies in response to environmental changes. In those relatively stable environmental times, relatively minor adjustments were often sufficient. For example, if a bank decided to focus exclusively on wealthy customers in the 1970s, this was a strategy adjustment compared to its previous focus on customers of all income levels. The bank was simply focusing on an existing customer segment. The **strategy adjustment** led to the bank's decision to exit the business of serving low-income customers. However, if this decision was motivated by yield considerations rather than changing customer needs, it had little to do with disruption.

In the 1980s and 1990s, as market dynamics intensified due to globalization, the term **strategy change** began to emerge [1]. The Internet, in particular, triggered such a change for many banks in the late 1990s. However, the extent of the change was primarily limited to sales. Changes did not occur in all dimensions of the value creation chain, which is also the decisive difference between a strategy change and a business model transformation. Both strategy adjustment and strategy change are based on changes in the corporate environment, but the scope of the change is limited (see Figure 3.2).

Figure 3.2 illustrates the magnitude of change involved in a business model transformation. Because the entire value creation process is being realigned, managers from all departments are affected. For this reason, the risk of failure is high, and the change process is not reversible: anyone who initiates a business model transformation cannot return to the original state. Banks that today successfully serve wealthy private clients are facing competition from fintechs. To meet this challenge, banks must adapt to changing customer needs, realign their services, improve their marketing strategy across all touchpoints (along the customer journey), partially replace their IT systems, reduce the number of physical branches, and make many other changes. The entire value creation process is being scrutinized, and therefore the business model as a whole must be transformed.

Disruptive market changes challenge companies to act comprehensively and quickly. Optimization in individual areas is usually not enough. However, the need for comprehensive adaptation appears unavoidable, but this change process is an extremely difficult undertaking. Machiavelli explained the reason for this 500 years ago:

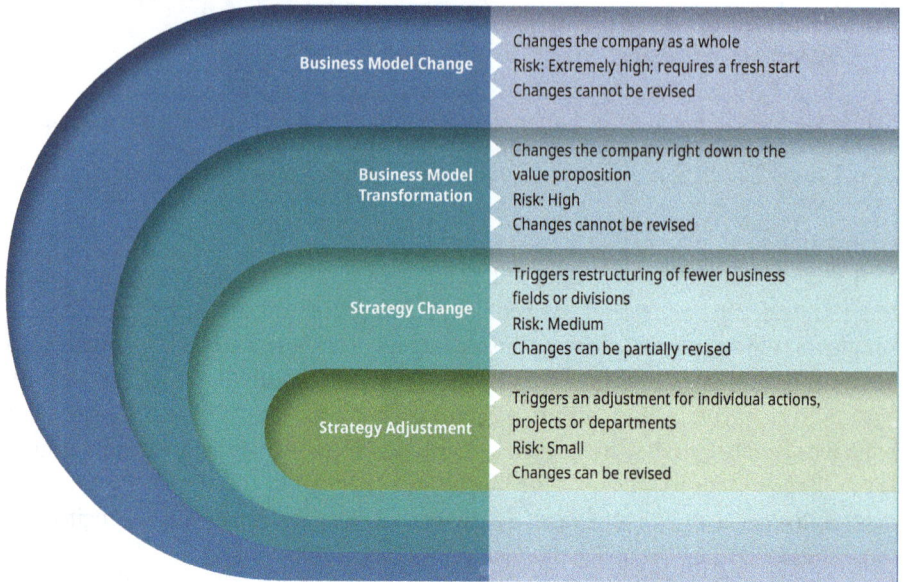

Figure 3.2: Strategy adjustment, strategy change, business model transformation and change.

It must also be remembered that no project is more difficult to execute, more uncertain of its success, and more dangerous to realize than the introduction of a new order; for those who want to introduce innovations have all those who benefit from the old order as enemies, and only weak defenders among those who would benefit from the new order. [2]

This new order means giving a new direction to the strategy, structure, processes, and, above all, the employees of a company. It affects value creation as a whole. Not only production and product range need to be reconsidered, but distribution and marketing also need to be realigned. A business model transformation occurs when internal and/or external factors require a change to several components of a business model [3], and the aim of these changes is to ensure the company's ability to survive [4]. Companies would not take such high risks if their economic existence were not at stake. This is often manifested in a combination of forecasts predicting dramatic change and a significant deterioration in business results. When this results in a new state for a company, we speak of a business model transformation [5].

The risk of failure in a business model transformation increases the more key drivers undergo change. A complete overhaul is usually required by a completely new value proposition. This results in a considerable need to adapt all the other key drivers in a business model.

In the case of a new value proposition, the term **business model change** should be used, especially as a completely new company needs to be developed in this case. This case occurs much less frequently, especially in established companies, than a business model transformation, in which the existing value proposition is retained or at most slightly adapted. With this book, we are addressing all companies that are planning such a business model transformation.

Figure 3.3 describes the results of an empirical study on business model transformations. In 2016, Safaric surveyed 74 managers from companies in the DACH region [6]. The companies surveyed had already implemented a business model transformation at the time of the survey. The data set provides valuable insights and guidance, especially as all of the companies surveyed had tackled these changes against the backdrop of digitalization.

Characteristics of Promising Business Models

While traditional strategic management literature emphasizes objectives like cost reduction, growth, and innovation, the discussion of business models delves deeper. According to Müller-Stevens and Fontin, it is about understanding how companies generate value for their customers (value creation) and derive revenue from that value (value capture). This focus has been a key driving force in the evolution of strategic management theory, making business models an essential tool for navigating today's dynamic landscape [7].

The roots of the modern business model discussion extend back to much earlier publications, notably those by Schumpeter in 1934 [8] and Drucker in 1954 [9]. As Markides [10] and Casadesus-Masanell & Ricart [11] observe, Drucker's perspective encompasses two key lenses. The first examines value creation from the customer's standpoint, asking "Who is the customer and what does the costumer value?" The second lens focuses on service delivery and its cost implications, guided by the question: "What is the underlying economic logic that allows us to deliver value to customers at an appropriate cost?" This holistic approach to "new ways to organize business" dates back nearly 70 years and forms the bedrock of every modern business model definition.

The recent wave of management literature has seen the emergence of a plethora of definitions for the business model approach [12]. This discourse on business models really ignited during the boom in innovative Internet ventures [13]. While the perspectives in the now vast (>1,000) body of scholarly work on the topic may diverge, they share a common thread: the systemic nature of business models. Management activities must be meticulously interlinked to ensure that the synergy of the whole is greater than the sum of its parts [14]. A business model is therefore much more than the mere aggregation of its components. Moreover, most authors agree that tactical and operational concerns do not directly constitute business model decisions; they are at best consequences of strategically sound model formulation. With this in mind, our definition below will emphasize the inherently strategic nature of business models.

Only Half of the Transformations Are Considered a Success

Only 54% of respondents reported a successful transformation. Since the sample included larger and more successful companies, the success rate may be even lower in the broader mass of companies.

Business ModelTransformation Typically Takes 2-3 Years

Although one in five companies completed the transformation in one year, the remaining 80% mostly took two to three years. This length of time is related to the complexity of the projects.

Changing Consumer Patterns as the Most Common Trigger

The most common reason for a BMT cited by respondents was a change in consumer patterns. This was followed by intense competition, the rapid adoption of new technologies, a change in strategy, declining consumer demand, internal innovation, and finally declining profitability. The results confirm the strong market orientation of the companies surveyed.

Customers Are at the Heart of the Transformation

Interestingly, profi t is only seventh on the list of most important BMT objectives. More important were identifying new market potential (#6), increasing sales (#5), improving customer satisfaction (#4), retaining existing customers (#3), increasing customer value (#2), and attracting new customers (#1).Clearly, most executives understand that improving customer perception is a prerequisite for better business results.

Most Companies Have a Proactive View of Their Approach

The majority of companies surveyed said they had averted a threat and recognized this as a proactive approach. By being proactive, they were able to consolidate their existing market position and seize new opportunities.

BMT Is Driven From the Top

According to nearly all managers surveyed, C-level executives are the catalyst for business model transformation. The scale of change requires a top-down approach.

IT Is Seen as the Greatest Barrier

Among the barriers to BMT, respondents ranked the delayed roll-out of IT systems as the most relevant, followed by conflicts with other group companies and an excessive customer focus at the expense of the company's financial goals. Conflicts between the old and new business models that arose during the transformation followed. Of similar importance was the failure to take into account the increased logistics requirements. Next came the wrong combination of price positioning and product range, and difficulties in building skills for the new business model.

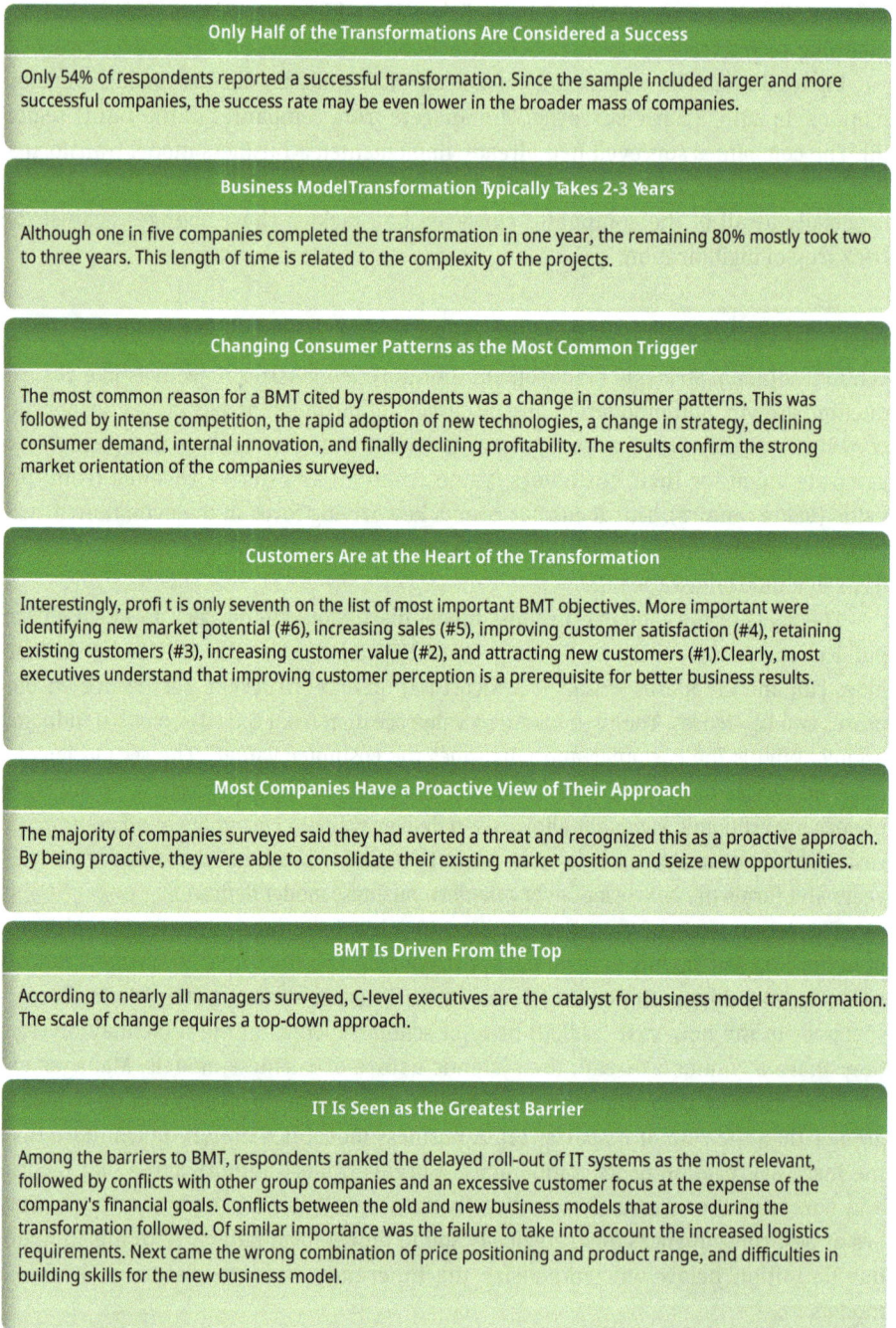

Figure 3.3: Findings from the manager survey.

We define a **business model** as the time-based strategic alignment and coordination of all value-creating activities to deliver a customer-focused and profitable value proposition, taking into account the resources required [15].

In contrast to other definitions, we assign the value proposition a 'primus inter pares function', with the task of creating coherence between all value-creating activities. The highlighting and coordinating role of the value proposition proves to be a key advantage, especially in turbulent markets. A focused value proposition that expresses a compelling market positionrelative to competitors also provides helpful guidance to employees and enables targeted and rapid implementation.

Our definition of a business model addresses the following constitutive characteristics of a business model [16]:

Customer Focus and Market Alignment: The core element of business model planning is the market and, within it, customer expectations. The value proposition exceeds customer expectations and lays the foundation for market success [17]. Focusing the value proposition on generating value for customers can help to strategically bundle existing capabilities and resources in a way that aligns with the market.

Strategic Alignment: Strategic alignment addresses the implementation of a specific business strategy. During business model planning, companies determine their market position in the competitive landscape and develop a market positioning strategy and implementation roadmap that outlines how they will achieve that position [18].

High-Level Direction: Managers set a high-level direction through the strategic alignment, without going into too much detail, maintaining flexibility to respond to environmental changes. Operational and tactical measures fall outside the scope of the business model itself [19].

Resource Leverage: As companies embrace market alignment, their ability to strategically deploy existing resources for maximum value creation and cultivate them [20] for the future becomes paramount especially during critical business model transformations.

Coordination focus: Business goals cannot be achieved without the alignment of business strategies, organizational units, and individuals [21]. Coordination requires consensus in management thinking and action. The formulation of a unified vision and a shared value proposition, especially during business model transformations, needs to be assured. Otherwise, departmental silos and turf wars can dominate, delaying development processes and paralyzing the organization.

Goal orientation: Business models, whether explicitly stated or implicitly practiced, are fundamentally about making a profit. Other goals certainly play a role, but without profit, a company's survival in the private sector is at risk [22].

Time orientation: Business models can be described in terms of the past, the present and the future. They are therefore in a static state that constantly needs to be adapted [23].

3.2 The Rationale Behind the High 5 Approach

Business models provide comprehensive guidance for various stakeholders. However, the focus is on employees. The description of a business model should provide them with a framework for understanding their daily operational and tactical activities. However, the question arises whether the often vague descriptions of a business model and the key drivers to be considered actually serve their purpose, as many employees simply do not understand how this description affects their work.

The challenge of transforming a business model is now compounded by this problem of understanding. It is no longer enough to simply create a business model and then leave it alone. Disruptive change increasingly requires companies to transform their business models. What was once a rare occurrence is now a regular part of management life.

For this reason, we derive from our broad definition of the business model concrete, understandable key drivers that play an essential role for management in a transformation [24]. These five key drivers, together with the associated goals, provide an approach that is easy to understand from an operational perspective compared to the more conceptual ideas of value creation and value capture. For business leaders navigating the imperative or desire to transform their business models from their current state to a target state, our High 5 Approach to Business Model Transformation offers a practical framework that facilitates successful self-disruption.

Companies observe disruptive market changes and at some point—often quite late—decide to turn things around and initiate major changes. Supported by consultants who usually leave the company after a short engagement, management is faced with a daunting challenge after the analysis and design phase. How can they make comprehensive adjustments in a short period of time and often even set a new course for the company?

Our High 5 Approach to Business Model Transformation answers this question. We use the term 'High 5' to encourage management to actively work on five key drivers in the course of a business model transformation. In addition, our approach explains how these focus areas can be coordinated. Figure 3.4 summarizes the rationale: The key driver of service delivery, service offering, and cost and earnings model must be aligned with the value proposition. The first four focus areas are equally important, while the value proposition has a special position—like the thumb on a hand. Without the thumb, our hand is of limited use. We cannot carry heavy weights or use the other fingers in a coordinated way. The same is true for major changes in companies. It is precisely then that a unifying idea is needed in the minds of leaders to guide the 'conversion' and describe the new direction a company is trying to take.

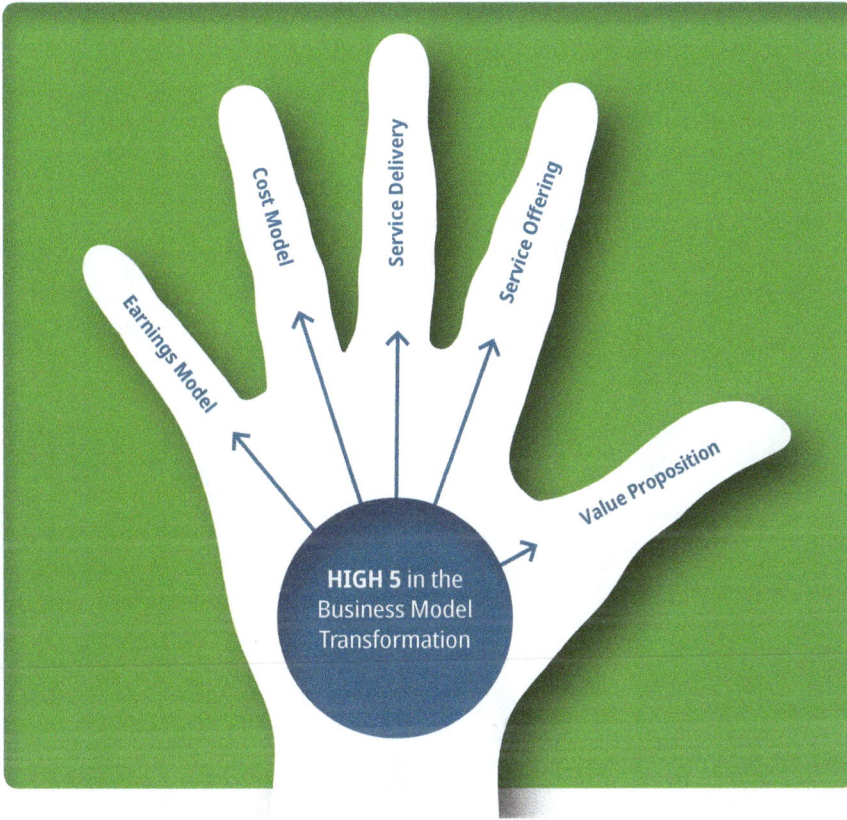

Figure 3.4: The High 5 Approach to Business Model Transformation.

In addition, our approach addresses specific objectives that companies should consider for each of these five key drivers. This creates a conceptual framework that both suggests strategic key drivers and the objectives associated with them. It also guides the operational search for company-specific projects.

The following chapters delve deeper into these key drivers and the ideally paired objectives and illustrate their application for companies in disruptive times.

3.3 Key Drivers and Associated Objectives

When a business model transformation is on the horizon, it seems like everything has to happen at once. Complexity is high and many managers feel that implementation is impossible, especially under increasing time pressure. Our breakdown into five key drivers is intended to provide an overview and help managers understand the situation and take the right action. We have refrained from providing a detailed derivation of the five business areas from the literature, as this would detract from the readability of this practical book. We refer interested readers to the comprehensive analyses in Alexander Safaric's thesis on this topic [25].

Numerous contributions from business model research recommend a holistic approach that takes into account **service delivery** and **service offering** in the wake of business model planning. In addition, disruptive market changes require managers to rethink their organization's **cost**and **earnings models**. The focus on costs is understandable: new competitors often attack on price, prompting incumbents to reduce costs. But costs cannot be reduced indefinitely. At some point, the old revenue or profit logic has to be expanded or replaced. For this reason, we first point out four key drivers with strategic links to day-to-day business.

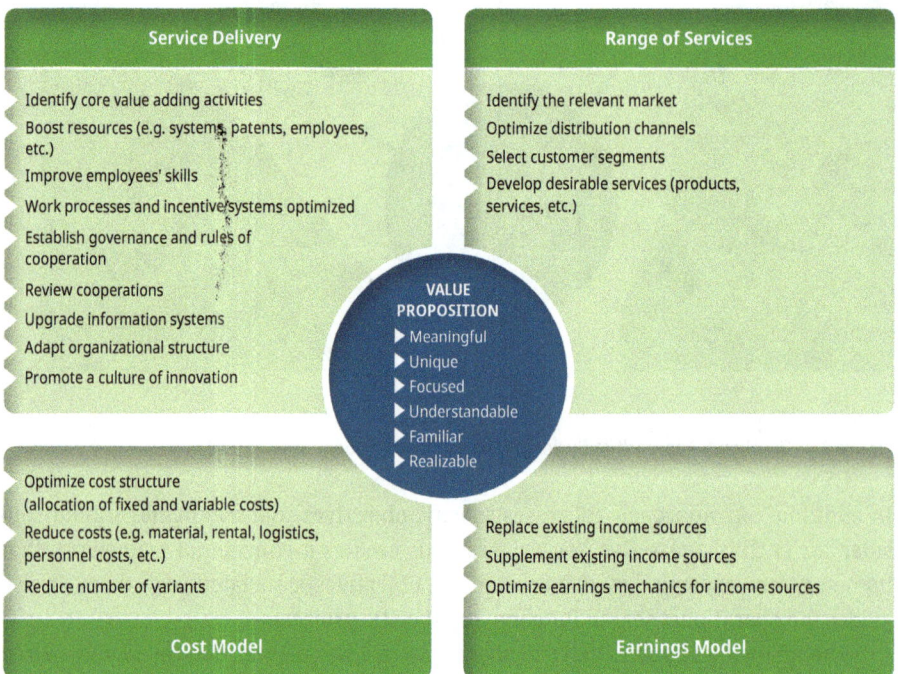

Figure 3.5: Description of the key drivers in the High 5 Approach with objectives.

Figure 3.5 suggests a link between these four key drivers. In addition, our business model definition emphasizes a coordination logic and introduces the **value proposition** to customers as a fifth key driver. In highly competitive markets, companies need to focus intensely on changing customer needs. Customer focus is recognized as the key to success. For this reason, the value proposition coordinates the four key drivers. In contrast, the value proposition is an overarching key driver that rarely changes at its core. It is the key to competitive advantage and thus determines the long-term direction of the company. Accordingly, it is placed at the center of Figure 3.5: The value proposition guides the other four key drivers.

When designing a business model, a company must first consider how it will create value (value creation) and then materialize it (value capture). This logic is reflected in the structure of Figure 3.5. The left-hand side deals with value generation through service delivery and the cost model. The key drivers on the right ensure sufficient profitability by focusing on an attractive offer and a working revenue logic. Let's look at the top two action areas, Service Delivery and Service Offering, which represent the relevance of the offering. The cost model and earnings model, on the other hand, create the conditions for profitability.

Value Proposition

"The most important attribute of a customer value proposition is its precision: how perfectly it nails the customer job to be done—and nothing else [26]."

The value proposition addresses both customers and employees alike. First, the value proposition should express a **company's competitive advantage from the customer's perspective** [27]. For target customers—consumers or customers who are highly attractive to a company— the value proposition should create excitement. To inspire enthusiasm, the promised service must be superior to competitive offerings and generate high customer value. Second, the value proposition acts as a guiding star for employees, helping them to see where a company wants to go and where their work is most needed. In other words, the value proposition serves as a guide for both customers and employees.

Many companies claim to offer a compelling value proposition. Yet, our experience shows that this assertion often proves inaccurate. We rarely find examples that meet the essential criteria for a truly convincing value proposition. The following six characteristics will help you refine and enhance your existing value proposition.

Make It Meaningful

The value proposition should capture the clear benefit your offering provides to customers. We can categorize these benefits into three types (see Figure 3.6). First, there is the **functional benefit**—the practical value that aligns with customers' buying motives. A functional value proposition emphasizes advantages in price, quality, and service. Think of Amazon— its promise of effortless shopping where convenience (service) is paramount. But functional benefits alone are often not enough. This is where the **emotional benefit** comes in. It is the emotional connection to a brand that drives desire and loyalty. Harley-Davidson, despite occasional functional hiccups, has mastered this game.

In addition to the two types of benefits mentioned above, the **social benefit** has become increasingly important in recent years [28]. This refers to the question of how a company can make our society a better place. Social responsibility, sustainable use of resources, climate protection and other issues play an important role in the way companies operate. For example, IKEA tries to provide as many people as possible in the world with a good place to live. With this value proposition, the company takes on social responsibility and automatically focuses on price as the only way to achieve its social mission.

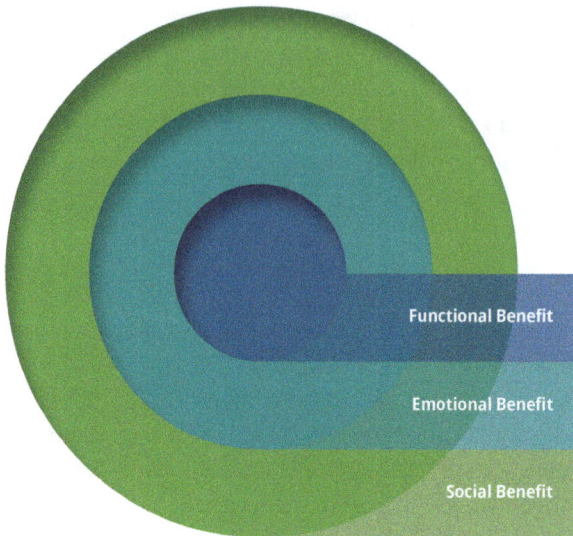

Figure 3.6: Functional benefits of a value proposition.

Creating meaning is gaining in traction, significantly amplifying functional and emotional benefits while increasing the appeal of a value proposition. Consider Migros, the Swiss supermarket chain. Its Culture Percentage (donating 1% of sales to cultural events), alcohol-free aisles, and Fair Trade labeling programs (ensuring better prices for coffee farmers in South America) cultivates high customer loyalty. Beyond low prices and its iconic private label brands (functional benefits), the Migros brand resonates emotionally because it is owned by its customers (cooperative structure) and champions social causes with its Culture Percentage (social benefit). Migros succeeds in creating meaning. Its commitment to purpose resonates with Swiss consumers, who reward the brand with unwavering loyalty.

Unique

Do companies want their service offering to clearly differentiate them from the competition and position them uniquely in the marketplace? Many companies have given up on this goal. In discussions with managers the following sentence is often heard: "The competition is basically offering the same thing". If you share this attitude, you have already taken the first step toward a lack of differentiation. Successful companies have ambitious plans in this regard. They determine where they want to be the best in class and review this regularly. Ryanair promises the lowest fares, Nespresso the best coffee, and the Ritz Carlton the best service. Value propositions must deliver on this 'best in class' claim unconditionally and through continuous innovation. A clothing manufacturer that chooses the interchangeable value proposition of "fashionable clothing at affordable prices" cannot differentiate itself from the competition. This value proposition is a matter of course that every fashion provider must offer. This interchangeable value proposition does not lead to growth or a good return on investment, unless it is a monopoly.

Focus
Focusing on a clear value proposition is often unappealing because it's perceived as limiting options. The conventional wisdom is that market leaders must excel in all dimensions. But this is far from the truth! Take Aldi and Lidl, for example. They deliberately don't strive to be the best in the industry in terms of service, store design, staff or product range. No, it is 'simply' the rock-bottom prices that make the difference [29]. This singular focus on price alone, the relentless pursuit of good quality at the lowest possible cost, is what has made Aldi and Lidl hard discount powerhouses in many countries and propelled them to global discount leadership.

Familiar
Value propositions are often included in annual reports and PowerPoint slides. But this is not enough because they are not known to the workforce. Companies mistakenly assume that everyone knows their value proposition, but they usually do nothing to actively communicate it. IKEA is again a notable exception. Employees are constantly reminded at work of IKEA's value proposition, which is to provide as many people as possible with beautiful home furnishings. Large posters in stairwells, elevators and even break rooms carry this message. The value proposition also plays an important role in day-to-day work. Many routines in work processes are designed to reinforce the value proposition.

Understandable
A value proposition must be clearly understood by employees. Employees should be able to see how they can achieve a competitive advantage. Unfortunately, companies are reluctant to choose the right words. Too much clarity is restrictive and overly prescriptive. Ambiguity provides the opportunity to respond flexibly to change, especially in turbulent times. This attitude is doubly misguided. First, clear market positioning encourages all employees to focus on the same competitive advantage. This creates synergy and positive energy. And because everyone knows what is important, on the other hand, centrifugal forces and negative energy are diminished. Second, a clear value proposition also allows for diversity and freedom. If Mercedes promises "The

best or nothing", then all employees—from the apprentice to the CEO—feel committed to it. All activities must be focused primarily on quality. Of course, this quality must be affordable as well, and this is central: Price must never take precedence over quality. But "The best or nothing" also leaves a lot of freedom to design all tasks. A high-quality engine alone is not enough to make the best car. The air conditioning system, the workshop service, the call center and the driver assistant must also live up to this brand promise.

Achievable

For a value proposition to truly resonate, employees and customers must believe it's achievable. Two major obstacles can hinder this belief: resource limitations and fierce competition. If you aspire to be a quality leader but lack the skilled engineers to develop it, fulfilling that promise becomes impossible. Similarly, setting goals that have already been achieved by competitors diminishes the impact of your proposition. Therefore, it is critical to evaluate your value proposition through the lens of potential customers. Do they trust your company to deliver on your value proposition? And which competitors could credibly claim the same promise?

The value proposition configures all other key drivers. It serves to bring order and orientation into a web of potential chaos [30]. Disruptive market changes provoke chaotic conditions in companies. A good value proposition can steer this fragile state back onto an orderly path. We therefore recommend that the value proposition be addressed and sharpened first in the course of a business model transformation. This view is shared by executives, as shown by the results of the executive survey in the DACH region mentioned in Chapter 3 [31]. 96% agreed with the statement that without a convincing value proposition, their own organization lacks the orientation for digital transformation. 94% supported the view that C level executives must drive digital transformation and act as a mentor and change leader.

Service Offering

Much of the business model literature that examines core key drivers assigns a critical role to the service offering [32]. This key driver asks what should be offered to whom in which market. The answers to these three questions are interdependent, as also illustrated in Figure 3.7 below.

The first step is to answer the question of whether the existing **market** or a new market should be the focus of future business activities. This question rarely arises in stable markets, but disruptive forces require it to be part of the business model planning. Companies that identify insurmountable difficulties in traditional markets at an early stage, whether due to new competitors or a change in technology, should focus on new markets at an early stage. Linde, for example, decided many years ago to exit the

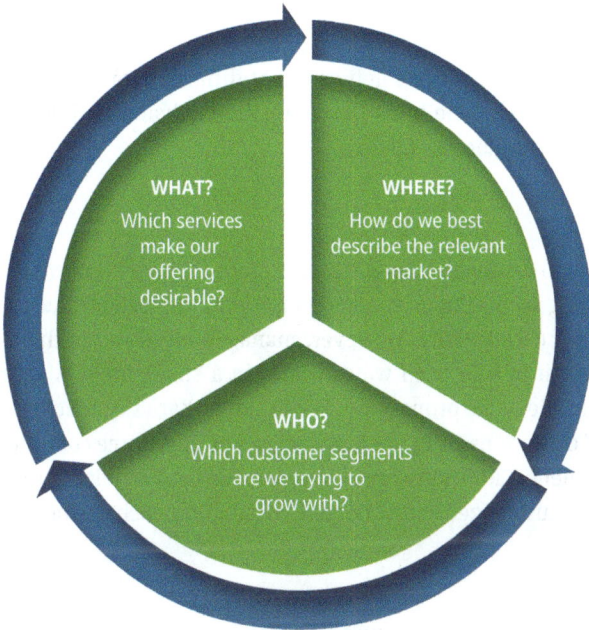

Figure 3.7: Issues affecting the definition of the service offering.

forklift truck business and focus entirely on the industrial gases market. The primary motivation for this decision was the prospect of profitability. The importance of market definition is further illustrated by the example of the American railroads: If they had not defined their market over 100 years ago as the transportation of people and goods by rail, but had simply left rail out of the sentence, they would have been involved in road building and the first airlines early on and would have survived.

Once the market has been defined, the next question to ask is which **customer segments and services are the most promising for the future**: Which customer segments offer the potential for sustainable growth? In this second step, customer segmentation is unavoidable, and the question of *what* products and services to offer is a recurring theme. Customer segments can only be identified if the future product and service offering can be described. In this sense, the questions of the target market, the customer segments, and the product and service offering for an upcoming business model transformation must be answered. Ideally, initial answers can be derived from the value proposition.

Service Delivery

Unique service offerings are built on a service delivery that differentiates the company from its competitors and provides the basis for competitive advantage. Managers should consider the following five success factors.

Core Activities

It is often difficult for managers to distinguish between core and support activities [33]. In day-to-day business, everything seems important, and employees can feel devalued if they are not given a task from a core activity. However, managers need to ask themselves this question and answer it in a focused way, at least in a small circle. A core activity significantly strengthens the value proposition. For example, Zara's core activity is the very fast production of collections in its own factories. For Salesforce.com, the customer relationship management (CRM) software developer, the core activity is providing individual consulting and customized software configuration for each customer.

Resources

Five essential types of resources play a role. **Physical** resources, such as excellent manufacturing facilities, ensure high quality production at Audi. **Legal** resources, such as patents, are the foundation of a pharmaceutical company's business. **Human resources and information** are equally important for all companies. Established companies face the challenge of finding and retaining well-trained employees in times of digital change. Motivation is another challenge.. If a well-trained employee does not see the point of the transformation project, their expertise is likely to be wasted. Information is not only about hardware and software, such as IT technology and programs, but also about the ability to use them wisely. The use of information based on modern data analysis methods is a major challenge for many companies [34]. In addition, **financial resources** are essential for comprehensive reorganization projects.

Work Processes and Incentive Systems

Work processes are the sequential linking of different value creating activities [35]. For example, at Zara, which activities, and in what order, contribute to the optimization of private label production? It may make sense for Zara to internationalize its Spanish-focused production process to a greater extent as Asian markets become more important. Such a decision would require Zara to make significant changes to its supply chain operations.

Incentives systems have a significant impact on the adaptation of work processes to new challenges. According to the results of our survey of executives in the DACH region on the topic of business model transformation, 81% of respondents called for new incentive systems for their organizations so that different departments and divisions could work together on disruptive change processes and thus create new work processes [36].

Organizational Structure

The organizational structure of challengers is often very different from that of incumbents. For example, Zalando in Berlin has more than 100 small teams working on countless software projects. This company does not subscribe to the philosophy of orderly and controlled (and slow) development. Instead, it relies on speed, initiative, and freedom, which results in a completely different organizational structure. This challenges incumbents to adopt a more agile approach. Hierarchies need to be broken down, decision paths shortened, and some decisions delegated to the grass roots.

Governance

Governance refers to the management and control of all parties involved in the service delivery process and the organization of the relationships between them. It includes issues related to contracts between parties, incentive systems, and key performance indicators used to manage the business. It also includes corporate culture as a non-formal tool [37].

Cost Model

"Clearly, though, the ability to translate value in the business into value for the shareholder requires the incorporation of the financial domain to the construct." [38]

The cost model is significantly influenced by the service offering and the required service delivery. The broader the service offering, the more complex it is and the higher the cost [39]. In a stable business environment, it is sufficient to optimize the cost model. However, disruptive market changes force incumbents to radically change their cost model. For example, Amazon does not have physical stores, so it does not have the cost of renting space or hiring store associates. Traditional retailers are therefore being forced to rethink their service offering while radically simplifying their cost model. In this context, the following success factors are important:

Cost Structure

This refers to the ratio of variable to fixed costs. The greater the variability in sales, the lower the fixed costs should be. Outsourcing and cooperation can help reduce fixed costs. In volatile markets, the question of whether a two-pronged strategy can achieve higher quality at lower cost is increasingly being asked. Singapore Airlines has been practicing this controversial approach for many years [40]. The airline is regularly awarded for its excellent cabin service, and does so with a significantly lower cost base than other airlines [41].

Digitalization can lead to significant cost savings and should be the aim of every company. Marketing is an area where significant cost savings can be achieved. If personalized promotional emails are made more relevant through improved big data algorithms or artificial intelligence, costs for traditional advertising and marketing staff can be saved. In light of these considerations, in March 2018, Zalando announced plans to cut 250 marketing jobs. The goal is to significantly reduce marketing costs as a percentage of sales in the coming years. The freed-up funds will be invested in better logistics processes to improve profitability [42].

Supplier Conditions

In manufacturing companies with little depth in value creation, cost savings can be achieved by negotiating better purchasing terms. The increasing interconnectedness of the economy and the sharp increase in cooperations offer further opportunities for cost savings beyond procurement. For example, Walmart saved inventory planning jobs by implementing an automated data exchange with its major supplier, Procter & Gamble.

Earnings Model

"Business models serve as a firm's organizing logic for value creation (for its customers) and value appropriation (for itself and its partners) . . . [43]"

This is a particularly challenging area for incumbent suppliers. They often face competition from digital aggressors with a different profit logic. Amazon, considered by many to be the most dangerous aggressor, makes little money in traditional retail. After costs, there is almost nothing left over from sales. However, the company is profitable overall thanks to significant surpluses generated by its web services and Amazon Prime. The annual membership fee for Amazon Prime includes free shipping on ordered goods as well as other services not directly related to retail such as music and movie streaming. The annual fee is relatively low for the more than 200 million Prime members worldwide [44], as it is paid only once a year and is quickly forgotten. As such, Prime represents an additional, profitable income source that complements the traditional transaction-based retail earnings model. In addition, Amazon's relentless and seemingly unstoppable growth has attracted cheap capital from investors, further fueling the company's growth [45].

In light of the literature on business models [46], we argue for a broader view of this key driver. Traditionally, the discussion around income sources has focused on revenue sources. The central question has been how to generate revenue. In the future, we believe that it is also important to consider which income sources can be expected to generate a stable (profit) margin. With a particular focus on profit, we advocate the development of a earnings model that is composed of promising income sources and offers the prospect of sufficient profit overall.

The following Figure 3.8 is a description of Amazon's earnings model. Classic transaction-based income sources are at its core. They are based on the sale of products from the Amazon product line (purchased by Amazon) and the brokerage of third-party products (not purchased by Amazon), for which Amazon charges commissions. Amazon rarely operates its own warehouses for third-party products, so this income source has low costs and a correspondingly high revenue potential. Income from services related to the core business include the Prime subscription, for example. Non-core income sources include Amazon Web Services, which are primarily cloud services. The classification of financial services is less clear. Does Amazon Pay count as another core service or is it a new business field? What about Amazon bank accounts, which the industry has been speculating about for a long time? Amazon has tapped into a third group of income sources through partnerships, for example in streaming or offering advertising space.

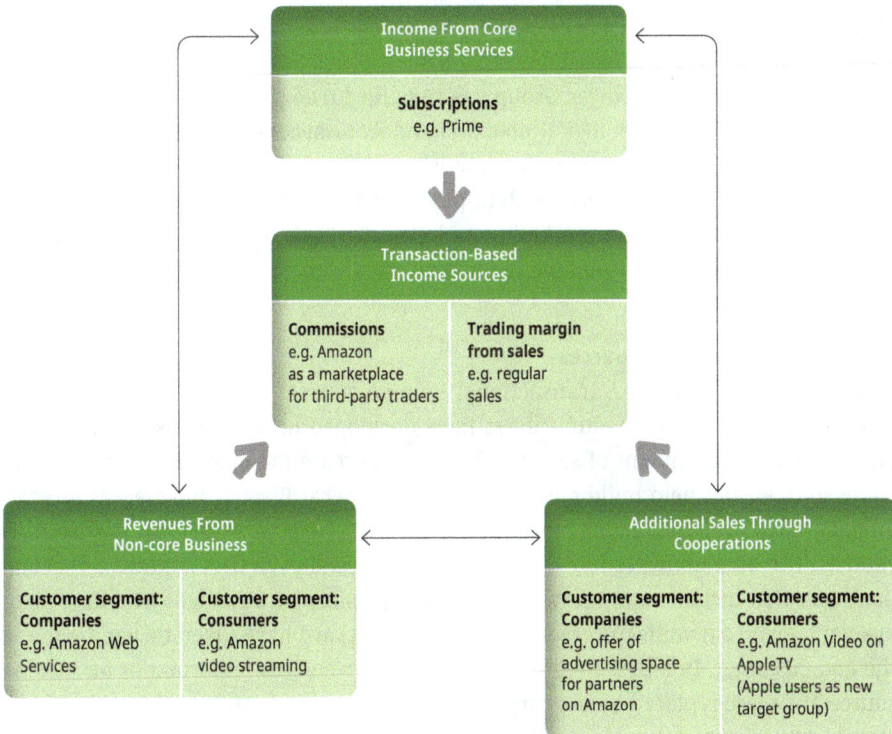

Figure 3.8: Amazon's earnings model and its income sources (source: own illustration based on Rudolph & Bischof [2017]).

For the sake of simplicity, the following discussion of management's options for optimizing its own earnings model will focus on actions and projects within the existing service offering. However, especially in times of disruptive technological change, it should be a matter of course to consider expanding business activities with new income sources.

Replacing Income Sources

Not long ago, streaming technology replaced music downloads. Companies that tried to continue to make money from music downloads have largely disappeared from the market or are making much less money. Companies like Spotify were early adopters of subscription models and have grown successfully as a result. In other industries, income sources have been replaced, often as a result of cutthroat price competition.

A wide range of ideas for alternative income sources can be found among the major Internet companies. Alibaba has chosen an income source that is not even visible to the end user: the company collects a commission from the seller for every purchase. Because Alibaba's business model does not involve a brick-and-mortar store with expensive logistics, profits are substantial due to the low cost structure. Google's income source is based on a per-click fee, Netflix's is based on a monthly subscription fee, and Axel Springer's is based on refinancing through advertisers.

Although the Axel Springer Group has remained true to its core business of print media, it has expanded its digital media channels to become the main source of income. Due to the prevailing freemium model, the company has replaced transaction-based revenue sources, where readers pay directly for articles and subscriptions, with revenue sources from marketing and classified ads (e.g. idealo, zanox, Immowelt). In the latter case, it is not the readers or users who pay, but the advertisers.

Supplementing Income Sources

As competition intensifies, transactional income sources can lead to unprofitable sales. As a result, many manufacturers have developed new income sources that include a significant amount of services. This can increase the profitability of these income sources and help build customer loyalty. General Electric now leases aircraft engines exclusively under long-term maintenance contracts, which can ensure high returns. The automotive industry enters into comprehensive fleet contracts for company cars that include many services such as inspections, tire changes, and fleet management. Printer manufacturers such as Hewlett-Packard have taken this approach to the end customer. In a first round, printer sales became less important as an income source and were replaced by ink cartridge sales. In a second round, the transition to a service subscription takes place with a fixed cost per printed page.

Netflix's income model is based on a monthly subscription fee. New users are attracted with a free trial subscription that automatically renews for a fee after one month. According to analysts, the conversion rate of free users to paying customers was an impressive 93% in 2011 [47].

Department store operator Karstadt is looking to diversify its income sources by expanding beyond its core business. Due to declining returns in the department store business, the company is opening up a new, promising income source by renting out unprofitable retail space to third parties. Karstadt is even willing to give e-commerce competitors access to its stores, charging a commission for goods that are ready for pickup. Tesla began as an electric car manufacturer, but has since expanded into solar cells and energy storage systems for homes and businesses. In 2021, Tesla generated nearly $1 billion US in revenue from these new businesses. Financial institutions are partnering with insurance brokers to create new income sources. Gone are the days of the 'all-finance' mantra that sought to merge banking and insurance under one roof. Today, the focus is on collaboration. For example, Deutsche Bank's mobile banking app now includes an 'Insurance Manager' tool that allows customers to manage their existing property insurance and explore new policies from various third-party providers—a welcome way to generate income in this era of low interest rates. Similarly, ING-Diba has seamlessly integrated a robo-advisor into its online banking platform, and in just two months, the commission-based investment volume has already exceeded €150 million [48].

In Switzerland, many companies have successfully entered into service contracts with owners for garden maintenance, flat roof inspections or property management, complementing income models that focus on individual transactions.

Optimizing Earnings Models

Earnings models consist of different income sources that need to be made profitable. To adapt a earnings model to a disruptive situation, the first step is to analyze the existing earnings sources. This analysis should calculate the profitability achieved for each individual earnings source. If the revenue generated is less than the attributable costs, that income source should be put to the test. The same applies to income sources that have little chance of increasing sales.

The result of the income source analysis is an income source portfolio that can also be managed like a portfolio. If a company rebalances its income sources and shifts sales, it can significantly improve its bottom line. For example, the aforementioned subscriptions (see the Amazon example in Figure 3.8) can in some cases generate more revenue and customer loyalty than single sales. What has long been the case with the sale of news and mobile phone subscriptions is slowly becoming a reality for car services, vehicle use, season passes for ski resorts, cosmetics, children's toys, food and fashion [49], often complementing existing income sources. IT companies such as Adobe or Cisco Systems are increasingly turning to the income source 'software as a service from the cloud' for profitability reasons. The old income source of 'software licenses on computers' is being systematically replaced by the cloud offering. Cisco

CEO Charles Robbins attributes a more stable revenue trend to the cloud income source. Customer loyalty is higher and not primarily dependent on price. In the fourth quarter of 2017, the cloud offering already accounted for 13% of Cisco Systems' total product revenue, more than double that of the previous year [50].

Field Test

The case studies in this book (see Chapter 4) analyze the business model transformations of companies from a wide range of industries and regions. The studies reveal not only a number of similarities with our framework model from Figure 3.5, but also some deviations that are related to the specific circumstances of each company. For this reason, we do not see our key drivers and the projects derived from them as a one-size-fits-all solution, but rather as a kind of checklist for management. In the case of a transformation the relevant projects must be determined on a case-by-case basis. For example, companies in the retail sector should add the project 'Optimizing Sales Floors' to their cost model. This is because online retailing is reducing the demand for brick-and-mortar stores, which means that the cost model for retailers needs to be adjusted to reflect the changes in the retail landscape.

The strengths of our framework model lie in its
– **holistic** approach: It takes a comprehensive view of value creation across the enterprise.
– It **focuses** on five key drivers with targeted tasks within each
– It identifies the interdependencies between the key drivers, highlighting the need for effective **coordination**.

3.4 The Coordination and Prioritization of Key Drivers

"Configuration . . . can be defined as the degree to which an organization's elements are orchestrated and connected by a single theme [51]."

In many situations in life, we can only achieve our goals by working closely with others. This is especially true when we work in teams: A soccer team, a sailing crew, and even a student team must coordinate the behavior of their members to achieve their goals. This insight can be applied to business management and is critical to success in times of change. During a business model transformation, managers must coordinate the five key drivers.

This coordination process should meet three requirements. First, the content and tasks of a transformation must be well aligned. Second, the key drivers must be prioritized in terms of timing. Third, all operational activities must be coordinated so that they 'fit together' as well as possible.

Requirement 1

Holistic Alignment of the Key Drivers

Systems theory provides the foundation for this call for alignment. It understands organizations as interactive value creation networks, where success hinges not on individual optimization of five key drivers, but on a synergistic interplay among them. This requires a cybernetic understanding of the interconnected effects of these functions on the part of employees, and an acknowledgment that transformation can only be mastered through cross-departmental collaboration. Vester emphasizes the need to consider the system context by including all problem areas [52]. Ackhoff illustrates this with the analogy of a car. No single component can move the car on its own. Just as the engine must be anchored to the body, the brakes fitted, the steering wheel mounted, and the wheels fitted, so too must a company's various departments all work together seamlessly for the transformation to realize its full potential. Tweaking each of these functions in isolation is like tinkering with individual parts of the car—it won't move the business forward [53].

The basic principles of systems theory also apply to configuration theory. Configuration theory is based on the premise that every business problem is unique, and therefore there are no universally applicable solutions [54]. Every transformation is different and will never follow exactly the same path. As the saying goes, "All roads lead to Rome". Therefore, each company should not seek an idealized path, but rather choose the configuration that is best suited to its own situation [55].

The interaction of the elements must therefore be situational, and configuration theory provides suggestions on how to do this, including for upcoming transformations from the current state to a planned configuration [56]. If we apply this core idea to our High 5 Approach to Business Model Transformation, each configuration of the five key drivers corresponds to a company-specific configuration. For example, Ratiopharm promises its customers affordable generics. This requires a manageable range of drugs, low cost structures and efficient production methods. The low margins require high sales volumes per item in order to achieve an adequate return on investment. The five key drivers are therefore closely coordinated, as they follow a configuration that is aligned with the value proposition of affordable prices. The value proposition therefore plays a leading role in the holistic alignment.

Requirement 2

Prioritizing the Individual Key Drivers Over Time

In addition to our fundamental belief that only a holistic approach can lead to successful business transformation, the need to prioritize key drivers over time brings additional benefits. Especially in times of disruption, the need to restructure a business can seem risky, lengthy, and often fraught with setbacks. Managers leading a transformation project are much more successful when initial successes occur quickly and continue throughout the project. Small wins ensure economic stability and high employee morale as well as prevent feelings of overload and excessive demands. Prioritizing key drivers and related activities is critical. Without focusing on or prioritizing the essentials, management runs the risk of getting bogged down and the transformation will fail. The following typology is intended to help companies prioritize their time. It is based on insights and tips from several workshops with executives from different companies.

All five key drivers are of great importance and must be addressed as part of a transformation. However, the question arises whether it is not sensible to prioritize certain areas of action. The main reasons for this suggestion are limited resources and the time pressure to succeed. Do all companies have the time to take a detailed look at their own value proposition in the first step of a business model transformation, or do they risk bankruptcy if costs continue to spiral out of control during this time? These and similar questions came up again and again in our workshops. Based on discussions with numerous managers, we propose a typology that describes the company's situation in the market and captures three different starting points (see Figure 3.9).

Risk of Bankruptcy In The Next 2 Years	Type A: High Risk of Bankruptcy	Type B: Low Risk of Bankruptcy	Type C: No Risk of Bankruptcy
Business fields at risk in the next 2 years	Many	Some	Few
Fluctuation in the workforce	Above-average	Average	Under-average
Competitive situation from customers' perspective	Poor	Medium	Good
Successful innovations of the last 2 years	Few	Some	Many
Risk of disruption from new competitors	High	Medium	Low

Figure 3.9: Three starting points for a business model transformation.

Type A companies face a high risk of bankruptcy in the next two years. They are in a very difficult situation, characterized by high staff turnover and a high risk of disruption. It is questionable whether a business transformation can be successful under these conditions, and there is a great deal of uncertainty. In the first phase of transformation, Type A companies need to focus on strict cost management and more efficient service delivery with regard to prioritizing the five key drivers. The goal is to reduce costs sustainably to ensure economic viability. Only then can the other key drivers be addressed. In the second phase, the focus is on service offerings. Companies must quickly realign their offerings, as several business areas are at stake. There is usually not enough time to drive innovation. The time pressure demands a strategy of observing competitors and copying their successful concepts as the best way to quickly develop new service offerings with high earnings potential. Ideally, in the third phase of a transformation, Type A companies can begin an orderly reorganization with a substantial value proposition and new earnings models. True to the motto "first secure your survival, then dare to make a new conceptual start," this requires turnaround management that radically challenges old beliefs and rapidly changes the corporate culture.

Depending on the precariousness of a Type A company's financial situation, painful measures may be necessary in the initial transformation phase. In severe cases, such as imminent or actual insolvency, decisive and radical action is the only option. The mantra here is: "Restructure, then transform." Cost reductions typically have a significant impact on profitability. Optimizing costs by one percentage point often improves profitability many times more than increasing revenue by the same amount. To reduce costs in the short term, companies can focus on operating costs. However, because cost structures vary widely from industry to industry and are highly dependent on the company itself, it is not possible to make universal recommendations.

Second, changes to a company's capital structure can help ensure its future viability. However, 'selling off the silverware' can only be a short-term measure to support other measures. However, divestments can only be made once. If necessary working capital or receivables are sold, this will result in an additional burden in the long term. It is therefore important to consider on a case-by-case basis whether divestitures will reduce fixed costs or contribute positively to the goal of raising new financial resources. Of course, in difficult restructuring situations, these considerations must give way to energetic pragmatism. If still available, Type A companies can release existing financial reserves. For most companies, this should be relatively straightforward and possible without negative consequences. In some cases, it may also make sense to factor long-term receivables to free up capital. In addition, assets such as real estate can be sold and then leased back (sale and leaseback). However, this is often at the expense of long-term profitability, as this arrangement must be worthwhile for the buyer of the assets. On the other hand, these assets are no longer depreciated and the cost of using them directly reduces the operating result, which can have tax advantages. Therefore, the appropriateness must be assessed on a case-by-case basis. Selling non-core businesses can also provide short-term relief. However, a well-founded fundamental decision must first be made as to what the company's future core business will be.

In all of this, it is essential that Type A companies use the success of cost-cutting measures to secure new financial resources from owners and financiers. This is important in order to gain enough time to reshape the company's future. Jörn Werner, a C level executive who has successfully led several companies through transformations, aptly describes this phase as "Fund the Journey". To be successful, owners, shareholders, investors, and lenders must gain new confidence in the company's future viability. This confidence comes from a compelling value proposition and a vision based on it. Thus, distressed companies must perform the balancing act of simultaneously reducing costs and developing a compelling, sustainable value proposition.

In contrast, **Type B** companies are not yet facing major economic difficulties. However, the medium-term risk of bankruptcy cannot be ignored. Some of the existing business fields are already being challenged and there is a risk of disruption from new competitors. The reduced time pressure allows a different prioritization of the key drivers. In one such situation, a company in one of our workshops reported that it had initially focused on new service offerings. By acquiring other companies and launching its own start-ups, the company was able to partially offset the risk of sales losses from weakening business areas. During this initial transformation phase, the company also focused on finding additional earnings sources and sharpening its value proposition. It was only in a second phase that the focus shifted to cost modeling and service delivery. These efforts did not involve radical cost reductions, but rather single-digit percentage cost reductions. In terms of service delivery, the company explored collaboration and outsourcing of supporting processes. Other companies in our workshops that fell into this second group took a slightly different approach. What they all had in common, however, was a much lower priority for strict cost management and the search for innovation on their own, which was made possible by their better economic situation.

Type C companies are not under pressure to act. The very good corporate culture, the many innovations of the past, and the good competitive situation do not create a sense of urgency. Instead, the company's good situation encourages management to maintain the status quo for as long as possible. There is also a lack of willingness among the workforce to support radical change. Accordingly, these companies find it difficult to initiate a transformation. One company reported an intensive review of its value proposition in the first phase. The goal of the project was to create a willingness to change. The company's image and the value proposition as perceived by customers were examined through extensive market research. The results significantly increased the willingness of employees to change. The company recognized a growing dissatisfaction among key customers, even though the figures were very good. This 'outside view' was the starting point for the second phase, in which the service offering was expanded. The focus was on expanding services and building an ecosystem with other providers. At the same time, the company changed its service delivery and earnings model. With the objective of offering certain services in partnership with other companies in the future, this prioritization triggered a realignment of many supply chain projects in the second transformation phase. From new services (e.g., subscription model), the company developed new earnings models that charged for services separately. The cost model was adapted only after the new service offerings had been developed. However, it is not possible to speak of a prioritization of the cost model in the third transformation phase. All Type C companies followed the maxim of adapting costs to service offerings and their delivery processes, not vice versa.

We have presented an ideal-typical approach to prioritization for three starting points. Of course, the typology presented is a simplification of reality. Not every company can be clearly assigned to a type, and not every prioritization can claim to be universally applicable. Therefore, we do not want to use the typology to present standard prioritization strategies, but rather to provide suggestions and ideas for finding a company-specific approach. Each company must find a prioritization that is appropriate to its specific circumstances and that best stabilizes profitability, motivates employees, and avoids management overload during a period of transformation.

Requirement 3

Alignment of All Activities to Ensure a Holistic Approach
The fit concept is used to assess configuration quality. Ackhof explains the basic idea of the concept with another example from the automotive industry. If you took the best parts from different manufacturers, such as the engine from BMW, the batteries from Tesla, and the seats from Mercedes, and put them together, the result would still be suboptimal because the parts would not fit together [57]. The coordination of the components, or the fit, plays a critical role in the performance of the vehicle. Doty, Glick, and Huber call for a maximum fit between context, structures, and strategy [58]. We try to put this literature reference into practice with our High 5 Approach to Business Model Transformation.

Porter also refers to the alignment of activities as activity fit [59]. He distinguishes between three different types of fit. With **first-order fit**, all activities contribute to a higher-level value proposition. For example, Ryanair's credo and value proposition is to offer the lowest possible fares. All of its activities are aligned with this goal, including online-only bookings, seat reservations for a fee, a limited number of flight attendants, and no free food or drinks because of cost reasons. **Second-order fit** occurs when activities complement each other. For example, the limited number of flight attendants is possible only because there are few tasks for them to perform on board. Demand for food and drinks for an additional charge is, for instance, low. Finally, **third-order fit** is achieved through information sharing between activities with the aim of becoming more effective. For example, Ryanair's connected database allows it to track demand for how many and what meals it serves and plan staffing levels accordingly. This helps to ensure that the right number of meals are carried, which helps to prevent excess inventory or waste and keeps prices low.

In the following section, we'll explore various business transformations, focusing on configurations that highlight the key orchestrating ideas of business model transformation.[86] In our High 5 Approach, the value proposition serves as the orchestrating idea. It embodies the driving force behind any successful business model transformation. All subsequent case studies follow this alignment logic in their basic structure. However, depending on the company's situation—from enjoying healthy returns to facing potential bankruptcy—the prioritization of these elements is critical and requires careful consideration. For a concise overview of our case studies, we will touch on prioritization only briefly.

3.5 Project Evaluation and Resource Planning[*]

When planning a transformation, companies generate many project ideas. These projects are intended to help drive the transformation in an effective and financially sustainable way. However, the goal of implementing large change projects as profitably as possible is often a huge challenge. This is due in part to the high cost of projects and the large number of project plans. Therefore, it is essential to evaluate project ideas based on their profitability and resource requirements. Projects with uncertain profitability should only be initiated if the company's financial situation allows it. In the case of companies with a high risk of bankruptcy (Type A), many of these project ideas should be canceled, while companies with a high equity ratio (Type C) can implement more projects.

Three key questions are at the forefront of project evaluation:
1. Do individual projects make economic sense? Can a positive capital value be achieved?
2. What are the capital requirements? Can the company afford the projects?
3. Does the company have the resources required to execute the projects?

The goal of project evaluation is to make an informed decision about whether to proceed with a project. In this chapter, we will explain the process of project evaluation using the fictional case study of Women's Wear.

Women's Wear is a clothing retailer with 100 stores in different cities and sales of 2.5 billion Swiss francs last year. Women's Wear is in crisis. The company is suffering from declining foot traffic in city centers, which has led to a massive drop in sales and severely impacted its liquidity. In addition, Women's Wear has invested in online sales in recent years, but the expected success has not yet materialized. The company is in crisis and faces insolvency in the medium term.

In order to secure the company's liquidity, Michael, the CEO, must initiate projects to save the company as quickly as possible. Corinne, the company's director of strategy, has worked with management to develop five projects that could help save the company. Women's Wear's finance department estimates that the company's liquidity will last for two years if Michael does not take action. These conditions must be taken into account when evaluating the five projects developed. At this point, Women's Wear cannot take on additional debt to finance the projects and will have to provide

[*]This chapter was written in collaboration with Nora Kralle (University of St. Gallen). We would also like to thank Dr. Philipp Dautzenberg for his suggestions.

the maximum 100 million Swiss francs from its already tight liquidity. Michael must now decide which of the five projects he will implement to lead Women's Wear out of its most serious corporate crisis to date.

Corinne presents Michael with the five projects. Three of the projects are aimed at reducing costs. The first project is to reduce labor costs by 10% by laying off some sales and corporate staff. The second project is for the company to renegotiate existing leases with landlords to reduce lease costs by 10%. A third project to cut costs is to close eight smaller stores. Corinne also proposes two projects that she hopes will increase sales. One is to optimize the online store. Although the company already has an online store, it is neither state-of-the-art nor integrated with other sales and marketing channels. Corinne sees this as the reason why Women's Wear has only achieved low sales online thus far. Finally, she suggests remodeling all the stores to increase sales. The last modernization took place many years ago and the store layout is very outdated.

The economic impact of these projects needs to be evaluated in line with their description. A number of financial metrics play an important role in this evaluation, which we describe below in Table 3.1 [60].

Table 3.1: Key Financial Metrics for Project Evaluation (source: Higgins, R. [2018]).

Metric	Description	Example
Top Line	Top line refers to total revenue, which is the amount a company earns from the sale of its products. The impact on the top line shows whether a project helps to maintain or increase sales.	Corinne predicts that in the first year after the project, Women's Wear will generate an additional CHF 40 million in gross profit by optimizing the online store, i.e., the top line will increase by CHF 40 million.
Gross Profit	Gross profit is the amount remaining after deducting the cost of goods sold from the total sales revenue. It is an indicator of the impact a project has on profitability.	The typical gross profit for women's apparel is 50%. An increase of CHF 40 million in top line by optimizing the online store therefore means an increase of CHF 20 million in gross profit in the first year.
Opex	Opex stands for 'operating expenses' and includes all expenses for running the business (e.g. rent, personnel, advertising). The impact of a project on operating expenses shows the extent to which the project affects the profitability of the business.	Corinne expects additional operating expenses of CHF 15 million over the next few years as a result of optimizing the online store (for IT, additional staff and logistics). Opex would therefore increase by CHF 15 million in future years.
Bottom Line	Bottom Line refers to the difference between gross profit and opex. It is an indicator of the impact of a project on profitability after deducting all the costs for purchasing goods and operating the business.	The online store optimization project would lead to an increase in the bottom line of CHF 5 million in the first year after implementation (additional gross profit of CHF 20 million less the additional opex of CHF 15 million).

Table 3.1 (continued)

Metric	Description	Example
Capex	Capex stands for 'capital expenditure' and refers to expenditures for investments. Capex for a project is typically incurred at the start of the project. This is the capital requirement for a project if it is immediately profitable (otherwise, start-up losses from opex must also be taken into account).	Corinne estimates an initial investment of CHF 20 million for the project, including software and logistics. This would immediately increase the capex by CHF 20 million. In the case of Women's Wear, the initial investment should not exceed CHF 100 million.
Free Cash Flow (FCF)	Free cash flow (FCF) is the cash flow after deducting all operating expenses and investments from the project's revenue. It is an important indicator of a company's financial health and shows how much money a company has available to repay debt, pay dividends or make further investments. The impact of a project on free cash flow indicates the extent to which a project affects liquidity.	The online store optimization project would today require Women's Wear to spend CHF 20 million. There would be no immediate additional income. The FCF for this project is therefore -20 million CHF today. In the following year, the company would earn an additional CHF 5 million after deducting all expenses, thus generating an additional FCF of CHF 5 million in the first year.
Discounted FCF	To calculate the discounted free cash flow (DCF), the expected future FCF is discounted to its present value. Discounting means converting the future value of monetary amounts to their present value. This is done to reflect the time value of money, as one Swiss franc today is worth more than one Swiss franc in the future. The discount rate depends on various factors, such as expected inflation or the risk of the investment.	Women's Wear uses a discount rate of 10%. The FCF of -20 million today does not need to be discounted because it will be paid out immediately. The FCF of 5 million Swiss francs is expected one year from now. Corinne discounts this amount using the 10% discount rate. The discounted FCF is then 4.55 million Swiss francs (5 million Swiss francs/(1 + 10%)).

Finally, the finance department calculates the capital value or net present value (NPV) of each project. The NPV is calculated by discounting all cash inflows and outflows for a project to their present value. Discounting takes into account the time value of money and the risk of the project. The time value of money means that one Swiss franc today is worth more than one Swiss franc a year from now because it can be invested today and earn a return tomorrow. The sum of the discounted free cash flow is the NPV.

$$NPV = -I_0 + \frac{FCF_1}{(1+i)} + \frac{FCF_2}{(1+i)^2}$$

This means:
- I_0 = Investment currently made for the project
- FCF_1 and FCF_2 = FCF generated by the project after one and two years respectively
- i = Discount factor

The NPV indicates whether a project is expected to generate positive or negative value for the company. A positive NPV means that a project is expected to generate more revenue than it costs over the assumed life of the project [61].

Project 1: To Reduce Personnel Costs

The first project is to reduce personnel costs by 10%. According to Corinne, there are currently too many people working in the physical stores, which is costly. There are also some jobs in logistics that are not strictly necessary. This project would not have a negative impact on sales. Last financial year, personnel costs amounted to CHF 375 million. A 10% reduction in personnel costs would result in annual savings of CHF 37.5 million (reduction in opex of CHF 37.5 million per year in years 1 and 2). However, this project requires the creation of a social plan and a one-time severance payment to the dismissed employees. The strategy department estimates the immediate costs at CHF 18.75 million (opex increase of CHF 18.75 million today).

It should be noted that the signs in Table 3.2 refer to the impact the position change has on FCF. Example: Today, opex increases by CHF 18.75 million, which has a negative impact on FCF of CHF −18.75 million. In years 1 and 2, opex decreases by CHF 37.5 million each year, which has a positive impact on FCF of CHF +37.5 million.

Table 3.2: Project 1: To Reduce Personnel Costs.

	Today	Year 1	Year 2	Total
Top Line	0	0	0	0
Gross Profit	0	0	0	0
Opex	−18,750,000	+37,500,000	+37,500,000	+56,250,000
Bottom Line	−18,750,000	+37,500,000	+37,500,000	+56,250,000
Capex	0	0	0	0
FCF	−18,750,000	+37,500,000	+37,500,000	+56,250,000
Discounted FCF	*−18,750,000*	*+34,090,909*	*+30,991,736*	**NPV = 46,332,645**

Project 2: To Reduce Rental Costs

Corinne Michael also suggests renegotiating leases to reduce rental costs. Women's Wear has a strong negotiating position because landlords may find it difficult to find a new tenant in certain locations. This project would result in legal fees of two million Swiss francs, which the company would have to pay immediately (an increase in opex of two million Swiss francs today). In the last financial year, rental costs amounted to 175 million Swiss francs. Corinne estimates that Women's Wear will be able to reduce its rental costs by 5% in the first year, or 8.75 million Swiss francs (a reduction in opex of 8.75 million Swiss francs in the first year). From the second year and in subsequent years, she even expects to be able to reduce rental costs by 10% through renegotiation. This corresponds to a saving of CHF 17.5 million (a reduction in opex of CHF 17.5 million in year 2; see Table 3.3).

Table 3.3: Project 2: To Reduce Rental Costs.

	Today	Year 1	Year 2	Total
Top Line	0	0	0	0
Gross Profit	0	0	0	0
Opex	−2,000,000	+8,750,000	+17,500,000	+24,250,000
Bottom Line	−2,000,000	+8,750,000	+17,500,000	+24,250,000
Capex	0	0	0	0
FCF	−2,000,000	+8,750,000	+17,500,000	+24,250,000
Discounted FCF	−2,000,000	+7,954,545	+14,462,810	NPV = 20,417,355

Project 3: To Close Branches

Next, Corinne suggests closing some stores. Specifically, eight small stores with low sales and high rental and personnel costs are considered. These eight stores had sales of 100 million Swiss francs in the last fiscal year. If they were closed immediately, this 100 million francs in sales would be lost starting the following year. Corinne expects that 40% of the lost sales from these eight stores, or 40 million Swiss francs, would be transferred to other Womens Wear stores or to the Womens Wear online store (leaving a top line reduction of 60 million Swiss francs in years 1 and 2). In her planning, she assumes the usual Women's Wear gross margin of 50% (with sales of 60 million, this means a reduction in profit margin of 30 million Swiss francs in years 1 and 2).

Corinne has already talked to the landlords. They are willing to release Women's Wear from the leases early as they are expiring anyway. This would eliminate CHF 17 million in rent and other building maintenance costs for the eight stores starting next year (a CHF 17 million annual reduction in opex in years 1 and 2). In return, Women's Wear would have to pay the landlords an advance of three months' rent. This would amount to CHF 1.75 million and would be due immediately (an increase in OPEX of CHF 1.75 million today).

In addition, staff in the stores to be closed would have to be laid off. Some head office positions would also be eliminated. The estimated savings in personnel costs is

CHF 20 million (a reduction in opex of CHF 20 million per year in years 1 and 2. In total, the reduction in opex due to the reduction in rental costs and personnel savings amounts to CHF 37 million). This requires a social plan and a one-time severance payment. Women's Wear would have to pay CHF 10 million for this today (an increase in opex of CHF 10 million today. Total opex decreases by CHF 27 million today). Table 3.4 summarizes the key financial figures for Project 3.

Table 3.4: Project 3: Branch Closures.

	Today	Year 1	Year 2	Total
Top Line	0	−60,000,000	−60,000,000	−120,000,000
Gross Profit	0	−30,000,000	−30,000,000	−60,000,000
Opex	−11,750,000	+37,000,000	+37,000,000	+62,250,000
Bottom Line	−11,750,000	+7,000,000	+7,000,000	+2,250,000
Capex	0	0	0	0
FCF	−11,750,000	+7,000,000	+7,000,000	+2,250,000
Discounted FCF	*−11,750,000*	*+6,363,636*	*+5,785,124*	**NPV = 398,760**

Project 4: To Optimize the Online Store

Women's Wear currently has an online store, but it generates only a small amount of sales. Corinne suggests a project to optimize the online store in order to increase online sales and strengthen the market position. This project requires an initial investment of 20 million Swiss francs (an increase in capex of 20 million Swiss francs today), mainly in software and logistics. Corinne expects the improved online store to generate additional sales of 40 million Swiss francs in the first year and 70 million Swiss francs in the second year after the start of the project (a top line increase of 40 million Swiss francs in year 1 and 70 million Swiss francs in year 2). It assumes the usual gross margin of 50% (an increase in gross profit of 20 million Swiss francs in year 1 and 35 million Swiss francs in year 2). It also anticipates additional ongoing costs for IT, additional personnel and logistics of 15 million Swiss francs in the following years (an increase in opex of 15 million Swiss francs in years 1 and 2). Table 3.5 summarizes the key financial figures for Project 4.

Project 5: To Remodel the Stores

The layout of the Women's Wear stores is very outdated and has not been updated in a long time. To become more attractive to customers, Corinne suggest modernizing the stores. The remodeling of the stores requires an initial investment of 100 million Swiss francs (an increase in capex of 100 million Swiss francs today). The 100 million

Table 3.5: Project 4: To Optimize the Online Store.

	Today	Year 1	Year 2	Total
Top Line	0	+40,000,000	+70,000,000	+110,000,000
Gross Profit	0	+20,000,000	+35,000,000	+55,000,000
Opex	0	−15,000,000	−15,000,000	−30,000,000
Bottom Line	0	+5,000,000	+20,000,000	+25,000,000
Capex	−20,000,000	0	0	0
FCF	−20,000,000	+5,000,000	+20,000,000	+5,000,000
Discounted FCF	−20,000,000	+4,545,455	+1,075,380	**NPV = 1,074,380**

francs can be used to refresh the layout of all stores and to renovate a few stores. Corinne expects the remodel to increase sales by 100 million Swiss francs after the first year, as it will take twelve months to remodel the stores (a top line increase of 100 million Swiss francs in year 2). There will be no increase or decrease in sales during the remodeling period. It assumes the usual gross profit of 50% (an increase in gross profit of CHF 50 million in year 2). The increase in sales can also be achieved because a major competitor has filed for bankruptcy. Table 3.6 summarizes the key financial figures for Project 5.

Table 3.6: Project 5: To Remodel the Stores.

	Today	Year 1	Year 2	Total
Top Line	0	0	+100,000,000	+100,000,000
Gross Profit	0	0	+50,000,000	+50,000,000
Opex	0	0	0	0
Bottom Line	0	0	+50,000,000	+50,000,000
Capex	−100,000,000	0	0	−100,000,000
FCF	−100,000,000	0	+50,000,000	−50,000,000
Discounted FCF	−100,000,000	0	+41,322,314	**NPV = −58,677,686**

To decide which projects Women's Wear should pursue, Corinne and Michael answer the three questions we introduced at the beginning of this chapter.

1. Do the individual projects make economic sense, and can a positive capital valuebe achieved?
Table 3.7 below summarizes the results of the NPV analysis for each of the five projects.

Since Project 5, the store remodeling, has a negative NPV for a project duration of two years, Michael decides against the project. However, the remaining projects, 1

Table 3.7: Results of the NPV analysis for each of the five projects.

	Project 1 (Reduce Personnel Costs)	Project 2 (Reduce Rental Costs)	Project 3 (Close Stores)	Project 4 (Expand the Online Store)	Project 5 (Remodel the Stores)
NPV	+46,332,645	+20,417,355	+398,760	+1,074,380	−58,677,686

through 4, are all projected to have positive NPVs over a two-year period and would therefore make good business sense.

It is important to note that the abbreviated two-year observation period in this case study is simplified for the reader's understanding. In reality, a longer multi-year analysis would be helpful. In addition to our NPV analysis, good liquidity planning is required to avoid potential bankruptcy in the next 24 months. Due to space limitations, these considerations were not addressed in this case study. However, they should be taken into account when evaluating projects in practice.

2. How much capital is required to implement the projects and can we afford it?
Table 3.8 below shows the capital requirements (capex) at the start of the five projects.

Table 3.8: Capital requirements at the start of the projects.

	Project 1 (Reduce Personnel Costs)	Project 2 (Reduce Rental Costs)	Project 3 (Close Stores)	Project 4 (Expand the Online Store)	Project 5 (Remodel the Stores)
Capex	−18,750,000	−2,000,000	−11,750,000	−20,000,000	−100,000,000

In total, the company needs 52.5 million Swiss francs in capex and opex (Projects 1–3) to implement the remaining four projects (Projects 1–4). Woman's Wear currently has an investment capacity of 100 million Swiss francs, so Projects 1–4 would be financially feasible.

3. Does the Company Have the Resources Required to Carry out the Projects?
In addition to the financial impact of the remaining four projects, Michael needs to assess whether these four projects can be supported with existing resources. In particular, he needs to consider IT and human resources. Many companies have difficulty finding sufficient staff, especially in IT. There are few specialists available on the job market, and existing IT departments are often overburdened and have little time for new projects. Table 3.9 compares the required IT and human resources of the four projects.

Table 3.9: Summary of the IT and human resources requirements.

	Project 1 (Reduce Personnel Costs)	Project 2 (Reduce Rental Costs)	Project 3 (Close Stores)	Project 4 (Expand the Online Store)
HR	No additional resources required	A lawyer is needed for the project	No additional resources required	40 programmers (CHF 200,000/year), 35 marketing FTEs (CHF 100,000/year), 35 logistics FTEs (CHF 100,000/year)
IT	No additional resources required	No additional resources required	No additional resources required	Additional servers as well as software

Corinne and Michael decide that projects one and three are feasible without additional resources. Project two requires a lawyer to renegotiate all the leases. Women's Wear has a long-standing relationship with a large law firm for such cases. Project four, the online shop, requires additional resources. The current labor market situation makes it unlikely that 40 programmers can be hired. This results in a bottleneck. The project is therefore not immediately feasible. Michael decides to put the project on hold for a year and to reassess its feasibility then. He could outsource the programming if necessary, but this would be more expensive.

The Bottom Line

The sample calculation presented concludes that, due to the current financial constraints, only projects one and three can be implemented immediately. While the 'Reduce Personnel Costs' and 'Close Stores' projects will provide some relief, they won't address the company's underlying strategic issues. In order to initiate a period of sustainable growth, the management has therefore decided to spend the next six months concretizing the company's value proposition and sharpening its overall profile.

References

[1]   See Burmann, C. (2002), "Strategische Flexibilität und Strategiewechsel als Determinanten des Unternehmenswertes" (Strategic Flexibility and Strategy Change as Determinants of Company Value), in: "neue betriebswirtschaftliche forschung" (new business management research), Vol. 292, Gabler Verlag, p. 100 ff.

[2]   See Machiavelli (2004), The Prince, Simon & Schuster, New York, NY.

[3]   See Levie, J./Lichtenstein, B. (2010), A Terminal Assessment of Stages Theory: Introducing a Dynamic States Approach to Entrepreneurship, in: Entrepreneurship Theory and Practice, Vol. 34 (2), pp. 317–350.

[4] See Cavalcante, S./Kesting, P./Ulhøi, J. (2011), Business model dynamics and innovation: (re) establishing the missing linkages, in: Management Decision, Vol. 49 (8), pp. 1327–1342.

[5] See Bieger, T./Reinhold, S. (2011), "Das wertbasierte Geschäftsmodell – Ein aktualisierter Strukturierungsansatz" (The Value-Based Business Model – An Updated Approach to Structuring), in: T. Bieger, D. zu Knyphausen-Aufseß/Krys (eds.), "Innovative Geschäftsmodelle" (Innovative Business Models), SpringerVerlag Berlin, Heidelberg.

[6] See Safaric, A. (2017), "Geschäftsmodelltransformation im Kontext von Cross-Channel Management" (Business Model Transformation in the Context of Cross-Channel Management), Dissertation at the University of St. Gallen.

[7] See Müller-Stewens, G./Fontin, M. (2003), "Die Innovation des Geschäftsmodells – der unterschätzte vierte Weg" (Business Model Innovation – The Underrated Fourth Way), in: Frankfurter Allgemeine Zeitung, p. 18, Frankfurt.

[8] See Schumpeter, J. A. (1934), The theory of economic development: an inquiry into profits, capital, credit, interest and the business cycle, London, Oxford University Press.

[9] See Drucker, P. F. (1954), The practice of management, New York, Harper and Row.

[10] See Markides, C. (2008), Game-changing strategies: how to create new market space in established industries by breaking the rules, San Francisco, Jossey-Bass.

[11] See Casadesus-Masanell, R./Ricart, J. E. (2010), From Strategy to Business Models and onto Tactics, Long Range Planning, Vol. 43 (2–3), pp. 195–215.

[12] A detailed overview is provided by Safaric (2017), "Geschäftsmodelltransformation im Kontext von Cross-Channel Management" (Business Model Transformation in the Context of Cross-Channel Management), dissertation no. 4623 at the University of St.Gallen, Difo-Druck GmbH, Bamberg, Germany, 2017.

[13] See Amit, R./Zott, C. (2001), Value creation in E-business, Strategic Management Journal, Vol. 22 (6–7), pp. 493–520.

[14] See Magretta, J. (2002), Why Business Models Matter, Harvard Business Review, Vol. 80 (5), pp. 86–92.

[15] See Rudolph, T./Loock, M./Kleinschrodt, A. (2008), "Strategisches Handelsmanagement – Grundlagen für den Erfolg auf internationalen Handelsmärkten" (Strategic Trade Management – Basics for Success in International Trade Markets), in: "St.Galler Schriften zum Handelsmanagement" (St. Gallen Publications on Trade Management), Volume 1, p. 59.

[16] Sourced and abridged from: Safaric, A. (2017), p. 80. Already cited in the text above.

[17] See Sorescu, A./Frambach, R. T./ Singh, J./Rangaswamy, A./Bridges, C. (2011), Innovations in Retail Business Models, in: Journal of Retailing, Vol. 87 (1), p. 5.

[18] See Teece, D. J. (2007), Explicating dynamic capabilities: the nature and microfoundations of (sustainable) enterprise performance, in: Strategic Management Journal, Vol. 28 (13), p. 1325.

[19] See Casadesus-Masanell, R./Ricart, J. E. (2010), From Strategy to Business Models and onto Tactics, in: Long Range Planning, 43(2–3), p. 2002.

[20] See Müller-Stewens, G./Lechner, C. (2011), "Strategisches Management" (Strategic Management). "Wie strategische Initiativen zum Wandel führen" (How Strategic Initiatives Lead to Change), Schäffer-Poeschel Verlag, Stuttgart, 4th Edition, p. 388 ff.

[21] See Zott, C./Amit, R. (2010), Business Model Design: An Activity System Perspective, in: Long Range Planning, Vol. 43(2–3), p. 217.

[22] See ibid. pp. 217.

[23] Breuer, S. (2004), "Beschreibung von Geschäftsmodellen internetbasierter Unternehmen. Konzeption – Umsetzung – Anwendung" (Description of Business Models for Internet Based Companies. Design – Implementation – Application). Bamberg: Difo-Druck, p.15.

[24] In the following, we refer to five key drivers that Alexander Safaric, a former doctoral student at our research center, developed from the literature in his thesis. See Safaric, A. (2017),

"Geschäftsmodelltransformation im Kontext von Cross-Channel Management" (Business Model Transformation in the Context of Cross-Channel Management). Specific tasks have been identified for these five key drivers. Our resulting High 5 Approach provides a concrete framework for management action.

[25] See footnote 24.

[26] See Johnson, M. W./Christensen, C. M./Kagermann, H. (2008), Reinventing your business model, in: Harvard Business Review, Vol. 86 (12), pp. 54.

[27] See Müller-Stewens, G./Lechner, C. (2011), "Strategisches Management" (Strategic Management). "Wie strategische Initiativen zum Wandel führen" (How Strategic Initiatives Lead to Change), Schäffer-Poeschel Verlag, Stuttgart, 4th Edition, p. 376 ff.

[28] Vershofen argues that corporate social responsibility and sustainable resource usage do not necessarily translate directly into societal benefit. Rather, they contribute to another form of emotional value for the buyer. This, in turn, can enhance the buyer's social standing and recognition within their social circle, positioning them as a conscious consumer contributing to a greater good. See Vershofen, Wilhelm, in: "Handbuch der Verbrauchsforschung" (Consumer Research Handbook), Berlin 1940.

[29] See Johnson, M. W./Christensen, C. M./Kagermann, H. (2008). Reinventing your business model, in: Harvard Business Review, Vol. 86 (12), p. 52.

[30] See Müller-Stewens, G./Lechner, C. (2011), "Strategisches Management" (Strategic Management). "Wie strategische Initiativen zum Wandel führen" (How Strategic Initiatives Lead to Change), Schäffer-Poeschel Verlag, Stuttgart, 4th Edition, p. 376 ff.

[31] See Rudolph 2016, paper presented at the "2016 St. Galler Handelstag" 2016 (St. Gallen Trade Congress) on disruption in trade based on a survey of 170 managers from different sectors.

[32] See Richardson, J. (2008), The business model: an integrative framework for strategy execution, in: Strategic Change, Vol. 17 (5–6), p. 139.

[33] Chatterje distinguishes between core, support, and peripheral activities. Since the core idea is a distinction between important and less important, we simplify this typology to just two categories. See Chatterjee, S. (2013), Simple Rules for Designing Business Models, in: California Management Review, Vol. 55(2), pp. 97–124.

[34] See Neslin, S. A./Grewal, D./Leghorn, R./Shankar, V./Teerling, M. L./Thomas, J. S./Verhoef, P. C. (2006), Challenges and Opportunities in Multichannel Customer Management, in: Journal of Service Research, Vol. 9 (2), pp. 95–112.

[35] See Zott, C./Amit, R. (2010), Business Model Design: An Activity System Perspective, in: Long Range Planning, Vol. 43 (2–3), pp. 216 ff.

[36] See Rudolph 2016, paper presented at the "2016 St. Galler Handelstag" 2016 (St. Gallen Trade Congress) on disruption in trade based on a survey of 170 managers from different sectors.

[37] See Müller-Stewens, G./Lechner, C. (2011), "Strategisches Management" (Strategic Management). "Wie strategische Initiativen zum Wandel führen" (How Strategic Initiatives Lead to Change), Schäffer-Poeschel Verlag, Stuttgart, 4th Edition, p. 395 ff.

[38] See Chesbrough, H./Rosenbloom, R. S. (2002), The role of the business model in capturing value from innovation: evidence from Xerox Corporation's technology spin-off companies, in: Industrial and Corporate Change, Vol. 11(3), pp. 535.

[39] See Osterwalder, A./Pigneur, Y. (2010), Business Model Generation: A Handbook for Visionaries, Game Changers, and Challengers, Hoboken, New Jersey, John Wiley & Sons, p. 5 ff.

[40] See Heracleous, L./Wirtz, J. (2012), Strategy and organisation at Singapore Airlines: achieving sustainable advantage through dual strategy. In: Energy, Transport, & the Environment, pp. 479–493. Springer, London.

[41] See Heracleous, L. T./Wirtz, J./Pangarkar, N. (2006), Flying high in a competitive industry: cost-effective service excellence at Singapore Airlines, McGraw-Hill.

[42] See Jansen, J. (2018), "Zalando ersetzt Mitarbeiter durch Algorithmen" (Zalando Swaps Employees for Algorithms), in: FAZ, No. 58, p. 24.

[43] See Sorescu, A./Frambach, R. T./ Singh, J./Rangaswamy, A./Bridges, C. (2011), Innovations in Retail Business Models, in: Journal of Retailing, Vol. 87(1), pp. 4.

[44] See Imre, M. (April 19, 2018): Amazon reports figures for the first time: More than 100 million Prime customers, handelsblatt.com, retrieved from: http://www.handelsblatt.com/unternehmen/handel-konsumgueter/aktionaersbrief-von-jeff-bezos-amazon-nennt-erstmals-zahlen-mehr-als-100-mil lionen-prime-kunden/21190388.html (in German only)

[45] See Markman, J. (May 23, 2017), The Amazon Era: No Profits, No Problem, Forbes.com, retrieved from: https://www.forbes.com/sites/jonmarkman/2017/05/23/the-amazon-era-no-profits-no-prob lem/#1d7b2f6b437a.

[46] See Morris, M./Schindehutte, M./Allen, J. (2005), The entrepreneur's business model: toward a unified perspective, in: Journal of Business Research, Vol. 58 (6), pp. 726–735.

[47] See Carr, A. (2011). Hulu Courts Buyers, While Netflix Streaming Surges, retrieved from https://www.fastcompany.com/1765434/hulu-courts-buyers-while-netflix-streaming-surges.

[48] See n.a., "Wenn die Versicherung von der Bank kommt" (When the Insurance Comes From the Bank), in: FAZ, No. 21, 2018-01-25, p. 23.

[49] Abdollahi, G./Leimstoll, U. (2011), A Classification for Business Model Types in E-commerce, in: AMCIS.

[50] See n.a. (2018), "Wir bewegen 20 Millionen vernetzte Fahrzeuge" (We Move 20 Million Connected Vehicles), in: FAZ, No. 67, p. 24.

[51] Cited from: Miller, D. (1996), Configurations Revisited, in: Strategic Management Journal, Vol. 17 (7), p. 509.

[52] See Vester, F (1999), "Die Kunst vernetzt zu denken – Ideen und Werkzeuge für einen neuen Umgang mit Komplexität, Der neue Bericht an den Club of Rome" (The Art of Networked Thinking – Ideas and Tools for a New Approach to Complexity, the New Report to the Club of Rome), DVA and dtv, Munich, 1st Edition.

[53] See Ackoff, R.L. (1994), Systems Thinking and Thinking Systems, in: System Dynamics Review, Vol. 10 (2–3) Summer – Autumn (Fall), pp. 175 ff.

[54] See Kumar, A./Sharma, R.(2000), Principles of Business Management, New Dehli.

[55] See Van de Ven, A./Drazin, R (1984), The Concept of Fit in Contingency Theory, Discussion Paper 19, Minnesota.

[56] See Mintzberg/H. Ahlstrand, B./Lampel, J. (1998), Strategy Safari – A guided Tour through the Wilds of Strategic Management, The free Press New York.

[57] See Ackoff, R.L. (1994), Systems Thinking and Thinking Systems, in: System Dynamics Review, Vol. 10 (2–3) Summer – Autumn (Fall), pp. 175 ff.

[58] See Doty, H./Glick, W./Huber, G.P. (1993), Fit, Equifinality and Organizational Effectiveness: A Test of Two Configurational Theories, in: Academy of Management, Vol. 36 (6), pp. 1196–1250.

[59] See Porter, M.E. (1996), What is Strategy?, in: Harvard Business Review, Nov/Dec, pp. 61–78.

[60] See Higgins, R. (2018), Analysis for Financial Management, McGraw Hill.

[61] See Volkart, R. (2011), "Corporate Finance – Grundlagen von Finanzierung und Investition" (Corporate Finance – Principles of Financing and Investment), Versus Verlag, Zurich.

4 Case Studies in Transformation

How does the High 5 Approach work in practice? Many publications on digital disruption mention the same companies: Amazon, Tesla, Airbnb, Uber and young start-ups from the Silicon Valley scene. However, established companies have limited ability to learn effectively from these game changers. They often hastily introduce idea labs, flat hierarchies, foosball tables in the cafeteria, or informal language in an attempt to replicate the success of Silicon Valley companies. But these isolated measures are usually extraneous and have little effect.

Instead, transformation requires a self-contained ecosystem. All five Key Drivers outlined in the High 5 Approach must be addressed in a comprehensive and coordinated manner, with a high degree of compatibility between them. While successful disruptors may seem like attractive benchmarks, their unique culture, structure, and processes operate in a completely different context, often without a long history, and make them unsuitable for comparison. Established companies should therefore look more often to the 'old economy' for benchmarks. In our case studies, we have given disproportionate weight to this type of company in order to provide a comprehensive overview.

Examples from different industries ensure a broad overview. They show how companies have addressed the five key drivers and which levers have led to success or failure. The goal of these case studies is to inspire and demonstrate different paths to transformation.

We have divided our case studies into three groups. Group 1: This group includes SHOULDICE and Flixbus, two companies that revolutionized their industries at different times by following the core principles of our High 5 Approach. Their success came from breaking new ground in all five key drivers. These cases illustrate the key elements of a business model that is superior to the competition and how to build one.

Group 2: This group features companies that have successfully transformed their business models. Many faced significant challenges during their transformation process, which we outline at the beginning of each case study. Following these challenges, we provide a concise description of the holistic High 5 Approach used in each case. Case descriptions from a variety of industries offer practical tips for implementing our approach.

Group 3: This group focuses on companies that failed in their transformations. These case studies provide a concise overview of their mistakes. In some cases, there was a lack of management commitment, and often there was poor coordination between the key drivers. In particular, many companies in this group failed to leverage an appropriate value proposition for their transformation. Accordingly, we value the

---

Note: The corresponding references can be found at the end of each case study.

https://doi.org/10.1515/9783110772111-004

learning opportunities offered by these cases, as even experienced managers can gain valuable insights from the mistakes of others.

4.1 Disruptive Industry Changes

Flixbus

Background and Objectives of the Case Study

How can a start-up secure a monopoly in an industry in less than five years? You might say it's impossible. But that is exactly what Flixbus has done. In 2018, the company achieved a market share of more than 90% in the long-distance coach market, and it was only launched in 2013. The success story began with a reform of the German Public Transportation Act (PBefG), which removed competition protection for the railroads. Since January 1, 2013, companies have been able to offer intercity coach services.

The main reason for this meteoric rise was and still is the price. Flixbus prices are extremely competitive compared to the railways and other coach companies. The average ticket costs only €10–20, even for coach trips lasting several hours. Customers have to pay considerably more for the good old railroad. Economically minded readers might say that such dumping prices are unsustainable in the long run and that it will not take long before bankruptcy comes 'a knockin' at the door. After all, the rules of simple cost accounting dictate that a company must cover its costs in order to survive. And even though Flixbus as a whole is not yet profitable, investors are still lining up because they believe the company will eventually break even and make a breakthrough. This attitude is highlighted by the investment round of $650 million US from June 2021. In the meantime, Flixbus is now valued at more than $3 billion US [1]. So where does this confidence come from? The answer comes from Managing Director Jochen Engert, who says: "The way we operate is fundamentally different from established transport companies". Flixbus does not own any buses. Instead, it works with small and medium-sized coach companies. The Munich-based company only develops timetables and service standards and handles online sales.

This strategy helped Flixbus attract more than 62 million passengers in more than 36 countries in 2019 before the COVID-19 pandemic. The company is also diversifying its services with the launch of Flixtrain, a long-distance train service. Expansion in the US received a strong boost with the acquisition of the heritage US brand Greyhound in 2021, with its 2,400 destinations and 16 million passengers annually. Flixbus went from number two to quasi-monopolist in the USA in one fell swoop [2]. The company, which now trades as FlixMobility GmbH, has disrupted the long-distance coach market. This case study explains how this happened.

Value Proposition

Flixbus describes itself as a unique combination of technology start-up, Internet company, and traditional transportation company. The company's value proposition underlines its competitive advantage: It can be found on the company website and reads: "We offer millions of travelers the opportunity to discover the world for less money, thanks to easy booking and a range of services that is growing every day" (see Table 4.1). Flixbus' green long-distance buses and trains offer an environmentally friendly and convenient alternative to private transportation and meet the highest comfort, safety and environmental standards [3]. In line with our chapter on value proposition, Flixbus excels in all three dimensions. Beyond the attractive price (functional benefit), the company cultivates an emotional green image (emotional benefit) and also prioritizes environmental responsibility (social benefit), and by doing so explicitly addresses social issues (social benefit). The value proposition inspires customers and guides employees, including those who work for subcontractors. This can significantly increase the brand value.

Table 4.1: Transformation of the Flixbus business model.

Value Proposition			
We offer travelers the opportunity to discover the world for less money.			
Service Delivery	**Service Offering**	**Cost Model**	**Earnings Model**
IT platform for booking transportation services with more than 3,000 buses and a few trains	Nationwide transportation at rock-bottom prices between major cities in Europe and North America	No-frills approach: Flixbus focuses on marketing city to city connections through a modern IT infrastructure	Dynamic pricing model for optimal coach utilization
Partnership with over than 500 regional coach companies	Comfortable coaches with on-board toilets and snack and beverage vending, free WLAN	Mileage-based reimbursement of travel costs to coach companies prevents unplanned cost overruns	Attractive commission model for affiliated coach operators and travel agencies
Environmental leadership through the introduction of electric buses	Attractive entertainment program		New income sources for express package delivery and package rental buses
Technologically mature delay management system	Convenient booking through app, website or travel agent.	Low fixed costs for IT and marketing personnel guarantee low ticket prices.	
	Information about delays, the location of coach stops, and the times of the next departures		Innovative service ideas that generate additional income

Service Offering

Disruption can succeed when incumbents fail to take a new business idea seriously. This was the case with Flixbus. With the deregulation of its rail monopoly, Deutsche Bahn (DB) showed little interest in entering the long-distance coach market. Although a number of competitors were interested in the new market segment, Flixbus prevailed after less than three years. This was primarily due to the company's compelling service offering. The most important argument was price. An example serves to illustrate this: A 2018 comparison by the car and transport portal Stau.info found that the price difference between sixteen return trips between Flixtrain and DB was 75% in favor of Flixtrain. Customers paid an average of €70.78 for a train trip, compared to just €17.42 for a Flixtrain trip [4]. The price difference between coach travel with Flixbus and rail travel was between 30% and 50% in favor of Flixbus [5].

The price advantage allowed Flixbus to quickly gain market share and build a comprehensive transportation network across Europe. The company also offered other value-added services such as comfortable coaches, free Wi-Fi, snacks, three items of luggage, and an easy booking process through its own app. Passengers also received reliable information about delays, departure times, and upcoming stops. Another competitive advantage was the development of a comprehensive entertainment program that offered passengers a wide range of series and movies to watch during their journey. If you can watch a movie during the journey, it's better to travel with Flixbus. This was particularly attractive to price-sensitive customer segments such as schoolchildren, young families, senior citizens, and singles.

Service Delivery

The performance of Flixbus is primarily due to the disruptive effect of its new business idea. The innovative concept is based on close cooperation between existing coach operators and a technology-savvy network developer. This allows Flixbus to bundle existing operators into a marketplace and market them with a compelling added value. The name Flixbus serves as a brand umbrella for many coach operators working together to create a nationwide transportation network in German-speaking countries. More than 500 local, medium-sized coach operators around the world provide the transport. Flixbus itself develops the network, organizes operations and handles bookings. Technology plays an important role in this.

With technological innovations such as the FlixBus app—a modern booking and ticketing system—the company has established a booking platform for more than 3,000 long-distance coaches and the first trains. In 2021, the first FlixTrains started running in Sweden, the first country after Germany. Through this platform, the connected coach operators can achieve a level of capacity utilization that a single operator cannot achieve. For FlixTrain's long-distance trains, the company cooperates with private train operators in Europe.

Free Wi-Fi for passengers and live GPS tracking enable automated delay management, which the competition on the railways cannot offer with the current forecasting quality. Dynamic pricing is also based on technological know-how. Prices are adjusted according to capacity utilization. Dynamic pricing also makes it possible to achieve profitability targets. As a further technological innovation, FlixMobility GmbH, together with Freudenberg and ZF, is planning to build Europe's first green long-distance coach with a fuel cell drive, which will be on the roads by 2024 [6].

Cost Model

The network concept, combined with the principle that each player in the network should focus on its core competencies, creates a significant cost advantage. For cost reasons, it was advantageous to leave transportation to experienced coach operators instead of building up this expertise at great expense. As mentioned above, this task is performed by medium-sized coach operators, which are also responsible for the maintenance of the buses. Although this is the largest cost item in Flixbus' income statement, the cost of transport is unrivaled. This is due to the low base prices. The following figures illustrate this: Flixbus pays 74% of ticket sales revenue to cooperating subcontractors in the form of a commission. The company keeps 26% for itself [7]. As small and medium-sized operators are dependent on cost-covering remuneration, Flixbus guarantees coach companies a remuneration of €1.10 per kilometer driven. If the minimum compensation of €1,100 for a 1,000-kilometer route is not collected through ticket sales, Flixbus grants the partner company a liquidity loan. This avoids financial bottlenecks for the subcontractor and does not cause any direct expenses for Flixbus, as the liquidity loan is reduced by the surplus if ticket sales increase at a later date.

The miles driven determine the transfer price. The actual travel time between two locations does not seem to play a role in the remuneration concept applicable in 2018. Long traffic jams are therefore borne by the coach operators companies and do not lead to negative surprises in the cost accounting, at least for Flixbus. However, the flat rate per mile should enable both sides—the coach operators and Flixbus—to make a viable living. This depends crucially on capacity utilization and pricing policy. Flixbus can influence the latter two factors through its centrally controlled marketing efforts, which means that the viability of the overall system is in its own hands.

Flixbus does not employ coach drivers, workshop staff, or call center staff. Flixbus' personnel costs are mainly for marketing and IT tasks. FlixMobility GmbH now has around 3,000 employees worldwide, in contrast to 10,000 drivers [8]. Fixed costs are correspondingly low in relation to the number of employees.

The stronger the Flixbus brand, the more customers are interested in the service. The company's high level of digitalization allows it to exploit economies of scale in marketing as it becomes better known. The digital marketplace for passenger transportation really comes into its own with its low transaction costs in mediating between supply and demand as its size, or 'traffic,' increases. This is due in part to direct sales without intermediaries, fully automated ticket sales, and low-cost social media activities.[1] Bloggers receive free tickets in exchange for posting about their experiences.

Earnings Model

Ticket sales are the main source of revenue. Profitability depends primarily on the design of the dynamic pricing model. As with rail or airline ticket sales, this model aims to create the lowest possible fare impression while still covering costs. To do this, prices are constantly adjusted, with the highest prices usually charged for remaining seats just before departure. For example, the first passenger pays only €9.90, while the last-minute customer pays €49.90. So far, Flixbus has not been able to cover its costs with the average price. From the founders' point of view, the goal of market penetration is still clearly ahead of the goal of running a profitable company. This attitude is made possible by investors, who agree with, and even demand, the prioritization of growth over profitability.

Flixcharter is another service, mainly used by travel groups, associations and clubs, that has generated very little revenue so far. The service's advantage over traditional coach companies could be its price, but this has not yet been clearly established. FlixMobility GmbH has entered the carpooling market with Flixcar, which is currently limited to France.

The extent to which the sale of snacks and drinks will be a profitable source of revenue remains to be seen. The company is certainly trying to attract customers with other services, such as a choice of better seats with more reclining function or table trays for computers. The introduction of an annual fee that includes certain services such as complimentary drinks, seat reservations or the latest movies could also help improve profitability.

The earnings model, with its various income sources, is still in its early stages of development. As the profitability target becomes more important and the growth targets become smaller, the earnings model will offer further potential for optimization.

The Bottom Line

Flixbus has not only opened up a new travel segment with its long-distance coach travel, but has also disrupted the passenger transport sector with more than 100 million passengers. Established players in other transport sectors, such as rail and air, have been hit hard and are responding by cutting prices. The trend of falling transportation prices

---

1 This accounts for over 90% of sales. The remaining 10% is sold through travel agencies, at bus stations or on the coach.

makes it more difficult for Flixbus to break even. The future remains uncertain and depends largely on the company's ability to seize new opportunities in an innovative way for the benefit of its many regular customers.

References

[1]   See Flixbus (2021), FlixMobility raises over $650M in Funding at $3B Valuation planning further global expansion, in: Flixbus website, 2021-06-02, https://corporate.flixbus.com/flixmobility-raises-over-650m-in-funding-at--3b-valuation-planning-further-global-expansion/.
[2]   See Flixbus (2021), FlixMobility acquires Greyhound to Expand US Intercity Bus Services, in: Flixbus website, 2021-10-21, https://corporate.flixbus.com/flixmobility-acquires-greyhound-to-expand-us-intercity-bus-services/.
[3]   See Flixbus (2021), "Klimaneutral reisen? Mit FlixBus und FlixTrain geht das!" (Climate-Neutral Travel? Flixbus and Flixtrain Make It Possible), in: Flixbus website, 2021-12-03, https://www.flixbus.de/unternehmen/umwelt (in German only).
[4]   See Heiniger, B. (2018), "Flixbus startet mit Kampfpreisen auf der Schiene" (Flixbus Launches Predatory Priced Rail Services), in: Handelszeitung, 2018-03-23, https://www.handelszeitung.ch/unternehmen/flixbus-startet-mit-kampfpreisen-auf-der-schiene (in German only).
[5]   See Weimer, M. (2017), "Ich habe lieber Flixbus als einen Doktortitel" (I'd Rather Have Flixbus Than a Doctorate), in: Gründerszene, 2017-02-21, https://www.gruenderszene.de/allgemein/flixbus-vier-jahre-schwaemlein-interview/2 (in German only).
[6]   See Flixbus (2021), HyFleet: FlixMobility, Freudenberg and ZF to build Europe´s first green hydrogen long distance bus, in: Flixbus-Website, 2021-11-10, https://corporate.flixbus.com/--hyfleet-flixmobility-freudenberg-and-zf-to-build-europes-first-green-hydrogen-long-distance-bus-/.
[7]   See Herbstreith, A. (2017), "FLIXBUS – DAS GESCHÄFTSMODELL DES FERNBUSGIGANTEN IM DETAIL" (THE LONG-DISTANCE COACH GIANT'S BUSINESS MODEL IN DETAIL), in: E-Business, 2017-05-10, https://ebusiness2020.wordpress.com/2017/05/10/flixbus-das-geschaeftsmodell-des-fernbusgiganten-im-detail/ (in Germany only).
[8]   See Götz, S. (2021), "Das grüne Imperium" (The Green Empire), in: Die Zeit, 2021-11-08, https://www.zeit.de/mobilitaet/2021-11/flixbus-preis-tickets-konkurrenz-busfahrt-expansion-europa-greyhound/komplettansicht (in German only).

SHOULDICE

Background and Objectives of the Case Study

SHOULDICE Hospital is a clinic in Toronto that has performed only hernia surgery since its founding in 1945 by physician Earle Shouldice [1]. From the beginning, and especially during its heyday in the late 20th century, it has revolutionized the market for hernia surgery in Canada, despite generating only single-digit millions in revenue. Patients can return to work as early as one week after surgery, while other clinics often require two weeks of recovery. The quality of the surgery is very high: only 1% of patients need to have another hernia operation later; other clinics have a recurrence rate of 10%. The costs are also surprisingly low: they are 50% lower per patient and procedure than the industry average. The staff is also very satisfied, with almost no turnover. Marketing expenditures were zero for a long time, as the company had good reason to fear that it would not be able to meet the demand that a successful marketing campaign would generate [2].

Too good to be true? No, but an example of the success that small businesses can achieve when they follow their own path with consistency, focus and innovation. SHOULDICE intuitively built a business model decades ago that has many disruptive features. The case study shows that cost leadership and quality leadership need not be mutually exclusive. In fact, many other disruptive business models resolve this contradiction.

This analysis refers to SHOULDICE's heyday, which occurred before the turn of the millennium. After that, new legislation for private clinics came into effect in Canada, and the founder's son reached retirement age. In 2012, the family sold the company to a hospital operator [3].

Value Proposition

SHOULDICE promises its patients that they can return to work just one week after their hernia surgery. The medical basis for this is a unique surgical technique developed by founder Edward Earle Shouldice that allows for a quick and complication-free recovery. In addition, patients receive professional care and preferential treatment. They walk away from the operating table without assistance and then relax in the atmosphere of a resort for another three days where they can play billiards, table shuffleboard or minigolf or go the solarium. The SHOULDICE team consists of twelve full-time and seven part-time surgeons, one anesthesiologist and 40 nurses. The team can perform up to 36 surgeries per day, and up to 8,000 patients are operated on each year. Table 4.2 shows SHOULDICE's value proposition and transformation actions in the key drivers:

Service Delivery

The hospital is designed in an atypical architecture in line with the value proposition. The reception and the restaurant are located on the first floor. The second floor is an inviting place to stay and houses the patients' rooms. Surgery is performed on the third floor. The whole building is designed to encourage people to move around and socialize. That is why there are no televisions anywhere. The lounges and catering facilities support this goal.

Work in the operating rooms begins in the morning and ends in the afternoon. A standardized process that has been optimized down to the last detail allows for an efficient workflow and a ten times higher success rate, with one attending physician, two specialists and sometimes an intern in five surgical teams operating on a patient in just 40

Table 4.2: Transformation of the SHOULDICE business model.

Value Proposition			
One week after your hernia operation you are back at work free of pain or complications.			
Service Delivery	**Service Offering**	**Cost Model**	**Earnings Model**
Clinic architecture gives patients a holiday feeling	Fast and efficient diagnostic system for remote patients	Email registration and initial examination upon admission	Very little legal leeway to change earnings model
Five surgical teams share one anesthesiologist	Pleasant reception at the clinic and contact between patients	Small but highly experienced surgical team	Cost leadership and high utilization as key factors for high profitability
Unique surgical technique ensures complication-free and rapid recovery			Commencement of marketing activities after 1997, as treatment of US citizens became much more expensive by law
Standardized processes facilitate efficient quality management	40-minute surgery with local anesthesia and quick recovery	Efficient operating room layout	
	Focused care and exercise program for rapid recovery	In-house laundry	
Convenient working hours and high salaries foster employee satisfaction		Full weekly utilization of the clinic with five operating days	
	Discharge on the fourth day		

minutes. The anesthesiologist is shared among the five teams operating simultaneously. Few patients receive general anesthesia, which speeds recovery and keeps costs down.

The Shouldice surgical procedure allows patients to walk immediately after surgery. The local anesthesia is well tolerated and allows the patient to start preliminary exercises on the same day. In order to guarantee such a fast recovery, quality management must function perfectly. Among other things, this is ensured by constantly changing surgical teams. Since the clinic only treats the most common types of hernia, the surgical technique is of very high quality. Complications are very rare; they are always solved as a team, which also promotes the exchange of experience. Doctors receive a slightly above-average fixed salary and variable compensation based on annual profit. The working hours are particularly motivating: Doctors work from 7 a.m. to 5 p.m. at the latest, and never on weekends.

Service Offering

Many patients come to the clinic on the recommendation of previous patients or their family doctor. Prior to 1997, there were no additional marketing efforts, which would have tended to increase patient waiting times. A detailed diagnostic system, the first step of which consists of a short questionnaire for patients living at a distance, selects relevant patients and suggests an operation date.

Patients are admitted to the clinic the day before surgery. Dinner is a mandatory meeting after preparing for surgery, and patients who arrived a day earlier and have already undergone surgery attend as well. This meeting relaxes the new arrivals as they can see how well the patients are doing on the day they had their surgery. The next day, the doctor collects the patient from their room and then brings them back after surgery. This marks the beginning of the exercise, training and care program designed to ensure a speedy recovery. In the evening, the patient goes to the dining room to eat with the new arrivals. The third day is for relaxation and wound care, if required. On the fourth day, patients are discharged home and return to work on the seventh day [4]. The exceptional food, beautiful cafeteria and recreational facilities contribute to a high level of patient satisfaction.

Cost Model

Various measures keep costs down without compromising quality. These include a very cost-effective diagnostic and assessment system. Most potential patients are identified and invited for surgery by computer, with almost no involvement of the staff. This means that patients who do not live in the Toronto area do not have to undergo costly preliminary examinations. The low cost structure for the four-day hospital stay allows, among other things, full capacity utilization with a maximum of 36 new patients per day, small surgical teams that share one anesthesiologist, the smart layout of the operating rooms, and very short surgery and post-operative care. With only two full-time employees in the laundry and streamlined kitchen management, Shouldice keeps overall costs 50% lower than other hospitals.

Earnings Model

Until 1997, the clinic enjoyed an above-average return. A superior cost structure and an excellent image were the cornerstones of its success. That year, however, legislative changes in Canada significantly increased the cost of care for US citizens, potentially leading to a 40% drop in patients.

In the highly regulated hospital sector, the ability to independently adjust prices to affect revenues is severely limited. As a result, SHOULDICE limited its price adjustments to an increase in the private patient overnight charge. Far more critical to the clinic's earnings model was its 1997 foray into Canadian marketing. This focused on chiropractors and referring physicians. In addition, publicizing successful surgeries on TV shows, participating in university case studies to raise awareness, and leveraging referrals from former patients helped offset the decline in foreign patients [5].

The Bottom Line

SHOULDICE has created a business model that is superior to competitors in many areas. Its value proposition requires a dual strategy that challenges Porter's traditional recommendations. The holistically structured approach as a part of this ensures both cost leadership and differentiation. With the exception of its earnings model, SHOULDICE is clearly differentiated from its competitors in all dimensions.

References

[1]   See Video at https://www.shouldice.com/about/.
[2]   See Haskett, J. (2003), Shouldice Hospital Limited, Harvard Business School Brief Case 9-683-068.
[3]   See Haskett, J. / Hallowell, R. (2013), Shouldice Hospital Limited (B), Harvard Business School Brief Case 9-913-405.
[4]   The video at https://www.youtube.com/watch?v=Yr1Jg9gC3QA provides an excellent overview.
[5]   See Pope, J./Stephenson, L. (1997), Shouldice Hospital Limited 1997, Richard Ivey School of Business Case Study No. 9A98D015.

N26*

Background and Objectives of the Case Study

In 2013, Valentin Stalf and Maximilian Tayenthal, former HSG graduates and longtime friends, decided to quit their jobs and start a business. They started with a credit card for teenagers, but quickly realized that customers wanted a better overall banking experience. This is how 'Papayer', the name of the credit card start-up, quickly became today's neobank 'N26'. N26 is part of a new wave of financial technology companies, such as Revolut, that are challenging and disrupting the traditional banking industry. Neobanks differ from traditional banks in that they have no bricks and mortar branches and are not part of a traditional banking group. Neobank services are offered exclusively through online channels. N26 was valued at more than €7.7 billion [1] in 2022 and $9 billion US in 2021, higher than the second largest listed bank in Germany (Commerzbank AG) [2]. More than 8 million customers in 24 countries and 19

---

*The case study was developed in collaboration with Michael Hoang and Christopher Schraml (University of St. Gallen).

global investors [3], including German insurance giant Allianz and Valar Ventures, founded by Silicon Valley legend Peter Thiel (co-founder of PayPal), already trust N26 with their money [4]. These investors have backed N26's mission to disrupt the banking industry with $819 million US in venture capital [5]. Despite N26's current losses, this case study illustrates the disruptive potential of so-called neobanks. These companies are relying on innovative technologies and leveraging customer trust to transform traditional banking services and meet the needs of a digitally savvy generation.

Value Proposition

N26 wants to build a bank "that the world loves to use" [6] and promises a user-friendly and transparent banking experience. The focus is on the customer experience [7]. The idea for N26 was born when the two founders realized that the digital products from many traditional banks were merely digitalized versions of traditional offerings, without focusing on the needs of online users. After all, in 2015, more than 70% of all millennials (people born between 1981 and 1997) would rather go to the dentist than to the bank [8]. CEO Valentin Stalf attributed the inability of traditional banks to innovate to inertia resulting from the use of legacy systems and technologies. Therefore, N26 set out to design a bank from the ground up and fill the gap with a customer-centric approach. The aim has always been to offer customers the best solution with the greatest convenience and the best service. The focus is on functional and emotional benefits.

The COVID-19 pandemic further accelerated N26's growth. During the pandemic, the company not only increased its user base by 2 million customers (40% growth compared to pre-pandemic figures), but also the number of customers using N26's current account as their main account. The average age has risen from the mid-20s to the mid-30s over the past five years because mobile banking has become a mainstream standard across all demographics [9]. Table 4.3 shows N26's value proposition and the transformation measures in the four key drivers.

Service Offering

By deploying of innovative technology, N26 offers a wide range of banking services that significantly simplify the complex issue of financial management. N26 offers current accounts that can be managed exclusively via smartphone or computer. Provided they have access to the Internet, users can open current accounts from anywhere at any time in just a few clicks. N26 promises that accounts can be opened in just eight minutes. Private users can choose from four types of current accounts:
1. The free N26 Standard current account: It offers a debit Mastercard and includes online banking access as well as payments and international transfers at signifi-

Table 4.3: Transformation of the N26 business model.

Value Proposition
We want to build the world's first digital bank. At the heart of this is a user-friendly app that simplifies your life with innovative technology. N26 helps you organize your banking and your life in the way you want.

Service Delivery	Service Offering	Cost Model	Earnings Model
Technologically advanced, state-of-the-art smartphone app	Digital account opening via video chat	N26 does not have brick-and-mortar branches	Traditional commission business (account management, payment and processing fees)
All services digitally mapped	Four different current accounts, for both personal and Business customers	No ATMs	Interest from lending
Cloud-based software applications	Payment by installments	Positive economies of scale with increasing number of users	Commissions from international transfers with Wise
Collaboration with partners to provide services (e.g. international transfers with Wise)	Insurance policies can be purchased directly from the app	Marginal costs close to zero	Insurance commissions
	Flexible credit options available		
	Innovative budgeting options		
	MoneyBeam function		

    cantly lower rates than traditional banks. All accounts offer free ATM withdrawals in the local currency. Customer service is only available through a chatbot.

2. N26 Smart: This account type costs €4.90 a month and, in addition to the 'Standard' account type, includes phone-based customer service, Spaces (creation of sub-accounts, e.g. for savings) and premium offers from partners.
3. N26 You: This account costs €9.90 a month and also promises unlimited free withdrawals abroad and includes travel and lifestyle insurance (e.g. for car sharing or winter sports).
4. N26 Metal: This account costs €16.90 a month and includes unlimited withdrawals in foreign currencies, insurance services (e.g. travel or mobile phone insurance), phone-based customer service, access to exclusive offers (e.g. discounted access to WeWork co-working spaces) and events.

N26 also offers the above accounts to business customers, such as the self-employed. The main characteristic of the business accounts is a simplified split between personal

and business expenses. All current account products are complemented by additional financial products, such as the option to:
- Pay in installments and split them flexibly,
- Trade cryptocurrencies,
- Take out insurance policies directly in the N26 app,
- Take out a loan of up to €25,000 without a waiting period,
- Take out flexible overdraft facilities in case an account becomes overdrawn, and open a flexible instant access savings account.

The direct bank operates in 24 European countries and appeals primarily to young customers. Approximately 60% of the bank's customers in Germany are under the age of 35 [10], reflecting this age group's affinity for digital solutions. The international orientation of the bank's services appeal to a customer segment that frequently travels abroad for business and leisure. The mobile banking app already has more than eight million users [11].

Service Delivery

Employees are a key success factor in developing and delivering key service offerings. All products are paperless and accessible with just a few clicks. N26 employs more than 1,500 people in ten locations, with offices in Berlin, New York and Barcelona, but no physical branches [12]. Since its inception, N26 has evolved from a single product provider to a platform provider. Today, customers can access a wide range of services from partner companies. For example, international money transfers are handled by the company Wise, and the N26 Savings product is based on a cooperation with the European interest rate portal WeltSparen, which allows customers to invest at attractive interest rates with five to ten different banks in Europe [13]. The vision of customer centricity throughout the entire offering provides the background to this platform idea. The customer should be offered the best possible service at the best possible terms. To achieve this goal, N26 is willing to integrate partners into its platform, while retaining control of the core infrastructure and acting as a one-stop shop for its customers. The customer therefore has a single point of contact and does not have to deal with different service providers. As N26 evolves into a platform provider, relationships with partner companies will become increasingly important, as this is the only way to realize the full value proposition for customers. Since 2016, N26 has been officially licensed as a bank, which strengthens its credibility and trust with customers.

Cost Model

Unlike traditional banks, N26 has no branch costs as all products and services are delivered digitally. The software-based business model has the decisive advantage that there are hardly any variable costs. The most important product-related cost factors are therefore limited to product development or 'first copy costs' [14]. However, as the bank is still relatively young and in a growth phase, there are high market development costs. Like many young digital companies, N26 is pursuing a fairly aggressive expansion policy. The focus is primarily on scaling up quickly to cover as broad a market as possible, rather than on becoming profitable as quickly as possible. Ideally, the business model will prove profitable in the medium term due to its low marginal costs [15]. Rapid customer acquisition enables a company to reach critical mass and to continuously expand its product and service portfolio. Aggressive customer acquisition is paying off for N26: between 2020 and 2022, the platform welcomed three million new users [16]. Each new user costs an average of €22 to acquire, resulting in marketing expenses of €66 million. In this relation, N26 aims to pass on the benefits of scaling to its customers [17]. As the number of users grows, the N26 platform becomes increasingly attractive to potential partner companies. With this strategy, N26 benefits from the resulting indirect network effects: The more users there are on the platform, the more attractive the platform becomes for other financial service providers. N26 expands its offering and saves development costs at the same time.

Earnings Model

The earnings model of traditional banks consists mainly of account management and service fees, as well as income from the difference between investment and debt interest [18]. In contrast, many young fintech companies, including N26, offer their basic product for free. According to the 2021 annual report, N26 has 3.7 million revenue-relevant customers, generating gross revenues of over €182 million. The majority of N26's revenue is generated through commissions. In 2021, N26 was able to generate net commission income (balance of commission income and commission expenses) of €90 million, an increase of almost 60% compared to 2020. By comparison, net interest income in 2021 was around €30 million. Commission income thus represents the majority of total revenues [19]. In addition, N26 offers loans of between €1,000 and €50,000 in selected markets (e.g. Germany, France) with an effective interest rate starting at 1.99% p.a. and a term of between six and 84 months. N26 also generates revenue by offering customers the option to split past payments of up to €1,000 into several installments (three to six months). In cooperation with the insurance company simplesurance, N26 also offers its customers electronics insurance and, in the future, liability and buyer protection insurance, which should further increase commission income [20].

Compared to the revenues of traditional banks, N26's revenues are still low, and due to its rapid expansion and hiring strategy, a loss of €172.4 million is reported for the fiscal year 2021, despite a 50% increase in revenues. However, the supposedly higher revenues of traditional banks do not necessarily promise economic success. Years of calls to increase capital ratios point to the critical state of the banking industry, and the case of Credit Suisse shows that even a traditional commercial bank is not immune to bankruptcy [21]. Despite its deficits, N26 is focused on expanding into new markets. The company aims to attract more than 100 million customers worldwide. It remains to be seen whether N26 will reach the critical mass of customers needed to operate profitably. Although many new customers are willing to try neobanks, the main account is rarely transferred to them [22].

The Bottom Line

N26's grand vision is to transform the banking industry by providing a superior customer experience. Without relying on outdated technologies, N26 offers financial products that are tailored to the needs of its customers. The online-only approach ensures cost leadership compared to traditional banks. At the same time, N26 is able to differentiate itself from traditional providers in the area of digital services. Only the earnings model is not yet mature enough to displace established banks from the market. It remains to be seen whether N26 will be able to establish itself as the main bank for many consumers, or whether traditional banks will be able to catch up with N26's digital service offering. The race is wide open. Despite its long history, Credit Suisse was also unable to avert the crisis in 2023.

References

[1]   See Martschin, M. (2023), "Neue Geschäftszahlen: N26 verdient mehr – und macht trotzdem höhere Verluste" (New Business Figures: N26 Earns More – And Still Makes Higher Losses), Gründerszene, https://www.businessinsider.de/gruenderszene/fintech/neue-geschaeftszahlen-n26-verdient-mehr-und-macht-trotzdem-hoehere-verluste/ (in German only).
[2]   See Browne, R. (2021), Fintech firm N26 is now worth more than Germany's second-largest bank, CNBC, https://www.cnbc.com/2021/10/18/n26-triples-valuation-to-9-billion-now-worth-more-than-commerzbank.html.
[3]   See N26 (2023), "Über N26" (About N26), https://n26.com/de-de/ueber-n26 (in German only).
[4]   See Crunchbase (2023), N26, https://www.crunchbase.com/organization/n26.
[5]   See CBInsights (2021), Berlin-Based Mobile-First Challenger Bank N26 Raises $900M To Break Into The Cryptocurrency Market, https://www.cbinsights.com/research/n26-series-e-funding/.
[6]   See N26 (2023), retrieved from: https://n26.com/en-eu.
[7]   See VentureTV (2017), "N26 – Das Geschäftsmodell der Online-Bank ist anders als du denkst" (N26 – The Online Bank's Business Model Is Different Than You Think), https://venturetv.de/n26-das-geschaeftsmodell-der-online-bank-ist-anders-als-du-denkst/ (in German only).

[8]   See BBVA (2015), The Millennial Disruption Index, retrieved from: https://www.bbva.com/wp-content/uploads/2015/08/millenials.pdf.

[9]   See W&V (2021), "N26 rüstet sich für Nach-Corona-Zeit" (N26 Gears up for Post-COVID Era), https://www.wuv.de/Archiv/N26-rüstet-sich-für-Nach-Corona-Zeit (in German only).

[10]   See Statista (2017), Share of N26 customers in Germany in 2017, by age group, https://www.statista.com/statistics/922408/customers-n26-by-age-germany/.

[11]   See N26 (2023), "Über N26" (About N26), https://n26.com/de-de/ueber-n26 (in German only).

[12]   See Mesch, S. et al. (2018). "Digitalisierung in Industrie-, Handels- und Dienstleistungsunternehmen. Bewegung in der Bankenbranche: FinTechs als Disruptoren und Hoffnungsträger" (Digitalization in Industry, Trade and Service Enterprises. Movement in the Banking Sector: Fintechs as Disruptors and Beacons of Hope), p. 391, Springer Gabler.

[13]   See VentureTV (2017), "N26 – Das Geschäftsmodell der Online-Bank ist anders als du denkst" (N26 – The Online Bank's Business Model Is Different Than You Think), https://venturetv.de/n26-das-geschaeftsmodell-der-online-bank-ist-anders-als-du-denkst/ (in German only).

[14]   See Gabler Wirtschaftslexikon (2023), "First-Copy-Cost-Effekt" (First Copy Cost Effect), https://wirtschaftslexikon.gabler.de/definition/first-copy-cost-effekt-52629 (in German only).

[15]   See DerStandard (2020), "Wie viel Bank in Online-Anbietern wie N26 steckt" (How Much Bank Is in Online Providers Like N26), https://www.derstandard.at/story/2000122246324/wie-viel-bank-in-online-anbietern-wie-n26-steckt (in German only).

[16]   See N26 (2022), "N26 gibt Konzernergebnis für 2021 bekannt – Fokus auf Kundenaktivität führt zu starkem Ertragswachstum" (N26 Announces Consolidated Results for 2021 – Focus on Customer Activity Leads to Strong Revenue Growth), https://n26.com/de-de/presse/pressemitteilung/n26-gibt-konzernergebnis-fuer-2021-bekannt-fokus-auf-kundenaktivitaet-fuehrt-zu-starkem-ertragswachstum (in German only).

[17]   See VentureTV (2017), "N26 – Das Geschäftsmodell der Online-Bank ist anders als du denkst" (N26 – The Online Bank's Business Model Is Different Than You Think), https://venturetv.de/n26-das-geschaeftsmodell-der-online-bank-ist-anders-als-du-denkst/ (in German only).

[18]   See Dimler, N. et al. (2018), "Unternehmensfinanzierung im Mittelstand. Lösungsansätze für eine maßgeschneiderte Finanzierung" (Corporate Financing in the SME Sector. Solutions for Customized Financing). Springer Gabler.

[19]   See N26 (2022), "N26 gibt Konzernergebnis für 2021 bekannt – Fokus auf Kundenaktivität führt zu starkem Ertragswachstum" (N26 Announces Consolidated Results for 2021 – Focus on Customer Activity Leads to Strong Revenue Growth), https://n26.com/de-de/presse/pressemitteilung/n26-gibt-konzernergebnis-fuer-2021-bekannt-fokus-auf-kundenaktivitaet-fuehrt-zu-starkem-ertragswachstum (in German only).

[20]   See N26 (2023), https://n26.com/en-eu.

[21]   See Büsser, H. (2022), "Die sichersten Banken der Welt" (The Safest Banks in the World), https://www.handelszeitung.ch/geld/konkurs-der-credit-suisse-mit-hohen-eigenkapitalquoten-wurden-geruchte-keine-bank-erschuttern-537139 (in German only).

[22]   See Ballard, B. (2018), The unstoppable rise of neobanks, https://www.worldfinance.com/banking/the-unstoppable-rise-of-neobanks.

4.2 Successful Business Model Transformations

LEGO

Background and Objectives of the Case Study

The emerging crisis in the toy industry was reflected in the company's figures for 1998: for the first time in the company's history, losses were recorded (around €40 million). The following years did not bring any significant recovery. Profits were reported in only three of the six years between 1998 and 2003. In 2003, the LEGO Group reached a low point and seemed to be heading for certain bankruptcy. Net sales were down 26% from the previous year, and toy sales fell by a whopping 29%. The annual result before taxes showed a loss equivalent to €188 million [1].

With the advent of computer game consoles and other digital games in particular, the virtual world increasingly displaced traditional toys. Digital games suddenly became a source of fascination. Sim City or RollerCoaster Tycoon, for example, enhanced the building experience with digital special effects. In contrast, good old LEGO bricks seemed like a relic of the past [2]. LEGO responded to this crisis with a number of measures:

– On the one hand, an efficiency program was launched to compensate for falling margins. Almost a tenth of the workforce fell victim to the Fitness Plan program.
– On the other hand, the number of new products was drastically increased in an attempt to anticipate gaming trends. New products quickly accounted for 75% of annual sales. However, attention to detail was an ingrained part of the company's culture, which had a negative impact on rapidly rising material and production costs. This culture negated the effects of the Fitness Plan efforts.
– In addition, the LEGO brand was expanded into new product areas (including books, clothing, watches, movies and computer games). Additional product lines were created, such as the Primo line for babies and the Scala line of Barbie-like dolls. LEGO opened up new distribution channels, new customer segments and entirely new product categories.

The company responded to market pressures on too many fronts at the same time. The result was an overstretched organization and exploding costs. For example, LEGO bricks were initially only available in the basic colors red, blue, green and yellow. After the innovation drive, there were more than 100 different colors. The number of product variations also increased significantly. The result was a dramatic increase in complexity. Within seven years, the number of components doubled from 6,000 to more than 14,000. Since approximately 90% of the new parts were only used for a single product set, production and inventory costs rose steadily.

Despite strong sales in the first half of 2001, driven by increasing demand for licensed products and collaborations with Disney on blockbuster films such as Star Wars and Harry Potter, LEGO was facing a fundamental change. What's more, Fortune magazine named the classic LEGO brick the toy of the century at the same time. At that time, LEGO was the fourth largest toy manufacturer in the world, with a turnover of €1 billion. However, this could not hide the fact that the current business model was about to undergo a fundamental change. The company's business model was no longer sustainable, as evidenced by poor financial performance and a lack of licensing revenue.

Kjeld Kirk Kristiansen, grandson of the company's founder and the man behind the business for 25 years, initiated the business model transformation. He handed over the reins to 34-year-old Jorgen Vig Knudstorp, a former McKinsey consultant who had been with the company since 2001 as head of strategic development and since 2003 as chief financial officer. Knudstorp took the helm in the fall of 2004.

Value Proposition

At LEGO, cost savings ensured the company's future viability and were effectively implemented thanks to a strong value proposition and a top-down approach. The tough cutbacks went hand in hand with a strong values-based approach at the top. LEGO was convinced that play is an essential part of a child's development and that LEGO's mission is to enrich children's lives by creating wonderful play experiences. The resulting strengthening of its value proposition helped the company to ensure the sustainability of the structural cuts. Change without purpose usually leads to resistance, internal resignation and a loss of good talent.

In the absence of strong internal conviction, systematic customer analysis can help to outline the value proposition based on the needs of the target customers. At LEGO, customer analysis and the search for a value proposition have complemented each other. Table 4.4 shows LEGO's value proposition and the transformation actions in the four key drivers.

Cost Model

Knudstorp explains in an interview that one of the reasons for the crisis was the long period of success, which created a feeling of invulnerability. Even at the height of the crisis, many managers were convinced that 'the storm would pass and better days would come'. In order to carry out the transformation, it was necessary to create an awareness of the crisis. So Knudstorp decided to start with a dose of harsh reality to, as he put it, 'break the backbone of the existing culture'. Managers were to forget about the existing visions for the time being and focus instead on operational and leadership tasks [3]. In the first phase, from 2004 to 2005, 'must-win battles' were defined to avert bankruptcy and immediately stabilize the company. In particular, this included fundamental work on the cost model:

Table 4.4: Transformation of the LEGO business model.

Value Proposition
– We nurture the child in each of us as a world leader in quality products and experiences that inspire creativity, imagination, fun and learning. – Even the best is never good enough.

Service Delivery	Service Offering	Cost Model	Earnings Model
Outsourcing of production to Eastern Europe	Consumer research to identify the typical LEGO child	Outsourcing of production to Eastern Europe	Neglected retailers rewarded with higher margins
Reorganization and simplification of executive board structures	Establishment of an ambassador program and Kid's Inner Circle to involve customers in the development process and to better understand customer needs	Reorganization and simplification of executive board structures	Multichannel strategy with several cooperation partners to stage the brand world
Teams given triangular function consisting of design, construction and marketing to achieve a holistic perspective		Teams given triangular responsibility for design, engineering and marketing	Highly attractive licensing business
	Bifocal perspective on maintaining the core product line and innovation		
	New skills set for employees (broad knowledge and profound expertise)		

A strict cost limit was introduced in 2004, assigning each development project a cost limit that could not be exceeded. This cost limit forced designers to innovate 'inside the box'. Instead of making products stand out with as many special parts as possible, designers had to creatively use existing standard parts. LEGO designers discovered that they could still be very creative with these limitations [4]. As a result, the number of different bricks was reduced from 13,000 to just under half. And because each brick requires an expensive injection mold, production costs were significantly reduced. Today, at least 70% of each LEGO set consists of standardized bricks that can be used in other sets.

LEGO had neither the expertise nor the resource to ensure the success of the theme parks. Accordingly, the sale of the LEGOLAND theme parks in the fall of 2004 was one of the first measures of the transformation, also in order to obtain the necessary liquidity for further restructuring. LEGOLAND was spun off into a newly established company in which LEGO retained a 30% shareholding [5].

Service Delivery

In 2005, LEGO's management decided to outsource most of its production to Eastern Europe and to consolidate its European distribution centers into a single location near Prague. This made LEGO the first major company to move all of its distribution to Eastern Europe. By 2009, LEGO had saved 40% of its distribution costs [6, 7].

The company's management, consisting of twelve board members who directly managed six market regions as well as other central functions such as the direct customer business and the global supply chain, worked largely in silos. Management was perceived as distant, and decision-making bottlenecks hampered development. As part of the transformation, the Executive Committee was reduced to nine members and the market regions to three, and clear decision-making channels were introduced.

This streamlining allowed the company to focus on the future. To drive the transformation forward, Knudstorp involved people from different departments in a two-stage approach: The management team, consisting of the Executive Board, developed the strategy, while a larger team of managers from sales, logistics, IT and production coordinated the change at the operational level. A war room was set up for the operational team to discuss decisions on a daily basis [8]. This ensured that silo thinking was avoided and decisions could be made quickly and in a coordinated manner.

To ensure holistic performance, each team was given a triangular responsibility for design, construction and marketing. For example, the Bionicle series created new characters that were embedded in a story and encouraged people to collect them. With an accompanying book series, comic books, and licensing revenue, a success story was born. Children were involved in the development of the story.

To implement the holistic approach, LEGO recruited employees with versatile skills, known as 'T-shaped' employees. LEGO also emphasized the importance of discipline which was essential for achieving the company's common goal of becoming more profitable.

Service Offering

LEGO recognized that it needed to find a new way to reach its customers. In the past, the company's designers had more or less worked in isolation, making it almost impossible to use the many creative minds in the company efficiently. There was also a lack of a shared vision of the future and a common understanding of the customer segment (s). To address these challenges, Knudstorp conducted a broad consumer study. The study identified the typical LEGO child as a five- to nine-year-old boy who loves to build toys. Each team was given a toolbox that included a description of the target customer, the company's strategy (less is more: back to core goods, core products and core customers), and a financial tool that calculated the financial effects. This ensured that all teams were working towards the same goal and using the same language.

LEGO also launched two new programs to integrate customers into the development process. The ambassador program for adults and the Kids Inner Circle for children gave LEGO valuable insights into the needs of its customers. Instead of asking children what they wanted, new designs were tested on them before being launched.

A bifocal approach ensured the maintenance of classic product lines (e.g. LEGO City) on the one hand, and the development of new games (e.g. LEGO Games) on the other. The question of how to make LEGO toys even more exciting laid the foundation for innovation and the unpretentious abandonment of routine.

Earnings Model

The high rate of innovation in recent years led to a slump in sales and slow sales of new series. The result was slow sellers that had to be reduced in price at the expense of the retailer's margin. This lost confidence had to be regained. Higher margins were an important first step here.

Rather than focusing on its own online channel, LEGO initiated partnerships with sales platforms. Since 2017, for example, LEGO has had its own LEGO brand world on the online marketplace eBay. The products can either be shipped directly to the customer's home or picked up at a local LEGO store via Click & Collect. LEGO thus offers a wide range of functionalities that have been implemented in a brand world on eBay for the first time. With this multichannel strategy, LEGO is tapping into new customer groups and can be found wherever people play.

Attempts to bring the LEGO universe to the virtual world have failed, most notably with the LEGO Universe project. In 2010, the platform was launched as a subscription-based massively multiplayer online game (MMOG). However, the market was not yet ready for building virtual worlds with LEGO bricks. In 2022, LEGO made another attempt to expand into video games when Kirkbi, the family-owned holding company behind the LEGO Group, invested $1 billion US in the US company Epic Games [9].

With its licensing business, LEGO has an interesting model for monetizing its theme worlds. The company has outsourced the production of products such as LEGO watches, sweaters and computer games and earns revenue from licensing fees.

The Bottom Line

Today, LEGO is once again a colorful world for children and adults who have remained children and love imaginative play. The crisis was overcome primarily by regaining control over the many innovations and bringing the organically grown activities back into a controllable system.

A critical factor in the crisis was that short-term successes (such as the Star Wars and Harry Potter licenses) masked operational shortcomings, making it difficult to recognize the need for realignment. Overcoming this inertia is one of the key success factors for traditional companies. It can only be achieved if the status quo is constantly challenged and the pursuit of excellence is embedded in the corporate culture. Otherwise, there is a tendency to defend the status quo and avoid change. Ultimately, the key to success is a coherent and consistent implementation of the strategy, led by a strong CEO.

References

[1] See Oliver, K./Samakh, E./Heckmann, P. (2007), Rebuilding LEGO, Brick by Brick, in: strategy & business magazine, 48, Autumn 2007, pp. 1–10.
[2] See Robertson, D./Breen, B. (2014), "Das Imperium der Steine: Wie LEGO den Kampf ums Kinderzimmer gewann" (Empire of Stones: How Lego Won the Battle for the Children's Room), Campus Verlag: Frankfurt/New York.
[3] See ibid.
[4] See ibid.
[5] See LEGO. (2005), Annual Report 2005. LEGO Group, 2005.
[6] Cooke, J. A. (2009), Lego's game-changing move, in: CSCMP's Supply Chain Quarterly, Quarter 3, pp. 38–41.
[7] See LEGO. (2005), Annual Report 2005. LEGO Group, 2005.
[8] See Oliver, K./Samakh, E./Heckmann, P. (2007), Rebuilding LEGO, Brick by Brick, in: strategy & business magazine, 48, Autumn 2007, pp. 1–10.
[9] see Hollenstein, E. (2022), "Lego investiert Milliarden in einen virtuellen Spielplatz" (Lego Invests Billions in a Virtual Playground), in: Tagesanzeiger, 2022-04-13, retrieved from: https://www.tagesan zeiger.ch/lego-investiert-milliarden-in-einen-virtuellen-spielplatz-185401356871 (in German only).

FC Bayern München AG*

Background and Objectives of the Case Study

Achieving excellence on the soccer pitch is in FC Bayern Munich's DNA. Founded in 1900, the club is not only Germany's all-time record champion with 28 titles, but also the world's largest soccer club with 295,000 members. Recently, the club underwent a major transformation, transforming itself into a multimedia entertainment company. This move has solidified its prominent position and extended its reach beyond Germany and Europe.

The transformation of FC Bayern Munich into a digital pioneer in the sports sector is a case study in how digital transformation can significantly expand a company's value proposition and thus squarely influence its entire business model. FC Bayern Munich is much more than a sports club today—it is a multimedia entertainment company that creates a sense of belonging for people around the world.

---

*The case study was developed in collaboration with Severin F. Bischof (University of St. Gallen).

Digital transformation has created a new playing field for institutions such as sports clubs, requiring them to acquire new skills in order to operate. These new skills have transformed the club's cost and earnings model. The service offering has also expanded, with a diverse entertainment offering for fans around the world. The same is true of service delivery, which only a few years ago was limited to player recruitment and training. In recent years, digital content has been added to the mix.

FC Bayern Munich is no longer driven by sporting success alone. Due to the global competition in the soccer business, the club is also focused on building its media presence. The digital transformation has provided people with an unprecedented range of entertainment content (e.g., YouTube, Netflix, Spotify, apps, and other digital content), and it has rearranged the chessboard for FC Bayern Munich. From that point on, the competition was no longer just other soccer clubs, but any entertainment offering to which people devote time and attention.

The new value proposition of delivering multimedia content beyond the soccer game itself also changed the way soccer and its players saw themselves. Transfer decisions were no longer based solely on a player's athletic ability, but also on his popularity on social media.

It is certainly questionable whether FC Bayern Munich would have the same social media relevance without its soccer success. The case presented here is therefore more of a strategy supplement than a complete transformation of the business model. Nevertheless, digitalization has permanently changed the value proposition, so that the entertainment factor has taken on a central role in addition to the sporting success.

Value Proposition

FC Bayern Munich's former value proposition was clear: sporting success. But it has not always been easy to deliver. From 2001 to 2009, the club was in crisis. The fall from international grace took its toll on the traditional club, and the situation was exacerbated by a merciless arms race between the international soccer leagues. In 1996/1997, the Bundesliga's revenues of €444 million were about 11% below the average of the five biggest European soccer leagues [1].

In order to catch up with the international top flight, the club needed a lot of money to buy international players. At the same time, digitalization was changing people's lives. While people have always looked for distractions from everyday life, since the turn of the millennium, they have increasingly used digital devices and spent more and more time on social media. In the 21st century, digitalization is increasingly capturing people's attention. Traditional media such as newspapers and magazines, once the mecca for sports enthusiasts, are losing influence.

To fit into this new structure of an all-encompassing entertainment culture, FC Bayern Munich had to change its self-image from a sports club to an entertainment company. This meant presenting the club to fans not just once a week, but seven days a week. The club therefore changed its value proposition. In addition to sporting success as a serial winner of numerous trophies and championships, the *spirit* of FC Bayern Munich was to be made accessible to every fan around the world at all times.

For 150 million fans worldwide, the idea of community and the feeling of belonging were to be emphasized even more. The previous value proposition of sporting success has therefore given way to an additional value proposition. This new value proposition requires sporting success, but also emphasizes the entertainment factor. The new value proposition addresses this objective: Communicate the spirit of FC Bayern Munich's success to every fan around the world, at any time (cf. Table 4.5).

Table 4.5: Transformation of the FC Bayern Munich business model.

Value Proposition

To communicate the spirit of FC Bayern Munich's success to every fan around the world, at any time.

Service Delivery	Service Offering	Cost Model	Earnings Model
27 outfield players and a multi-member coaching team create sporting success and the basis for commercializable content. More than 1,000 employees in FC Bayern's management and marketing department use the performance on the soccer pitch to create commercializable content. Media content before and after matches. Maintains facilities and offices on three continents (in Europe, the USA, China) to ensure localized content	Successful participation in national and international sporting competitions All-round entertainment with FC Bayern content on all channels Accessibility on social media channels with localized content The aim of the service offering is to deliver both services at the same time: Success on the soccer pitch while expanding the global media presence through increased reach.	Increased personnel costs due to the desire to be seen as an entertainment company, leading to increased demand for personnel to manage and create multimedia content (higher personnel costs). Player costs have increased. James Rodriguez on loan (from Real Madrid for one season) in 2017 is considered the most expensive player loan in German soccer history. The cost of a player is amortized not only through sporting success, but also through positive effects on FC Bayern Munich's reach (player followers on different continents).	Revenue from increased media coverage, advertising and sponsorships Increased attractiveness of FC Bayern Munich as a platform for businesses, fueled by the value proposition of being a central feature in fans' lives as an entertainment company. Higher ticket sale and merchandising revenues driven by players who have greater awareness and reach Revenues (2020/2021) of €643.9 million and earnings (EBT) of of €5 million

Service Offering

The motivational message of a successful FC Bayern Munich has always appealed to people. The team's success guarantees that the entertainment offers the fans can talk about between matches is filled with positive content. In order to achieve comprehensive communication, FC Bayern München has created a multi-layered entertainment structure.

Thanks to their digital transformation, FC Bayern Munich's service offering is no longer limited to sporting events in the stadium. The club now offers entertaining and informative content on digital channels to fill the gap between weekly sporting events. The club broadcasts individual reports in several languages on digital channels such as Facebook, X (Twitter), Instagram, Snapchat, Periscope, Soundcloud, etc. As of December 2017, the club already had 32 different international Facebook accounts with more than 60 million fans. Interestingly, less than 10% of these were from German-speaking countries. FC Bayern's new multimedia strategy has made the club the most popular soccer club in the world (measured by the number of members: 295,000) [2]. The club is also the sixth most valuable soccer brand in the world, valued at €1.1 billion [3]. In addition, the German Bundesliga is now the third-largest soccer league in Europe, with revenues of €3.1 billion for the 2021/2022 season [4].

In addition to retaining existing audiences, the new value proposition required the development of new audiences and the search for new sales opportunities for merchandising the club's own products and marketing sponsors' products. Digital media consumption made it necessary to reach out to consumers. Felix Lösner, head of social media at the time, confirmed that the club could not assume that fans would come on their own. On the contrary, FC Bayern had to go to the fans [5].

Service Delivery

The performance of a soccer club is measured primarily on the pitch. Some 27 outfield players form the core of the team, responsible for delivering results on the pitch. But to build the service offering of a global entertainment company like FC Bayern Munich, you also need people off the field. Approximately 1,000 employees manage the processes and procedures within the company and communicate the performance of the players to the entire world. Together, the 27 players and 1,000 other employees make FC Bayern Munich's extraordinary media presence possible.

The club combines the skills and strengths of its players and management and marketing staff to enhance its media presence. The resulting service delivery is expressed in a worldwide, professional media production. In this way, the one-way communication with the media was transformed into a 'communication loop' that actively involved the fans in the discussion about FC Bayern [6]. From that moment on, the fans were no longer mere recipients of news and advertising messages, but actively engaged with the brand. A fertile ground for communication with fans was the club's presence on Studi-

VZ, the now defunct social networking platform for students which was launched in 2010. By 2012, the club had three million fans on Facebook.

Cost Model

FC Bayern Munich's transformation into an entertainment company has significantly changed its cost model. Whereas in the past, the performance on the pitch was the only deciding factor when signing new players, today other factors are now important. This attitude stems from the fact that in FC Bayern Munich's two-pronged strategy, a soccer player acts not only as a service provider in the stadium, but also as a social media influencer and entertainer as part of the club's digital communication initiatives. While the service delivery seems to have remained the same, there is an recognizable trend toward signing more players who also contribute to the communication and internationalization strategy at the same time.

The cost model has changed to the extent that expensive investments in players are now more worthwhile than in the past, when shirt sales were the only source of income apart from ticket sales. The cost of 22 licensed players for the 2021/2022 season was approximately €275 million [7]. However, the marketing of the team and the associated cost accounting is not only based on sporting performance, but also on the team's marketing appeal. This is why the most expensive player on loan to a German club, in this case James Rodríguez, who was loaned by Real Madrid for €10 million in the 2017/2018 season, was suddenly considered a profitable investment when the communication-related influence on the internationalization of the club was taken into account [8].

The transfer on loan of James Rodríguez, who is undoubtedly an excellent player, was aimed at raising the profile of FC Bayern Munich, particularly in South America, in addition to providing sporting support. With 76 million followers on Facebook, Instagram and X (Twitter), the Colombian was the fifth most popular sporting personality in the world at the time. Professor Haupt from the Institute of Football Management put the weekly advertising value of James Rodriguez's Facebook posts at around €600,000. The transfer on loan of the Colombian player significantly raised the club's profile in South America. Rodriguez's posts and media presence brought FC Bayern to the attention of hundreds of thousands of fans in that part of the world [9]. Today, the individual presence of each player contributes directly to the club's media presence and supports its visibility on new media. Since the arrival of James Rodriguez, CEO Karl-Heinz Rummenigge has seen a six-figure increase in the club's social media accounts, most of which come from South America [10]. With two representative offices working as management teams in China, the second largest growth market in soccer, and the USA, the club is also underlining its value proposition to spread the *spirit* of FC Bayern Munich around the world [11, 12]. This media reach increases the awareness of FC Bayern Munich as well as the attractiveness of the club for sponsors. This makes it possible to significantly expand the earnings model.

Earnings Model

The expansion of the earnings model is largely based on FC Bayern's greater reach on digital media and the associated higher sponsorship revenues. Andreas Jung, Head of Marketing at FC Bayern Munich, emphasized the club's ability to generate greater reach through the creation of media content, making it more attractive to sponsors: "We can strengthen the [FC Bayern Munich] brand through social channels and position it ourselves." [13] Sponsors can benefit from this by communicating their individual content on dedicated channels.

In addition to traditional communication channels, the digitalized stadium offers added value to sponsors, so that part of the value proposition, namely sporting success, is directly linked to them. A variety of digital signage solutions, for example above the entrances to the stadium, offer the opportunity to link special moments where anticipation is central directly with the sponsors. Lufthansa in particular, whose product 'travel' is largely based on the customer's anticipation of their vacation, actively uses this opportunity. The anticipation before a sporting event can be transferred to the provider through clever measures. The comprehensive digitalization of FC Bayern Munich thus facilitates an extraordinary value-added product for sponsors that can appeal to potential customers in every situation.

In addition, traditional income sources such as jersey sales are benefiting from FC Bayern Munich's increased media presence. In the 2015/2016 season alone, more than one million jerseys bearing James Rodriguez's number and name were sold, second only to Lionel Messi's jersey (1.6 million). FC Bayern Munich's €600 million turnover will increase significantly in the future, allowing for further investment in players and sporting success [14].

The increased revenue will also allow the club to spend more money on potential player signings, thus providing the team with strong players. This will gradually increase the team's competitiveness and lead to further triumphs in various soccer championships and trophy races. Reaching the finals of the Champions League, for example, is associated with a higher payout in television revenue. Sporting success leads to increased revenues, fueling the upward spiral. FC Bayern Munich's 360-degree communication is therefore not just an end in itself, but also offers added value to the ecosystem of sponsors, fans and players, thus ensuring the club's future success.

The Bottom Line

FC Bayern Munich has successfully embarked on a digital transformation. The one-way communication from 2006 through FCB.de, FCB magazines, SMS service and press releases has developed into a 'loop' communication in 2017 (FCB.com, SOM channels, apps, matchday show, e-magazines, CRM database, etc.). The expansion of the value proposition has not turned the business model of Germany's most successful soccer club upside down, but has complemented it in key areas. The club has taken advantage of the great opportunities offered by digitalization to the benefit of its brand awareness and economic prosperity. According to a study conducted by nexum AG and kicker business solutions, FC Bayern Munich was named Digital Champion in March/April 2022. The club took first place in the Online Store and Professional Networks categories, received the silver medal in the Website and Social Media categories, and achieved an overall lead of almost ten percentage points over second-placed FC Barcelona, underscoring the success of the club's digital transformation and internationalization strategy [15].

References

[1]   See Deloitte (2017), Annual Review of Football Finance 2017, in: Deloitte, 2018-02-13, https://www2. deloitte.com/uk/en/pages/sports-business-group/articles/annual-review-of-football-finance.html.
[2]   See FC Bayern München AG (2017), 2016/2017 Annual Financial Statements of FC Bayern München AG – Separate Financial Statements, in: FC Bayern, 2018-02-18, https://fcbayern.com/binaries/con tent/assets/downloads/homepage/jhv/jahresabschluss_ag_16-17.pdf (in German only).
[3]   See Statista (2022), The Top 10 Most Valuable International Soccer Brands in 2022, in: Statista, 2022-06-01, https://de.statista.com/statistik/daten/studie/511008/umfrage/die-wertvollsten-marken-im-fussball/#:~:text=Wertvollste%20Marken%20im%20weltweiten%20Fu%C3%9Fball%20in% 202022&text=Im%20Jahr%202022%20wurde%20der,1%2C1%20Milliarden%20Euro%20gesch%C3% A4tzt. (in German only).
[4]   See Statista (2022), Revenue of the Big Five soccer leagues in Europe from 2011/12 to 2020/21, with a forecast to 2022/23, by country, in: Statista, 2022-10-05, https://www.statista.com/statistics/261218/ big-five-european-soccer-leagues-revenue/.
[5]   See Ansorge, K. (2016), "FC Bayern München – der deutsche (Social-Media) Meister" (FC Bayern Munich – The German (Social Media) Champion), in: Horizont, 2016-11-10, http://www.horizont.net/ medien/nachrichten/HORIZONT-Bewegtbildgipfel-FC-Bayern-Muenchen---der-deutsche-Social-Media -Meister-144030 (in German only).
[6]   See ibid.
[7]   See fcbinside.de(2022), "Die neue Gehaltstabelle des FC Bayern – So viel verdienen Mané, de Ligt, Gnabry & Co." (FC Bayern's New Salary Table – How Much Mané, de Ligt, Gnabry & Co. Earn), in: fcbinside.de, 2022-08-05, https://fcbinside.de/2022/08/05/die-gehaltstabelle-des-fc-bayern-so-viel-verdienen-mane-de-ligt-gnabry-co/ (in German only).
[8]   See Fischer, J. (2017), James: "Bayerns neue Gelddruckmaschine" (Bayern's New Money-Printing Machine), in: Sport1.de, 2017-07-13, http://www.sport1.de/fussball/bundesliga/2017/07/fc-bayern-transfer-von-james-rodriguez-loest-social-media-ansturm-aus (in German only).
[9]   See ibid.
[10]   See Kessler, P./ Verhoff D. (2017), "Mit James erobert Bayern die Welt" (Bayern Takes the World by Storm With James), in: Bild, 2017-07-12 https://www.bild.de/sport/fussball/transfer/mit-james-erobert-bayern-die-welt-52528582.bild.html.
[11]   See Rentz, I. (2014), "Rudolf Vidal leitet Büro in New York" (Rudolf Vidal Heads Office in New York), in: Horizont, 2014-02-25, http://www.horizont.net/marketing/nachrichten/FC-Bayern-Muenchen-Rudolf-Vidal-leitet-Buero-in-New-York-119385 (in German only).
[12]   See Rentz, I. (2016), "Fussball-Bundesliga behauptet Platz 2 unter Europas Top-Ligen" (Bundesliga Wins 2nd Place in Europe's Top Leagues), in: Horizont, 2016-06-02, http://www.horizont.net/market

ing/nachrichten/Deloitte-Umsatzranking-Fussball-Bundesliga-behauptet-Platz-2-unter-Europas-Top-Ligen-140573 (in German only).

[13] See Rondinella, G. (2017), "Wie sich der FC Bayern München über Social Media vermarktet" (How FC Bayern Munich Markets Itself Through Social Media), in: Horizont, 2017-01-18, http://www.horizont.net/marketing/nachrichten/Marketingvorstand-Andreas-Jung-Wie-sich-der-FC-Bayern-Muenchen-ueber-Social-Media-vermarktet-145470 (in German only).

[14] See FC Bayern (2017), "Die Miglieder-Entwicklung des FC Bayern München e.V." (Membership Trends at FC Bayern München e.V.), in: FC Bayern, 2017-11-23, https://fcbayern.com/binaries/content/assets/downloads/homepage/jhv/mitglieder_fanclubs_kidsclub_16-17.pdf (in German only).

[15] See FC Bayern (2022), "FC Bayern holt Platz 1 in der Digitalen Champions League" (FC Bayern Takes First Place in the Digital Champions League), 2022-05-23, https://fcbayern.com/de/news/2022/05/studie-der-nexum-ag-und-kicker-fc-bayern-holt-platz-1-in-der-digitalen-champions-league (in German only).

Netflix*

Background and Objectives of the Case Study

In Europe, Netflix is best known as a successful video-on-demand platform that offers unlimited movies, documentaries and series for a monthly fee. But it wasn't always like that. Netflix's success story has its origins in the classic movie rental business. In 1997, the year Netflix was founded, the movie rental market was clearly dominated by the franchise chain Blockbuster Inc. But while Blockbuster Inc. filed for bankruptcy in September 2010, Netflix is now an international success. Netflix was quick to recognize the new customer needs in video rental and adapted its business model early on. Its competitor Blockbuster, on the other hand, underestimated the potential of the online channel for too long, treating online movie rentals as a niche market—a mistake with serious consequences, as it turned out.

Value Proposition

One of the main reasons for the successful transformation of the business model from DVD rental in the US to a globally popular streaming service is the strong value proposition offered by Netflix. Even in the company's early years, when DVD rentals were booming, co-founder Reed Hastings repeatedly stated that Netflix was not just about renting DVDs over the Internet. Rather, he wanted his company to provide customers with the best video viewing experience [1]; a value proposition that Netflix now delivers to millions of users worldwide.

---

*The case study was developed in collaboration with Gianluca Scheidegger (University of St. Gallen).

This customer-centric value proposition meant that the company was constantly looking for innovative ways to improve the customer experience. The 'best in class' claim was consistently pursued: Hastings and his team had a vision of delivering movies directly to customers' televisions without the need for an additional device. They were convinced that this would one day be possible thanks to the advances in digitalization. Accordingly, they began to prepare Netflix for this fundamental change. Settling for a tried and tested solution for their customers was not in line with their value proposition. The company's management recognized early on the consumers need to consume media whenever they wish. They adapted the business model based on the value proposition. By January 23, 2013, when Netflix was already a popular streaming provider, the company aptly expressed in a letter to investors the customer need it had successfully identified and met with its streaming service: "Imagine if books were only released in one chapter a week, and you could only read them for a short time on Thursdays at 8 pm. And then someone changed the law and suddenly people were able read an entire book at their own speed. That's the change we're making. That's the future of television. "This is Internet TV." [2] Table 4.6 shows Netflix's value proposition and the transformation actions in the four key drivers.

Table 4.6: Transformation of the Netflix business model.

Value Proposition			
To offer customers the best possible video playback.			
Service Delivery	**Service Offering**	**Cost Model**	**Earnings Model**
Recommendation algorithm	Technology solution for movie consumption at any time	Cost reduction through innovative technology solutions (e.g. recommendation algorithm)	Increase in subscription fees
Sourcing the required expertise through new hires	Subscription to thousands of series, documentaries and movies	Conversion of fixed costs into variable costs when purchasing DVDs for rental	Expansion abroad is slowly paying off
Purchase of exclusive licenses	Reduction in the size and increase in the quality of the video library	Increasing production of original content instead of expensive bidding wars	
Production of own content			
	Local productions for international markets		
Unbureaucratic corporate structure			

Service Offering

In early 2007, Netflix announced that subscribers could now access a limited selection of 1,000 titles directly on their PCs over the Internet. Unlike unlimited DVD rentals, playback was limited to 6–18 hours per month, depending on the subscription model [3]. Entry into a partnership with Samsung made it possible to stream the expanded Internet content of 12,000 titles directly to the TV over a Samsung Blu-ray box [4, 5]. More and more partnerships, such as with Xbox 360 and Sony Playstation, led to the proliferation of direct-to-TV streaming through Netflix-enabled devices. The final breakthrough came with smart TVs, which allowed Netflix to be installed without an additional device.

Contrary to expectations, Netflix now offers its subscribers an increasingly reduced and carefully curated selection of titles. The number of TV shows available in the US has dropped from 1,609 (2014) to 1,197 (2016). The number of movies dropped from 6,494 to 4,335 over the same period [6]. While competitors Amazon and Hulu offer significantly more titles, the strategy still seems to be working. Netflix focuses on quality rather than quantity in its service offering and is particularly notable for its in-house productions, which are described in the following section on service delivery. Netflix's excellence speaks for itself, with its productions consistently winning international film and series awards. In 2022, it dominated the Golden Globe Awards nominations with an impressive 17 nominations [7].

To capture the foreign market, Netflix is increasingly investing in local productions. In particular, on December 1, 2017, it launched "Dark," the first television series developed, produced, and filmed entirely in Germany. This investment is in line with the company's clear international strategy, as evidenced by its reported $2 billion US investment in European film and series production in 2017 alone [8]. In late 2018, Netflix surprised audiences with the meticulously crafted interactive film "Bandersnatch." This innovative offering thrust viewers into the heart of the story, demanding their active participation through crucial decisions that shaped the direction of the narrative. "Bandersnatch" captivated users and generated international buzz.

Service Delivery

To address the fluctuating demand for DVDs, a cost concern in the past, Netflix ingeniously developed a consumer favorite recommendation system. This system uses user data from past rentals to make personalized suggestions. The key differentiator? Prioritizing lower-demand movies over new releases. This strategy facilitated increased rentals of lesser-known, lower-cost productions from independent studios, effectively spreading demand across the entire catalog and minimizing frustrating delivery bottlenecks. The recommendation technology, which continues to be refined, remains a cornerstone of Netflix's streaming service and is highly popular with users.

Months before video-on-demand became technologically feasible on television sets, Netflix was investing heavily in the development of an online streaming channel. In 2006, the company invested $10 million US in this new technology, and by 2007, that investment had grown to $40 million US [9]. In addition to investing in technology, Netflix also made a concerted effort to recruit top talent in the field. One key hire in 2007 was Anthony Wood, the founder of ReplayTV, a technology that allowed users to record television shows to an internal hard drive for later viewing. Wood's expertise was instrumental in developing Netflix's proprietary software for third-party TV boxes.

In 2002, Netflix suddenly faced a major challenge when a bottleneck in staffing occurred. The dot-com bubble bursting and 9/11 made the situation precarious at Netflix. The company was forced to delay its planned IPO and cut its workforce by one-third. In the same year around Christmastime the demand for DVD players was skyrocketing. Netflix, which at that time still specialized in DVD rentals, gained many new customers. As a result, fewer employees had to do more work. During this time, Netflix leaders realized that talented employees were their company's most important resource. In 2009, Hastings and Patty McCord created one of the company's most important documents. The PowerPoint presentation, titled "Netflix Culture," redefined human resources at Netflix. In the presentation, the two describe how as a company grows, it typically increases complexity and decreases the density of talented employees. If the density of talent is not increased in proportion to the increase in complexity, chaos threatens. This is why Netflix implemented a strict 'hire and fire' policy to constantly replace the right people with the right talent. What sounds very reprehensible is, according to Netflix, the best option for both parties. It is better to pay employees who are overwhelmed by the new technology a good, better than average severance package than to retrain them in a manner that consumes resources or to keep them at the company where they would be unhappy. At the same time, employee red tape was minimized to increase productivity and job satisfaction. Vacation days could be taken at will, and a complicated and time-consuming expense policy was simply replaced with the following sentence: "Act in Netflix's best interests." Standard employee meetings with managers were replaced with informal face-to-face team meetings [10].

In addition to an innovative approach to employee organization, Netflix also reverted on its own initiative when it came to content. Today's streaming market is highly competitive, especially in the US. Netflix's biggest competitors are no longer Blockbuster Inc. but Amazon, HBO, Walt Disney, YouTube, and Hulu. In order to stand out from the crowd of streaming providers and not become interchangeable, it is no longer enough to license third-party productions. So Netflix took a bigger risk. In January 2013, the company launched two seasons of the political drama "House of Cards," its first series produced in-house at a cost of $100 million US.

Spurred on by the enormous success of this in-house production and the increasing pressure from competitors - Amazon and HBO are now also successfully producing their own content - Netflix's Chief Content Officer, Ted Sarandos, is investing ever larger sums in the production of so-called 'Netflix Originals'. In 2018, Netflix's spending on original content was already estimated at $12 to $13 billion US—more than any movie studio or TV network spent on content. By 2022, the spending had grown to $17 billion US [11].

The goal is to increase the amount of exclusive content in Netflix's video library to 50% in the near future, clearly differentiating Netflix from its competitors [12].

Cost Model

Physical video and DVD rental is a capital-intensive business. Because the majority of customers demand new releases, a distributor must stock up on as many copies as possible in the first few days after a title is released. After a few months, demand for the title tapers off, and the expensive DVDs and videos sit on the shelves gathering dust. This fact inspired many of the key features of Netflix's service delivery: The smart recommendation algorithm, the in-house content production and the wide selection of films from independent producers.

Unlike traditional movie rental companies like Blockbuster, Netflix never had a physical presence. During the DVD rental period, DVDs were shipped directly from the distribution center to customers. This saved on rental and labor costs, which are significant for a distributor with a dense, nationwide store network. At its peak, Blockbuster operated about 4,500 stores. At the same time, Netflix was able to ship DVDs to customers in just one day from 44 distribution centers across the country [13].

Netflix had long suffered from its small market position. This weak negotiating position meant that the company typically had to pay higher prices to movie studios for new DVDs than its competitors. To combat this problem, newly appointed Chief Content Officer Ted Sarandos negotiated new variable contracts with the major studios. This meant that instead of paying a fixed price for each DVD, Netflix would pay a percentage each time the title was rented. This turned fixed costs into variable costs. This gave the company more flexibility in a market that was subject to significant fluctuations in demand.

In the US, Netflix continues to operate a DVD rental service in addition to its streaming service. The acquisition of licenses for the new core business of streaming has dominated costs since the transformation of the business model.. Exclusive rights for online content are becoming increasingly expensive due to the high competitive pressure in the streaming market. In most cases, exclusive rights have to be acquired in bidding wars with competitors (e.g. HBO or Hulu). For this reason, Netflix is increasingly relying on in-house productions to secure exclusive content.

Earnings Model

The earnings model introduced in the days of DVD rentals will remain in place even after the streaming service is established. For a monthly fee, Netflix users can stream an unlimited number of series, documentaries, movies and stand-up comedy directly to their TVs. Initially, subscribers paid $7.99 US per month for the standard subscription. In May 2014 and October 2015, this was increased by $1 each to $9.99 US for new subscribers. While this resulted in a slight decline in growth figures, contribution margins improved significantly: from 22.6% (2013) to 38.0% (2017) [14].

Depending on the subscription model, Netflix allows users to share their account within the same household and use it on multiple devices at the same time. However, this also means that many subscribers share their password with friends or acquaintances. Analysts at Citi Bank estimate that about 65% of users in the US and UK use a 'shared' account outside the household to avoid the subscription fee [15]. While Netflix currently tacitly tolerates this practice, new technologies could prevent it in the future. The company Synamedia specializes in streaming providers and uses artificial intelligence to detect shared accounts [16].

The international market is becoming increasingly important for Netflix. In the first quarter of 2017, the company managed to achieve a positive contribution margin of 4.1% ($42.7 million US) with its international streaming business, after expanding to more than a hundred new markets [17]. This positive result has been a long time coming, as each new market entry has been costly. In each country, the company had to acquire the rights to third-party content and make massive investments in marketing; costs that only pay off once a certain number of users per market is reached. Netflix sees significant growth potential in its international business and is targeting a combined operating margin of 19–20% in 2022 and 2023 [18].

The Bottom Line

The Netflix story is a successful example of disruptive business model transformation in the age of digitalization. To transform itself from a niche DVD rental company to the dominant video-on-demand provider, Netflix had to adapt all four dimensions (service delivery and service offering, revenue and cost model) under the banner of its value proposition. The transformation did not take place overnight across all dimensions, but step by step. First, the cost model was adapted before the service offering was expanded in a second step. In order to offer customers the best possible video playback, the service offering was continuously expanded. Only in the final step did Netflix change its earnings model. The entire transformation was further facilitated by an unbureaucratic corporate structure made up of highly qualified employees.

References

[1]   See Netflix (2007), Netflix Offers Subscribers the Option of Instantly Watching Movies on Their PCs, 2017-01-16, https://media.netflix.com/en/press-releases/netflix-offers-subscribers-the-option-of-instantly-watching-movies-on-their-pcs-migration-1

[2]   Netflix (2013), Netflix 4Q 2012 Investor Letter, 2013-01-23, https://de.scribd.com/document/121853053/Netflix-4Q-2012-Investor-Letter?ad_group=35871X943606Xcadf4064821386ac440ec8cf4adfe2b3&campaign=Skimbit%2C+Ltd.&content=10079&irgwc=1&keyword=ft750noi&medium=affiliate&source=impactradius

[3]   See Netflix (2007), Netflix Offers Subscribers the Option of Instantly Watching Movies on Their PCs, 2017-01-16, https://media.netflix.com/en/press-releases/netflix-offers-subscribers-the-option-of-instantly-watching-movies-on-their-pcs-migration-1

[4]   See Netflix (2008), Netflix and Samsung Partner to Instantly Stream Movies on Next Generation Blu-ray Disc Players, 2008-10-22, https://media.netflix.com/en/press-releases/netflix-and-samsung-partner-to-instantly-stream-movies-on-next-generation-blu-ray-disc-players-migration-1.

[5]   See Netflix (2008), Netflix Begins Roll-Out of 2nd Generation Media Player for Instant Streaming on Windows PCs and Intel Macs, 2008-10-27, https://media.netflix.com/en/press-releases/netflix-begins-roll-out-of-2nd-generation-media-player-for-instant-streaming-on-windows-pcs-and-intel-macs-migration-1.

[6]   See Van Voorhis, G. (2016), Everything You Always Wondered About Netflix But They Refuse To Tell You, https://moviepilot.com/posts/3932999.

[7]   See Golden Globes. (2022). Golden Globes 2023: Nominations for the 80th Golden Globes Have Been Announced, 2022-12-12, https://www.goldenglobes.com/articles/golden-globes-2023-nominations-80th-golden-globes-have-been-announced.

[8]   See Feldman, D. (2017), Why Netflix Is Investing Nearly $2 Billion Into More Than 90 European Productions, in: Forbes, 2017-03-02, https://www.forbes.com/sites/danafeldman/2017/03/02/why-netflix-is-investing-billions-into-more-than-90-european-productions/#2e2f1dfd6b82.

[9]   See Netflix (2007), Netflix Annual Report 2007.

[10]   McCord, P. (2014), How Netflix Reinvented HR. In: Harvard Business Review, January/February 2014, https://hbr.org/2014/01/how-netflix-reinvented-hr.

[11]   See Variety, (2022), Netflix's Ted Sarandos Is Feeling 'Better and Better' About $17 Billion Content Budget: 'We're Spending at About the Right Level', in: https://variety.com/2022/tv/news/netflix-content-spend-17-billion-subscriber-growth-1235407818/.

[12]   See McCormick, R. (2016), Netflix planning to fill half of its catalog with originals in the next few years, in: The Verge, 2016-09-21, https://www.theverge.com/2016/9/21/12997058/netflix-originals-half-catalog-streaming.

[13]   See Shih, W./Kaufman, S./Spinola, D. (2009), Netflix, Harvard Business School Case.

[14]   See Netflix (2017), Consolidated Segment Information, https://ir.netflix.com/static-files/37587286-62c8-4621-a39e-cc1e303a8159.

[15]   See Stern, C. (2015). Wall Street doesn't think using your friend's Netflix account is a problem, in Business Insider, 2015-07-25.

[16]   See Synamedia. (2018). Synamedia launches Credentials Sharing Insight – turns casual password sharing into incremental revenues for service providers, 2018-12-17, https://www.synamedia.com/synamedia-launches-credentials-sharing-insight-turns-casual-password-sharing-into-incremental-revenues-for-service-providers/.

[17]   See Netflix (2017), Consolidated Segment Information, https://ir.netflix.com/static-files/37587286-62c8-4621-a39e-cc1e303a8159.

[18]   See Netflix (2022), Top Investor Questions, 2023-01-18, https://ir.netflix.net/ir-overview/top-investor-questions/default.aspx.

Dell

Background and Objectives of the Case Study

When Michael Dell started selling computers as a student at the University of Texas in 1984, he was a disruptor. He cut out the middleman by going directly to retail and whole-sale customers. One of his advantages was low-cost inventory because he built computers only after orders were received. This cost leadership strategy worked through a combination of outsourcing to third-party service providers and customized mass production of low-cost PCs with high-quality components. Despite this just-in-time production, Dell was able to deliver products within seven days by bypassing intermediaries. This also had the advantage of making technological innovations available to customers without delay.

Traditional computer manufacturers stuck to their traditional business model. They built computers to order from retail customers and based their on own sales forecasts. Once produced, the computers were typically stored in warehouses. The cost of tying up capital was significantly higher than Dell's business model. Dell achieved annual sales of more than $70 million US in its first year of operation due to its significantly lower selling prices as a result of its costs.

In 1988, the company went public and began its international success story that lasted until 2004. The direct sales of PCs especially and later also of notebooks made Dell the market leader for many years. Over the years, Dell has expanded its standard product range to include peripherals such as printers and monitors, as well as PDAs and services. Despite this increased complexity, the service level of delivery within two weeks has been maintained. Processes were continuously optimized, and the number of suppliers was greatly reduced and structured.

The trend toward smartphones and tablets brought Dell's success story to an abrupt end. The company was unable to establish itself in this new market segment. The former disruptor was now in danger of becoming a victim of disruptive change itself. In 2005, the stock lost about 25% of its value. After a three-year hiatus from operational management, the board brought the Dell founder back as CEO in 2007. Although the company emphasized long-term thinking, diversification into more services (including extensive acquisitions), and a strong customer focus, the transformation process was very slow [1]. To make matters worse, PC sales slumped again in 2013. Consumers worldwide preferred to use tablet computers or were content to use their smartphones to access the Internet. Dell was still barely able to compete in these device categories. Notebook sales fell 25% and desktop sales fell 13%. Profits shrunk by 31% as a result. Dell lost its position as the world's largest computer maker to Hewlett-Packard and even fell behind its Chinese rival Lenovo.

In 2013, CEO Michael Dell announced that, with the help of investors, he would buy back the company founded in 1984 and delist it from the stock exchange. Without having to consider other shareholders, he was able to accelerate the ongoing restructuring. The deal was valued at $24.4 billion US.

The privatization of the company was a particularly strong move, allowing the costly transformation to be carried out without external pressure. The often short-sighted sensitivities of shareholders do not have to be taken into account, and long-term planning becomes possible. The goal of the transformation is to make the company an end-to-end IT provider.

Value Proposition

With the ongoing digital transformation, disciplines such as artificial intelligence and self-learning machines are becoming increasingly important. This is creating an enormous amount of data that needs to be stored, protected, and most importantly, analyzed and turned into value [2]. This is where Dell comes in with its broadly diversified portfolio of companies. Michel Dell explained that delivering new and increasingly powerful servers is no longer enough today. Customers have specific business challenges that need to be solved. In the future, Dell will become a partner in the search for solutions. The focus is not on IT components, but on how they can best be used in a company's specific

Table 4.7: Transformation of the Dell business model.

Value Proposition
– We cover all of our customers' IT issues.
– We achieve this through our expertise in both hardware and software, coupled with our unwavering focus on the customer.
– We are dedicated to transforming and constantly challenging our product offerings so that our customers can count on the latest and greatest solutions.

Service Delivery	Service Offering	Cost Model	Earnings Model
Expansion of global partnering with retailers Strengthening of our own end-to-end IT portfolio through acquisitions (including the $67 billion US acquisition of EMC)	Stronger focus on small and medium-sized enterprises Stronger focus on servers, storage and security, particularly in the healthcare and public sectors Expansion of activities outside the USA Particularly in the growth markets of Ghana, Kazakhstan, Ivory Coast, Croatia and Nigeria	Initiation of a long-term cost reduction program by laying off 8,800 employees Sale of our own factories and gradual shift of production to even lower-cost suppliers	Continued expansion into new business fields that require technological expertise (e.g., artificial intelligence). This move cushions the performance of weaker divisions

environment. Table 4.7 below shows Dell's value proposition and the transformation actions in the key drivers.

Service Delivery

Dell moved away from its direct sales model and began to reach new customer groups through retail, for example by selling through Walmart. In the B2B space, Dell increasingly positioned itself as an enabler for digital transformation, for example at Volkswagen, Mercedes or BMW through the development of connected car platforms.

Dell's $67 billion US acquisition of the Electric Membership Corporation (EMC), its largest technology acquisition to date, accelerated Dell's transformation into a service provider for sophisticated end-to-end IT projects. The combination with virtualization and cloud specialists VM-Ware and Pivotal, as well as cybersecurity providers RSA and Secureworks, has created a market leader in infrastructure to help companies with their digital transformation. The group now employs approximately 160,000 people. This has allowed the company to pursue longer-term and lucrative service contracts with larger companies such as hotel chains and hospitals.

Nevertheless, Dell remains active in its core business as a PC provider alongside its new pillars as a cloud, analytics, security and mobility provider. The company continues to gain market share in a consolidating market. According to Michael Dell, it really is possible to be successful in a shrinking space. This insight is at the heart of self-disruption. A company's own transformation often fails because it clings desperately to its old business model and perceives cannibalization by the new business model as a threat to its success. This inhibition creates a state of shock paralysis, and the focus remains on the original business model.

Service Offering

By focusing on small and medium-sized businesses, Dell has identified growth potential in a shrinking market. In particular, the expansion of the service and software business for relationship customers (with annual sales of at least $1 million US) has made the technology group less dependent on PC sales. In the past, consumers and small businesses were served with the same product line. This was changed because it was recognized that these two customer groups have different needs. The product lines were differentiated, and product development and marketing were reorganized. In particular, PC as a Service (PCaaS) has become an attractive value proposition for SMBs. Hardware, software, lifecycle services and financing are offered in a comprehensive solution at a predictable monthly flat rate per workstation. This gives companies a single point of contact for their entire IT management, allowing them to focus on their core business.

The company generates half of its revenue outside the United States. By strengthening its presence in high-growth regions, Dell aims to provide government agencies, authorities, government institutions and telecommunications providers with modern IT, for example in Ghana, Kazakhstan, Ivory Coast, Croatia, and Nigeria.

In addition to hardware and software services, Dell is increasingly trying to gain a foothold in the consulting business. This involves supporting companies in the development and implementation of their IT strategy. This includes the IoT Solutions Partner Program as an ecosystem with 90 partners to date, including Intel, SAP and Microsoft. Start-ups are also involved in the program. This service helps SMBs find the right technologies for their solutions in the fragmented IoT landscape, for example in the area of predictive maintenance. Business customers will benefit from the market expertise of a leading global technology provider. For Dell, as the platform owner, this opens up a lock-in model.

Dell recognizes that it is becoming increasingly difficult for companies to attract and retain qualified IT professionals. As a result, the company's internal human resources policy is based on four pillars to help the company attract, retain and share talent:
1. Developing leaders who inspire.
2. Commitment to team members.
3. Listening and sharing information.
4. Being an employer of choice.

What sounds like a list of trivialities is actually one of the basic rules of successful human resources management—rules that are often not sufficiently followed.

Cost Model

In the wake of the reprivatization, all the business units worldwide were streamlined. In-house production was scaled back and production outsourced to low-cost suppliers. The EMC acquisition was accompanied by another major wave of layoffs to eliminate duplication and consolidate and reorganize the sales structure.

Earnings Model

In the early days of direct sales, the earnings model was based on the company's innovative financial structure. Customers paid for their PCs before Dell had to pay its suppliers. Instead of having to finance working capital, Dell was able to use the cash to finance other areas on favorable terms.

With the PCaaS service and the comprehensive IoT ecosystem, Dell has discovered two business models that make the company independent of PC sales and facilitate a long-term relationship with customers. In the case of the IoT ecosystem, a lock-in system can be assumed, as customers can only change platforms with increased effort (see also Amazon Prime in the B2C sector).

The Bottom Line

Dell's success is based in particular on the agility of its strategy: in recognizing and exploiting the opportunities presented by changing conditions. Before the Internet era, Dell used telemarketing and direct mail as its primary sales channels. As the Internet began to establish itself as a sales channel in 1993, Dell invested heavily in this technology. By 1995, more than 50% of sales were made through this channel. In addition, Dell's website has evolved from a shopping cart solution for standard components to a configuration system that allows customers to assemble their own PC according to their needs. In this way, each PC is ordered individually. The results of this differentiation strategy are customer loyalty and production optimization. Finally, the last step in the company's development was to become a full-service IT provider. This equips companies with the systems they require and supports them throughout the entire lifecycle.

According to Michael Dell, long-term thinking was neglected during the period of rapid growth. And that is exactly what is catching up with many successful companies. Looking to the future in certain circumstances may be institutionalized, but the willingness to change the current successful business model is often lacking. Changing the formula for success is seen as too risky. The result is a strategy of small adjustments that is no longer sufficient in times of disruption.

References

[1]   See Jahn, T. (2010), "Dem alten Erfolg hinterher" (Chasing Old Success), in: Die Zeit, No. 42, 2010-10-14.
[2]   See Heeg, T. (2017), "Der Glaube an den Computer bleibt" (Faith in the Computer Remains), in: Frankfurter Allgemeine Zeitung, No. 19, 2017-01-23, p. 22.

Amazon Web Services*

Background and Objectives

Amazon is one of the most valuable companies in the world today. Founded under the name "Cadabra," it reached a market capitalization of nearly $800 billion US in March 2018. This was the second highest stock market valuation in the world at the

*The case study was developed in collaboration with Tim Lersch (University of St. Gallen).

time, after Apple [1]. Amazon has reinvented itself many times over the years, and in the process has expanded beyond retail into other businesses. Cloud infrastructure solutions for consumers and businesses—known as Amazon Web Services (AWS)—contributed the lion's share of the company's free cash flow. Amazon has demonstrated its ability to transform: With AWS, the company has quickly created a profitable income source to support its low-margin retail business.

The company has successfully embraced self-disruption by significantly expanding its retail-only business model. This case study describes how Amazon was able to strengthen its position in the cloud services market by opening up its own infrastructure to other companies. It explains how a company that sought to be disruptive opened up a new, highly profitable business. In 2021, AWS generated $62.2 billion US in revenue and a remarkable $18.5 billion US in operating profit [2]. This highly profitable market position was based on a low cost structure and a profitable earnings model that ensured high utilization of available server capacity. This case study also illustrates how a very large company made a virtue out of necessity, successfully self-disrupting to create the most profitable business segment in the group.

Value Proposition

Jeff Bezos founded Amazon in 1995 with a focus on online bookselling. Amazon radically changed the book market and disrupted the industry. Since its founding, the company has continued to set new trends by expanding into new business segments. It has continually reinvented itself. Opening up its own sales platform to third-party sellers via the Amazon Marketplace alone shows that Amazon is not afraid to take unconventional paths and even make the advantages of its own platform available to its competitors.

In 2006, Amazon launched AWS as the first provider of distributed, cloud-based server infrastructure solutions. Previously, Infrastructure as a Service (IaaS) was only viable for large enterprises and was offered by vendors such as HP or IBM through on-premises solutions (company-owned server farms). With AWS, companies could now add computing power on the fly without having to build their own server farms. This made the service attractive to smaller companies that could not afford their own data centers. In addition, Amazon offered an unbeatable price ($0.15 US per gigabyte per month), which was 70–80% below the cost of on-premises solutions. This made AWS a cost-effective solution even for large enterprises. The reliability and security of Amazon's cloud infrastructure help make AWS an all-inclusive, worry-free package for businesses of all sizes. AWS promises "the most scalable, secure, and reliable cloud infrastructure for any size business at the best price". Over the past years, this value proposition has driven a very successful business model transformation (see Table 4.8).

Table 4.8: Transformation of the AWS business model.

Value Proposition			
To deliver scalable, secure, and reliable cloud infrastructures for businesses of all sizes at the best price.			
Service Delivery	**Service Offering**	**Cost Model**	**Earnings Model**
Continuous expansion of server farms facilitates close to infinite computing capacity	Cafeteria model: AWS offers more than 70 different IT services that customers can configure as needed	Amazon's commercial business ensures high server park base utilization as well as continuous development	Marketplace character generates revenue based on a classic transaction-based earnings model
Distributed, cloud-based service makes it easier for maintenance teams to efficiently maintain servers	Multiple pricing models allow customers to build the most cost-effective package	Leasing of unused capacity to other companies	Third-party merchants pay a sales commission per item sold
AWS continues to expand and improve its global cloud-based product offerings, including compute, storage, database, analytics, networking, mobile, developer, management, IoT, security, and enterprise applications		Synergies reduce the average cost per computing power	AWS customers pay only for the services they use on a pay-as-you-go basis
		Decentralization of the offering leads to cost reductions from server maintenance savings	Additional revenue from offerings including Amazon Sponsored Products and Amazon Pay

Service Delivery

AWS is a service born of necessity. At the turn of the millennium, Amazon's IT processes were not particularly efficient. IT application development was slow and sometimes unpredictable. Marketplace development could have been faster, and there were recurring problems with project management. Amazon addressed these issues systematically and fundamentally as part of a transformation process. The company turned disorganized and confusing development platforms into decentralized and reliable infrastructures. This made it possible for the company to develop IT solutions more efficiently and scale more quickly. In the early stages of the project, Amazon managers had a visionary idea that would prove extremely important to other companies in the future. Because local server solutions (IaaS) were only an option for large companies due to their high cost, smaller companies (e.g., retailers selling goods on the Amazon Marketplace) were at a particular disadvantage. There was no such affordable IT infrastructure solution for them. With its cloud-based, low-cost, scalable server solutions, Amazon opened up the possibility of renting out the infrastructure it was not using to other companies, thus scaling its own IT infrastructure.

From the beginning, AWS was especially appreciated by small businesses with a small turnover. The aforementioned disadvantage over large enterprises disappeared, and AWS sales flourished. Expanding server farms created more and more computing capacity to rent to customers. Therefore it was only a matter of time before large enterprises with above-average capacity needs moved to AWS. The high security and performance of AWS server farms also served as an incentive.

Service Offering

By offering web services solutions, Amazon created a highly cost-effective way for companies of all sizes to outsource computing power and storage to the cloud. In keeping with the value proposition, AWS customers range from individual consumers who store personal data such as photos, videos, and documents securely in the Amazon cloud, to small and medium-sized businesses, to large corporations such as General Electric. Even Netflix, Amazon's biggest competitor in video streaming, uses AWS servers to store its movies and shows [3]. This diverse customer base is reflected in the variety of AWS products. Customers can choose from nearly 240 different AWS cloud products and mix and match [4]. Gone are the days of painstakingly installing and maintaining each new application on dedicated servers. The service offering is diverse and ranges from basic computing power and storage to database creation, analytics, and machine learning applications. In addition, AWS stands out for the infinite scalability of its applications. It is within the services offered that the value proposition shines as a guiding light. It acts as a coordinating tool across all domains. All available services serve to strengthen the value proposition, e.g. by minimizing costs. Companies can add additional server capacity on demand (short or long term) to ensure an efficient workflow. In addition, Amazon is constantly developing the platform and introducing new application options (e.g. Internet of Things solutions). As a result, customers can meet more of their cloud service needs with AWS. Gone are the days of being forced to remain loyal to one provider because of the high upfront costs of installing your own servers. Amazon achieves high customer loyalty through easy scalability, unbeatable pricing, and global offerings.

Cost Model

Since its 2006 debut, AWS sales have seen a continuous upward trajectory. In Q1 2022, its services claimed a 33% market share in cloud-based web services, leaving Microsoft Azure in second place with 21% [5]. But how did AWS achieve such dominance in such a short time, all while maintaining a return on sales exceeding 20%? This remarkable feat is attributed to Amazon's unique synergistic approach. Firstly,

Amazon's retail business ensured high base utilization of its server farms. This not only provided constant development opportunities but also allowed them to rent out unused infrastructure to external companies for a premium. Sophisticated capacity planning prevented bottlenecks and enabled AWS to consistently lower average computing costs. This combination of internal use and external rental, unmatched by any competitor in the retail space, explains Amazon's significant lead. Secondly, the unique synergy between Amazon and external companies resulted in unparalleled low IT costs.

Competitors like IBM and HP had to solely build their server farms for rental purposes, hindering optimal capacity utilization like that achieved by AWS.

Additionally, Amazon's cloud infrastructure stood out from traditional on-premises solutions. Its decentralized nature minimized costs by eliminating the need for on-site maintenance technicians. Only smooth operation within their own server farms was essential, resulting in significantly lower personnel costs compared to local solutions.

Looking back, AWS's disruptive impact on the industry becomes clear. They embodied the principle once again that the rapid acquisition of market share is only possible for those companies that achieve cost-efficiency and leverage cost advantages.

Earnings Model

Prior to the launch of Amazon Web Services (AWS), Amazon's profits came primarily from two sources. First, its core retail business on the Amazon website followed a traditional transaction-based model, generating revenue through margins like any other retailer. Despite being a disruptor in the bookselling industry, even Amazon faced the challenge of declining margins in traditional retail. In fact, outside of its home market of the United States, its retail business was losing money in some areas. Second, the company operated a marketplace where third-party sellers offered their products. For each sale, Amazon received a percentage commission on the sale price that varied by product category, ranging from 6% for PCs to 45% for accessories for its own devices such as the Kindle [6]. The launch of the marketplace in 2000 marked a first step away from complete reliance on retail.

However, Amazon's leadership likely already recognized the need for further diversification. By embracing one of its core leadership principles of 'frugality,' or resourceful innovation, demanded from its employees, a new earnings model was born out of necessity [7]. Amazon turned its existing cloud infrastructure into a business model that initially served small and medium-sized businesses. It then expanded to offer solutions for large enterprises. Customers pay for various services such as computing power, storage, and analytics tools based on a chosen usage-based pricing model [8]. Instead of fixed monthly fees, customers are charged only for the resources they actually use [9]. This combination of affordability and flexible billing models makes AWS attractive to virtually any business, regardless of size, and even to individual users. As a result, Amazon is maximizing its market potential. This is evident not only in its impressive market share, but also in its rapidly growing revenues. From just $3.1 billion US in 2014, AWS revenue has grown nearly twenty-fold in seven years, reaching a staggering $62.2 billion US in 2021 [10].

Amazon's income sources extend beyond its core retail business to include other sources such as Amazon Sponsored Products and Amazon Pay. These recent additions significantly bolster profitability, especially in light of doubts about the long-term viability of the marketplace's own business outside the US. This uncertainty stems from intense price competition for the products offered and heavy investments, such as those in logistics, that fuel annual growth of up to 30%. Against this backdrop, Amazon has strategically added these highly profitable income sources to its existing model.

The Bottom Line

AWS is another example of Amazon conquering a market that didn't exist just a few years ago.

Early entry into this fast-growing segment of cloud-based Internet services was critical to its current market share. In addition, the combination of cost leadership and service excellence has been critical to its success. This competitive advantage has been continuously strengthened over the years. Like no other company, Amazon can leverage economies of scale to outsource server services that are critical to its core business and continually improve their efficiency. AWS offers pay-as-you-go pricing for more than 90 cloud services, ensuring that customers pay only for what they use, for as long as they need it, without long-term commitments or complex licensing. This unwavering value proposition has guided management over the past several years, serving as the guiding principle for expanding and capturing the market in the four key drivers.

This still relatively new business segment for Amazon expands upon its initial marketplace operations. While perhaps less strategically planned than originally thought, this serendipitously conceived idea has blossomed into a cash cow. Beyond its core retail business, Amazon has demonstrated its ability to create further disruption in Internet-driven businesses segments. In particular, the high profitability of its cloud-based services has been a major driving force of the company's stock price.

References

[1]   See Finance.yahoo.com (2018), AMZN : Summary for Amazon.com, Inc. – Yahoo Finance, 2018-04-01, https://finance.yahoo.com/quote/AMZN/.

[2]   See Amazon (2022), Amazon Annual Report 2021, 2023-01-18, retrieved from: https://s2.q4cdn.com/299287126/files/doc_financials/2022/ar/Amazon-2021-Annual-Report.pdf (in German only).

[3]   see Amazon Web Services, Inc. (2023), cloud products from AWS, 2023-01-18, retrieved from: https://aws.amazon.com/products/.

[4]   See Amazon Web Services, Inc. (2018), "Fallstudien und Kundenerfolge – Amazon Web Services" (Case Studies and Customer Success – Amazon Web Services), 2018-04-04, retrieved from: https://aws.amazon.com/de/solutions/case-studies/all/ (in German only).

[5]   See Statista (2022), Cloud infrastructure services vendor market share worldwide from 4th quarter 2017 to 1st quarter 2022, in: Statista, 2022-08-05, https://www.statista.com/statistics/967365/world wide-cloud-infrastructure-services-market-share-vendor/.

[6]   See Sellercentral.amazon.com (2018), Selling on Amazon Fee Schedule – Amazon Seller Central, 2018-04-04, https://sellercentral.amazon.com/gp/help/external/200336920/ref=asus_soa_p_reffees? Id=NSGoogle.

[7]   See Amazon.com (2018), About Amazon – Working at Amazon – Our Leadership Principles, 5.4.2018, https://www.amazon.com/p/feature/p34qgjcv93n37yd.

[8]   See Amazon Web Services, Inc. (2018), "Preisprinzipien für AWS Cloud – Amazon Web Services (AWS)" (Pricing Principles for AWS Cloud – Amazon Web Services (AWS)), 2018-04-04, https://aws.amazon.com/de/pricing/?nc2=h_ql_pr&awsm=ql-3 (in German only).

[9]   See Amazon Web Services, Inc. (2018), "AWS-Fakturierung und Kostenmanagment" (AWS Billing and Cost Management), 2018-04-04, https://aws.amazon.com/de/documentation/account-billing/. (in German only).

[10]   See Amazon Inc. (2022), Amazon.com Annual Report 2021, retrieved fom: https://s2.q4cdn.com/299287126/files/doc_financials/2022/ar/Amazon-2021-Annual-Report.pdf.

IBM*

Background and Objectives of the Case Study

Legend has it that former IBM CEO Thomas J. Watson Jr. proclaimed in the mid-20th century that global demand for computers would be limited to just five buyers and units [1]. Though misinterpreted and out of context, this anecdote has survived as a reminder about failed market analyses and the critical importance of in-depth customer and market knowledge that is indispensable for forward-thinking leadership.

Nonetheless, IBM has undergone a fundamental transformation in recent decades. From its original role as a hardware manufacturer, the company has evolved into an integrated service provider that supports clients across the IT landscape through a vertically integrated value creation chain.

While this transformation may not be readily apparent, IBM's core mission of helping corporate clients with their IT needs remains the same. However, the way in which it delivers this value proposition in the 21st century has changed fundamentally.

Value Proposition

The transformation that began in the 1990s fundamentally changed IBM's value proposition. Once focused solely on building data management machines, IBM trans-

---

*The case study was developed in collaboration with Severin F. Bischof (University of St. Gallen).

formed itself into a partner and advisor to its clients. Its new value proposition proclaims: IBM enables companies to break through the boundaries of IT and realize its potential before it becomes an industry standard (see Table 4.9).

A critical success factor in IBM's transformation has been recognizing and harnessing the potential of the Internet since the mid-1990s. While only 16 million people surfed the Web in 1995, the number of Internet users worldwide skyrocketed to nearly 4.9 billion by 2021. IBM strategically aligned itself with this burgeoning technology by seamlessly integrating hardware sales with services-a concept known as 'consultative selling'. This shift to services, consulting and support helped IBM avoid further revenue and margin declines amid the ongoing commoditization of the IT industry. Since 1998, services and software revenue has surpassed hardware revenue [2].

Table 4.9: Transformation of the IBM business model.

Value Proposition			
IBM gives companies the power to break through the boundaries of IT and realize the potential before it becomes an industry standard.			
Service Delivery	**Service Offering**	**Cost Model**	**Earnings Model**
Technically skilled employees (19 research labs staffed by 3,000 researchers on six continents; more than 9,000 patents in 2020) Increasingly business-centric employees (business economists, strategy, consultative sales) Consistent divestiture of unprofitable business divisions, even those with market dominance	IBM partners with customers to help them use IT and implement new technologies Integration of hardware, software and consulting services Bespoke, highly innovative solutions for every need (IBM Cognitive Solutions, Watson, Quantum Computing)	Lean processes without unnecessary redundancies and complexities (shared services that country organizations can source from the back office as needed) Highly efficient use of resources (nine out of ten employees are dedicated to product development, processing, and sales; only one out of ten positions is in the back office)	Consistent focus on highly profitable business areas, especially consulting services Hardly any pure hardware sales without consulting services

Service Offering

IBM positions itself as a trusted partner, guiding clients through the complexities of emerging technologies. By offering hardware, software and consulting services under one roof, IBM delivers customized, cutting-edge solutions based on a three-pronged service offering that exceed industry standards. Imagine quantum computers and AI (like Watson) autonomously analyzing your data and uncovering hidden insights from individual data points. While still rare, these big data solutions give IBM clients a significant competitive advantage.

This comprehensive service offering has evolved from an earlier model rooted in IBM's historic technology leadership. Like the American dream, IBM's journey is a testament to perseverance and innovation. From its humble beginnings in 1911, the company, officially renamed International Business Machines in 1924, relentlessly pursued technological leadership. Its focus on industrial mainframes led it to become a renowned manufacturer of components and equipment. Throughout the mid-1980s, IBM remained an investor favorite [3], even supporting John F. Kennedy's mission to the moon and boasting several Nobel Prize winners among its alumni.

But just as every peak is followed by a trough, IBM's success story took a dramatic turn in the late 1980s. As the mainframe business approached commoditization and profit margins dwindled, the company suffered an eight-billion-dollar loss in 1993, the largest in American corporate history at the time. This near-death experience forced a major reckoning [4]. Rather than fall into a state of shock paralysis, IBM embarked on a transformational journey marked by cultural change and a redefined value proposition. Recognizing the need to navigate the complexities of the IT landscape, they transformed their service offerings, moving beyond the sale of pure IT infrastructure to a comprehensive suite of technology-driven consulting services. Today, IBM is a global leader in both consulting and services.

Service Delivery

To ensure a smooth transformation of the service offering, the company has carefully adapted its service delivery capabilities. Since the 1990s, IBM has strategically acquired resources on a constant basis, investing more than $30 billion US in the acquisition of 200 companies. It also divested itself of low-growth, low-margin businesses, even shedding iconic products such as computer monitors and printers even though IBM invented some of them and they were steeped in sentimental value.

Following this transformation, management reshaped the composition of the workforce. To solidify its service-oriented image, IBM began attracting more science-oriented talent [5]. MBAs and strategy consultants joined the ranks, skillfully combining hardware sales with expert consulting services. A service offering made up of comprehensive technology consulting was critical to maintaining its pioneering role in IT. To maintain this position, IBM developed technically skilled researchers as key service providers. Today, with 19 research labs on six continents and 3,000 researchers, IBM filed more than 9,000 patents in 2020 alone, solidifying its leadership in technology innovation.

Cost Model

In addition to overhauling its service offering, IBM has fundamentally changed its cost model. The company now prioritizes reducing redundancies and complexities [6], with a focus on achieving economies of scale. This included implementing a 'shared services model' that consolidated back-office activities such as human resources and accounting across countries and divisions. Various geographical regions share the costs of the HR and accounting departments. Standard processes were consolidated into centers for all internal functions so that, for example, all human capital needs are now met from a global talent pool. These efficiencies reduced back-office costs by 25% between 2005 and 2010 [7]. Simultaneously, the Group's overall productivity reached more efficient levels, with nine out of 10 employees dedicated to developing or selling IBM's offerings. Lean central administration and the elimination of redundancies have resulted in highly efficient capacity utilization, which has been instrumental in supporting the development of the service offering.

Earnings Model

This transformation sparked a dramatic shift in IBM's earnings model. A relentless focus on high-margin areas, particularly consulting services, pushed the record loss of 1993 further into the past. As consulting services grew as a percentage of total revenue, so did profitability. Nearly every hardware sale was bundled with a service, making IBM's sales efforts much more lucrative.

Diverse acquisitions such as the $3.9 billion US purchase of the PricewaterhouseCoopers' consulting arm in 2002, fueled by the Enron scandal and the subsequent Sarbanes-Oxley Act, accelerated this shift toward services. In one fell swoop, IBM's consulting workforce doubled to 60,000 in 52 countries. Today, consulting is divided into distinct areas: strategy (IBM Global Business Services), infrastructure (IBM Global Technology Services) and cloud.

The Bottom Line

Today, IBM offers end-to-end service solutions that support businesses across their entire operations. With revenues of $57 billion US in 2021, IBM remains a global leader in IT and services. The spirit of transformation continues to define the company. As Bridget van Kralingen, former General Manager of IBM North America, said, "Your ability to change is not just an expression of your wish to survive, it is about actively shaping you future. You must accept that complacency is a business killer and banish it from your thinking. You must understand that transformation is a constant and continuous process that can never end. And you must embrace the notion that when faced with tough times your goal must be not merely to survive but to succeed, and success comes through leadership." [8]

References

[1]   See Shapiro, F. R. (Ed.). (2006),The Yale book of quotations, Yale University Press.
[2]   See Applegate, L., Austin, R., & Collins, E. (2009), IBM's decade of transformation: Turnaround to growth,in: Harvard Business School Case, 9-805-130.
[3]   See Forbes (2010) IBM's Transformation – From Survival to Success, in: Forbes, 2010-07-07, https://www.forbes.com/2010/07/07/ibm-transformation-lessons-leadership-managing-change. html#5bb836043afb.
[4]   See IBM (2018), Chronological History of IBM, in: IBM Archives, 2018-01-25, https://www-03.ibm. com/ibm/history/history/history_intro.html.
[5]   See Forbes (2010), IBM's Transformation – From Survival to Success, in: Forbes, 2010-07-07, https://www.forbes.com/2010/07/07/ibm-transformation-lessons-leadership-managing-change. html#5bb836043afb.
[6]   See ibid.
[7]   See ibid.
[8]   See ibid.

Nordstrom*

Background and Objectives of the Case Study

Few could have predicted that young John W. Nordstrom, who arrived in New York from Sweden in 1887 with little money and no knowledge of English, would one day build one of the world's most successful retail empires. He spent his early years in America far from the world of department stores, toiling as a lumberjack and miner in California and Washington. The Klondike Gold Rush of the 1890s drew him far to the north to Canada, where he struck gold two years later and returned to the US with $13,000 US in his pack to invest in his long hankered for entrepreneurial dreams. Partnering with shoemaker Carl F. Wallin, he opened the Wallin & Nordstrom shoe store in Seattle in 1890 only a short time later. Business boomed and a second store was opened in 1923, and in 1929, both founders went into retirement and sold their shares to John's sons, Everett and Elmer, who took over and renamed the company Nordstrom [1]. For decades, Nordstrom thrived. But in the late 1990s, the fourth generation faced a significant challenge. While overall sales increased with new store openings, individual store performance stagnated. Sales per square foot fell 13% between 1995 and 2001 [2], margins were squeezed by price cuts, and debt levels soared to 49% by 2000 [3]. Dissatisfied with the Nordstrom experi-

---

*The case study was developed in collaboration with Gianluca Scheidegger (University of St. Gallen).

ence, long-term customers began to drift away. After losing around half its market value in one year (1999–2000), the supervisory board took decisive action in August 2000: CEO John Whitacre was replaced by Blake Nordstrom, and 66-year-old former CEO Bruce Nordstrom returned as chairman of the supervisory board. To reverse the downward spiral, Blake und Bruce Nordstrom and the rest of the management team had to undertake a comprehensive transformation across all key drivers. At the core of this strategy stood their sales associates. The following sections of this case study explore Nordstrom's successful transformative journey from 2000 to 2005.

Value Proposition

After taking the helm of the company, Blake and Bruce Nordstrom embarked on a nationwide journey to connect with the people who know their customers best: Nordstrom's associates on the sales floor [4]. Since the company's founding by John W. Nordstrom, sales associates have been central to Nordstrom's customer-centric culture. This focus stems from the company's core value proposition, which can only be fulfilled by dedicated associates: "We provide the best possible service to our customers and help them live their lives with ease" (see Table 4.10).

Nordstrom is widely recognized today as a model of customer service. Over the years, the company has learned that a value proposition focused on excellent cus-

Table 4.10: Transformation of the Nordstrom business model.

Value Proposition			
To provide the best possible service to our customers and help them live their lives with ease.			
Service Delivery	**Service Offering**	**Cost Model**	**Earnings Model**
Empowerment of employees	Attractive and clear store design and fashionable assortment at competitive prices	Centralization of the back office and buying process to achieve economies of scale and reduce costs	No discounted goods Sale at regular price
Frequent exchange of information and experience between management and employees	Excellent customer service	Installation of an inventory tool to generate demand forecasts	Introduction of the GMROI metric to explain the key profit drivers
	– e.g. very accommodating when it comes to returns		
Introduction of a 'Personal Book' service tool on the sales floor	Right of return assessed on a case-by-case basis		
Involvement of store associates in the buying process			

tomer service pays off handsomely. The service ethos is deeply embedded in Nordstrom's DNA, embraced by every associate, and guiding every aspect of the business. All decisions are evaluated from the customer's perspective. Even as a publicly traded company, Nordstrom puts customer needs ahead of shareholder demands. Only in this way can Nordstrom provide the best possible customer service.

Service Offering

During their trip, Blake and Bruce Nordstrom interviewed more than 2,000 associates in 77 stores. Many associates expressed concern that the merchandise assortment was out of touch with customer preferences. In addition, long-time, mostly older customers felt unwelcome in the stores. This sentiment stemmed in part from Nordstrom's "Reinvent Yourself" campaign, which targeted a younger demographic. The 40 million dollar campaign, which featured pop music, bright colors, trendy fashions and young models, confused longtime customers instead of attracting new ones [5]. So it was terminated. In response, Nordstrom invested in a more targeted in-store experience. In 2005, customers were greeted by soft piano music and a luxurious interior.

Recognizing that many loyal customers had difficulty navigating the stores, the new Nordstrom team prioritized easy in-store navigation. In the huge women's shoe department, for example, high heels were organized by heel height and color. While most fashion retailers today organize their assortments by traditional categories such as brand or demographic criteria, Nordstrom sought to inspire shoppers through unique categories. Based on different price points (moderate to designer) and styles (classic to contemporary), Nordstrom created unique categories such as 'Studio 121' and 'Narrative' [6]. This concept encouraged customers to discover new products and be inspired by the assortment.

Despite its commitment to excellent customer service, Nordstrom also strives to offer competitive prices. The company's website promises to match the price of any product if a customer finds it cheaper elsewhere at a competitor [7].

Service Delivery

Nordstrom associates have long enjoyed a high degree of autonomy in the stores, with responsibility at the same time for ensuring that customer leave the store satisfied. For example, there are no rigid return policies; associates handle each case and make independent decisions. This fosters a high level of staff engagement, which is critical for a service-centric company like Nordstrom.

During their store visits, however, Bruce and Blake Nordstrom noticed a significant decline in staff morale. Staff felt disenfranchised by the management, because key decisions about merchandise assortment and store layout were being made without their input. Blake committed to increasing dialogue with the associates in future, involving them more in the process and spending nearly half of his time in the stores interacting with them. His approachable style, greeting everyone with a simple "Hi, I'm Blake," resonated with associates [8].

The rapid expansion of the 1990s meant that new stores were neglected, which affected service levels. Nordstrom responded by making significant investments to improve these. In 2004, the 'Personal Book' software developed in-house was deployed on the sales floor [9], allowing sales associates to store customer preferences, enabling personalization and better responsiveness to individual needs. Customers were identified by name or loyalty card. Sales associates could also use the Personal Book to reorder out-of-stock sizes and colors or track alteration orders, with the data stored centrally and accessible to any Nordstrom sales associate.

A critical change in the new merchandise buying process gave sales associates on the floor a voice in selecting the merchandise. The newly created role of regional merchandiser in each regional buying department was responsible for connecting buyers and sales associates on the floor [10]. Buyers gained clearer insight into customer needs, and sales associates felt empowered to provide customers with better explanations and presentations.

Cost Model

Nordstrom's customer-centric focus aimed to make decisions as close to the customer as possible. In Nordstrom's early days with few stores, this was easy. Over time, the local focus led to a decentralized organizational structure with major redundancies and limited collaboration.

Selling, general and administrative (SG&A) expenses reached 31.6% of sales in 2000 [11]. For example, each division (private label, Internet, etc.) had its own human resources and finance departments. From 2000 to 2003, the consolidation of back-office functions across the divisions provided cost savings and an added subsidiary benefit: store managers had more time to focus on exceptional customer service rather than administrative tasks.

One of the most significant actions taken by Nordstrom's new management was to restructure its decentralized buying process. In 1999, Nordstrom employed 730 buyers, more than four times the number of its competitors [12]. Not only was this expensive, but it also weakened Nordstrom's bargaining power with suppliers. Instead of ordering large quantities in a single process, orders were distributed among several dozen buyers. Because a decentralized purchasing department can respond more quickly and flexibly to customer needs, not all areas were merged during the restructuring. Instead, an analysis was conducted to determine which product groups were suitable for centralized purchasing: the buying of jewelry, hosiery, socks and housewares was centralized as a first step. These categories were considered appropriate because customer preferences did not vary significantly from store to store. In other categories, such as women's apparel, the company wanted to continue to make local adjustments to the assortment based on demand.

At the same time as the restructuring, an inventory tool was installed in 2000 to provide buyers with an overview of daily inventory figures per store and product. This enabled them to make demand estimates to minimize inventory and supply shortages. Using the proprietary tool, Nordstrom also identified top and bottom performing products and strategically removed the latter from its assortment. This streamlining approach reduced inventory per square meter from $5.85 to $4.74 US in four years [13].

Earnings Model

In the years of turbulence, Nordstrom held steadfast to its old profit model, recognizing that the decentralized structure, not the model itself, was the root cause of its challenging situation. It continued to offer attractive merchandise and exceptional service at competitive prices and, unlike its competitors, eschewed price promotions.

CFO Michael Koppel and his team introduced a new metric after 2000 that made it easier for the management to understand how it could influence the return on invested capital (ROIC). Gross margin and inventory turns are popular KPIs for analyzing department stores, but when viewed in isolation, this analysis has major weaknesses. High margins alone are meaningless if products sit on the shelves for months, while high sales can yield minimal profit for a store. GMROI (gross margin return on investment) takes into account both margin and turnover, and is calculated by dividing average margin (in USD) by average inventory. Koppel described the introduction of GMROI as an 'aha moment' for the company's leadership, pinpointing the levers for improving profitability: inventory and margins [14]. This insight significantly shaped Nordstrom's future decisions. The increased management focus on GMROI likely led Nordstrom to optimize its cost model by reducing inventory and, unlike its competitors, avoiding price cuts.

The Bottom Line

As the old adage about family businesses goes, "The father creates, the son maintains, and the grandson dismantles." In the late 1990s, Nordstrom, a fourth-generation family business, faced a similar fate. Rapid expansion coupled with a decentralized structure exacerbated the complexity of the company enormously. Costs and the debt ratio soared, undermining investor and customer confidence. Fortunately, the board recognized the need for a holistic transformation just in time. Feedback from the sale associates informed efforts to improve product assortment and store layout, while communication between the staff in general and management was improved. Selected processes were centralized for cost savings, and new technology was introduced to streamline inventory management and demand forecasting. In addition, customer service received a personalized boost with the introduction of the 'Personal Book' software. These initiatives quickly produced positive results. Sales climbed from $5.6 billion in 2001 to $7.1 billion US in 2004. At the same time, sales per square meter at store level increased by 8% [15]. By 2022, Nordstrom's total sales had reached a staggering $15.53 billion US, a remarkable growth of $8.43 billion US from 2004. This robust increase underscores the company's impressive sales trajectory over the years [16].

References

[1]   See Nordstrom, (2017), Nordstrom Company History, 2018-02-27, https://shop.nordstrom.com/c/company-history.
[2]   See Nordstrom, (2001), 2001 Annual Report.
[3]   See Lal, R./Arar, H, (2005), Nordstrom: The Turnaround. Harvard Business School Case.
[4]   See Mulady, K., (2001), Back in the family: The Nordstroms reassume control after a brief change in leadership, in: The Seattle Post-Intelligencer Reporter, 2001-06-26, https://www.seattlepi.com/business/article/Back-in-the-family-1058196.php.
[5]   See Ouchi, M.S., (2007), Nordstrom: A fashion-forward future, in: The Seattle Times, 2017-05-23, https://www.seattletimes.com/business/nordstrom-a-fashion-forward-future/.
[6]   See Nordstrom, (2000), Press releases: Nordstrom to Begin Construction of Its New Store at Fashion Show, 2000-08-06, http://press.nordstrom.com/phoenix.zhtml?c=211996&p=irol-newsarticle&ID=1022608.
[7]   See Nordstrom, (2018), Pricing Policy, 2018-03-23, https://shop.nordstrom.com/c/pricing-policy.
[8]   See Lal, R./Arar, H, (2005), Nordstrom: The Turnaround. Harvard Business School Case.
[9]   See Ross, J.W./Beath, C.M./Sebastian, I., (2015), Why Nordstrom's Digital Strategy Works (and Yours Probably Doesn't), in: Harvard Business Review, 2015-01-14, https://hbr.org/2015/01/why-nordstroms-digital-strategy-works-and-yours-probably-doesnt.
[10] See Lal, R./Arar, H, (2005), Nordstrom: The Turnaround. Harvard Business School Case.
[11] See Nordstrom, (2000), 2000 Annual Report.
[12] See Lal, R./Arar, H, (2005), Nordstrom: The Turnaround. Harvard Business School Case.
[13] See ibid.
[14] See ibid.
[15] See Nordstrom, (2004), Annual Report 2004.
[16] See Nordstrom (2023), Quarterly Results Q4 2022, 23-03-02, https://investor.nordstrom.com/static-files/373ef026-7361-4c47-b171-90c52c9646d3.

Best Buy[*]

Background and Objectives of the Case Study

Despite a dominant 23.7% market share as continuing industry leader in American electronics retail in 2011, unease permeated Best Buy's executive suite [1]. A glance at

---

[*]The case study was developed in collaboration with Elias Barth (University of St. Gallen) and Marcus Tengler (MediaMarktSaturn Retail Cooperation).

the balance sheet revealed the cause. Since 2008, operating income had halved despite rising sales, pushing the company into the red.

Digitalization was also driving changes in customer behavior, with the customer journey often starting online rather than in a store. Phenomena such as 'showrooming' and the 'ROPO' effect (research online, purchase offline) illustrated this trend [2]. As a result, online retailers, epitomized by Amazon, gained market share and squeezed margins for established players like Best Buy. The company's 10% revenue growth in 2010 slowed to just 1% in 2011 [3]. In stark contrast, Amazon's market share jumped to 4% in a short period of time, while Best Buy's online sales stagnated at 7%. This was particularly worrisome for Best Buy given that online electronics sales had doubled between 2008 and 2012, representing missed growth from an investor perspective. These fears translated into a plummeting stock price, which fell from $49 to $31 US per share in 2010 [4]. In the midst of this tense situation, Hubert Joly was appointed CEO. The Frenchman's lack of experience in the industry caused initial skepticism among investors and analysts, so his actions were observed critically and intensively. His turnaround strategy, 'Renew Blue' addressed the following critical challenges.

Stagnant market share and declining margins were Best Buy's overarching concerns. Changing customer preferences toward online retailing had triggered the profit decline. Many consumers sought advice in-store but then purchased online from competitors, highlighting the 'showrooming' phenomenon. This negatively impacted Best Buy's price image and customer satisfaction.

To gain control of the situation, the turnaround strategy focused on two key areas. A better 'customer experience' in terms of omnichannel buying behavior and service offerings became the focus of differentiation efforts [5].

In terms of the business model transformation pursued, the'Renew Blue' strategyfirst focused on the value propositionand then on the service offering. In retrospect, the changes to the earnings model that were not part of the original turnaround plan paid off in particular.

Value Proposition

Best Buy's traditional value proposition of offering a wide selection of electronics at fair prices was increasingly challenged in the age of online retailing. Online giants like Amazon, which leveraged third-party sellers, offered much broader product assortments. In addition, their lower fixed costs, without physical stores and sales staff, translated into more competitive pricing than Best Buy. Best Buy therefore presented a revamped value proposition to differentiate itself from other electronics retailers. To turn around its business, Best Buy first needed to make its value proposition clearer. Second, the company needed to emphasize its service nature, which Amazon could not offer. Third, Best Buy decided to rely on a curated selection of products, products that met Best Buy's quality standards. These three aspects led to a more precise value proposition: "The best selection of curated consumer electronics products/services at unbeatable prices." (see Table 4.11).

The revised value proposition summarized Hubert Joly's 'Renew Blue' turnaround plan and clarified the approach to the business model transformation.

Table 4.11: Transformation of the Best Buy business model.

Value Proposition

To deliver the best selection of curated electrical products/services at unbeatable prices.

Service Delivery	Service Offering	Cost Model	Earnings Model
Existing stores expanded to create logistics centers	New store layout introduced to emphasize product/service offering	Closure of unprofitable stores in the USA and Canada	Introduction of price matching
Product/service training introduced for employees	Product mix adjusted with focus on own and premium brands	Withdrawal from unprofitable markets (China and Europe)	Service-based earnings models established (fee-based advice)
'Net Promoter Score' introduced to monitor customer focus	New services introduced (cell phone tariff, advice, etc.)	Downsizing in middle management	New source of earnings opened up by renting out retail space
		Cost redistribution through store-in-store concepts	

Service Offering

Best Buy sought to differentiate itself from the competition through a combination of both online and brick-and-mortar stores. Their focus shifted to areas where online-only retailers like Amazon fell short: Customer experience and service-driven offerings.

A key focus was the redesign of store layouts. Best Buy abandoned its previous strategy of displaying as many products as possible. Instead, the store layout communicated the concept of service and the customer experience. The space was divided into clear product/service areas that were easy to navigate. A 'Solution Central Help Desk', reminiscent of Apple's 'Genius Bar', encouraged interaction between customers and sales staff [6]. In keeping with the service aspect, customers could also pick up their orders at the stores (click and collect).

As part of the 'Renew Blue' strategy, Best Buy adjusted its product mix. Product categories that were not growing or had low margins (e.g., CDs, DVDs, etc.) were eliminated. Instead, the company focused on premium and brand own products to replace existing products. These became the focus of the new assortment. In 2009, Best Buy's own brand sales increased by 40% [7]. Best Buy also focused on improving in-store customer service. For example, the company helped customers sign up for mobile phone contracts. By 2015, more than 1 million customers had taken advantage of this offer, saving an average of $35 US per contract [8]. This development was also reflected in the share of sales of products that require a lot of advice, such as mobile phones (including contracts) or major household appliances (washing machines, etc.). In 2018, the combined sales share of these two categories was 55%, compared to just 38% in 2010 [9]. Best Buy continues to embrace this trend by offering in-store advisory services, such as topic-specific training or personalized technology solutions.

Service Delivery

Best Buy also used its stores as fulfillment centers to provide better delivery service. Stores acted as 'ship from store' stations so customers could receive their products the same day [10]. The company relied on a high level of employee expertise to ensure a consistent focus on service. Employees, especially front-line staff, were encouraged to take on the role of concierge, providing expert assistance to customers. Staff were trained to better explain the benefits of new products. For the Windows 8 launch, Best Buy consultants received approximately 50,000 hours of product training [11]. This shifted the service creation process. Service was no longer created by a broad product offering, but by product advice (service) and a curated product selection.

Best Buy monitored and managed customer focus by introducing the 'Net Promoter Score'. This metric measures customer loyalty and can be thought of as the dependent variable of all the factors that increase customer loyalty.

Cost Model

Best Buy also launched a cost savings program as part of its 'Renew Blue' strategy. First, the retailer consolidated its weak international business, ending its joint venture with Carphone Warehouse in Europe in 2013 [12]. In Canada, 66 stores were closed and the 'Future Shop' brand was discontinued [13]. In 2014, Best Buy exited the Chinese market, selling its 184 stores there [14]. The company also closed 50 big-box stores in its home market and reduced its average store size by 20 % [15]. In addition, Joly decided to cut middle management, eliminating 2,000 management positions [16].

Store-in-store concepts allowed Best Buy to externalize some of its labor costs. Leasing partners contributed financially to the new store concepts and often provided the sales associates. This shifted some of the costs to external partners. The cost savings from 'Renew Blue' already amounted to $860 million US in 2014 [17].

Earnings Model

From a customer perspective, Best Buy's pricing policy proved to be its Achilles' heel compared to online retailers. Only 23% of customers surveyed said Best Buy offers attractive prices (compared to 71% at Walmart and 56% at Amazon) [18]. On average, the electronics retailer's prices were about 8% higher than Amazon's [19]. After some controversy, Best Buy implemented a new pricing policy. The retailer offered customers a price-matching option, guaranteeing them the lowest price if another retailer was cheaper than Best Buy. In this way, Best Buy limited the incentives to simply 'showroom' and buy from cheaper vendors. Of course, this pricing policy came at the expense of the previous earnings model. Best Buy had to look for alternatives to protect its margins.

The answer lay in the service concept. By strengthening its service offering (e.g., in-store technology training, mobile phone contract advice, repairs, etc.), the company moved away from its transaction-based earnings model. It generated revenue through additional free and paid services. The company also focused on store-in-store concepts. By leasing retail space to companies (e.g., AT&T, Samsung, Microsoft), Best Buy increased space utilization and created a new income source (retail space leasing). The company benefited from regular and consistent revenue [20]. By 2014, Samsung had opened 1,600 and Microsoft more than 600 store-in-store concepts in Best Buy stores [21].

The Bottom Line

In August 2015, CEO of Best Buy, Hubert Joly, commented on the company's financial situation: "Our strategy of offering advice, service and convenience at competitive prices is paying off" [22]. The financial development indicated for 2015 has been confirmed so far. The share price doubled from $35 in January 2011 to $78 US in January 2018. ROIC[2] returned to a competitive level of 18.9% in 2017 (2013 = 10.85%). Best Buy has returned to annual domestic sales growth since 2014. The 'Net Promotor Score', which was also introduced as part of Renew Blue to measure customer loyalty, improved again in 2017 by 350 basis points to 35[3]. This continues to place the company above the retail industry average (NPS Retail = 7) [23]. This shows that Best Buy's customer focus is bearing fruit [24].

The fears of many experts and analysts that Best Buy would not be able to cope with online retailing have not been confirmed. On the contrary, Best Buy has emerged stronger than ever, proving that brick-and-mortar retail has a future despite Amazon and other online players. Those who recognize and build on the strengths of their existing business

---

2 Return on Invested Capital (ROIC) is a profitability measure. It measures the return that an investment generates for investors. ROIC explains how well a company is able to turn capital into profit.
3 A Net Promoter Score of 30 or more is considered high. The average in retail was 7 in 2017.

model can thrive in the age of Amazon. Best Buy's positive revenue trajectory from 2017 to 2022, with sales increasing from $39.4 billion to $51.8 billion US in the 2022 financial year, is a testament to the company's successful transformation efforts [25]. These efforts have allowed Best Buy to adapt and thrive in an ever-changing retail landscape, positioning itself as an industry leader and delivering added value to its customers.

References

[1]   See Rosenberg, A. (2013), Deutsche Bank Doubles Down on Best Buy, in: CNBC, 2013-03-31, https://www.cnbc.com/id/100780675.

[2]   See Teixeira, T./Watikins, E. (2015), Showrooming at Best Buy, Harvard Business School Brief Case 9-515-019.

[3]   See Best Buy (2012), 10-K Report 2012, in: Best Buy, 2012-05-01, http://s2.q4cdn.com/785564492/files/doc_financials/2012/annual/FY12-Annual-Report-on-Form-10-K.PDF.

[4]   See Yahoo! Finance (2018), Best Buy Co., Inc. (BBY), in: Yahoo! Finance, 2018-04-26, https://finance.yahoo.com/quote/BBY/?guccounter=1.

[5]   See Wells, J./Ellsworth, G. (2017), Reinventing Best Buy, Harvard Business School Brief Case 9-716-455.

[6]   See Zimmermann, A. (2012), Can Retailers Halt «Showrooming», in: The Wall Street Journal, 2012-04-11, https://www.wsj.com/articles/SB10001424052702304587704577334370670243032.

[7]   See Bustillo, M./Lawton, C. (2009), Best Buy Expands Private-Label Brands, in: The Wall Street Journal, 2009-04-27, https://www.wsj.com/articles/SB124078866665357525.

[8]   See Vomhof, J. (2016), Half Of People Are On The Wrong Mobile Plan, Best Buy Data Shows, in: Best Buy Blog, 2016-01-29, https://corporate.bestbuy.com/half-of-people-are-on-the-wrong-mobile-plan-best-buy-data-shows/.

[9]   See Best Buy (2018), 10-K Report 2018, in: Best Buy, 2018-04-02, http://d18rn0p25nwr6d.cloudfront.net/CIK-0000764478/853fa6b6-72de-4529-8ccb-9469780df3e2.pdf.

[10]   See Wells, J./Ellsworth, G. (2017), Reinventing Best Buy, Harvard Business School Brief Case 9-716-455.

[11]   See Gallo, C. (2012), Best Buy Invests 50000 Hours of Employee Training To Attract Windows 8 Customers, in: Forbes, 2012-11-09, https://www.forbes.com/sites/carminegallo/2012/11/09/best-buy-invests-50000-hours-of-employee-training-to-attract-windows-8-customers/#66391e112fd.

[12]   See Thompson, M. (2013), Best Buy quits Europe, in: CNN Money, 2013-04-30, http://money.cnn.com/2013/04/30/news/companies/best-buy-europe/index.html.

[13]   See Chain Store Age (2015), Best Buy eyes a different 'future' in Canada, in: Chain Store Age, 2015-03-30, https://www.chainstoreage.com/article/best-buy-eyes-different-future-canada/.

[14]   See Reuters (2014), Best Buy Co Inc to exit China, sells 184 stores as it seeks to focus on North America, in: Financial Post, 2014-12-04, http://business.financialpost.com/news/retail-marketing/best-buy-co-inc-to-exit-china-sells-184-stores-as-it-seeks-to-focus-on-north-america.

[15]   See Zimmermann, A. (2012), Can Retailers Halt «Showrooming», in: The Wall Street Journal, 2012-04-11, https://www.wsj.com/articles/SB10001424052702304587704577334370670243032.

[16]   See Covert, J. (2014), Best Buy cutting 2000 managers, in: New York Post, 2014-02-26, https://nypost.com/2014/02/26/best-buy-cutting-2000-managers/.

[17]   See Trefis, (2014), Best Buy suffers from lower electronic sales, but cost savings improve profits, in: Forbes, 2014-05-23, https://www.forbes.com/sites/greatspeculations/2014/05/23/best-buy-suffers-from-lower-electronic-sales-but-cost-savings-improve-profits/#75ceaae56062.

[18] See Stewart, J. (2013), Underdog Against Amazon, Best Buy Charges Ahead, in: New York Times, 2013-12-13, https://www.nytimes.com/2013/12/14/business/fast-rise-of-best-buy-in-the-face-of-amazon.html.

[19] See Zimmermann, A. (2012), Can Retailers Halt «Showrooming», in: The Wall Street Journal, 2012-04-11, https://www.wsj.com/articles/SB10001424052702304587704577334370670243032.

[20] See Loeb, W. (2016), Best Buy Focuses On Shop-In-Shop Sales and Makes Changes For Growth, in: Forbes, 2016-08-08, https://www.forbes.com/sites/walterloeb/2016/08/08/best-buy-focuses-on-shop-in-shop-sales-and-is-making-changes-for-growth/#1d72f3b15bca.

[21] See MarketWatch (2014), Best Buy Reports Fourth Quarter Results, in: MarketWatch, 2014-02-27, https://www.marketwatch.com/story/western-gas-announces-marcellus-acquisitions-and-fourth-quarter-and-full-year-2012-resultsprovides-outlook-for-2013-2013-02-27.

[22] See Kilgore, T. (2018), Best Buy's stock surges after blow out earnings, upbeat outlook and raised dividend, in: MarketWatch, 2018-03-01, https://www.marketwatch.com/story/best-buys-stock-surges-after-blow-out-earnings-upbeat-outlook-and-raised-dividend-2018-03-01.

[23] See Index NPS (2018), Best Buy Net Promoter Score (NPS), in: Index NPS, 2018, http://indexnps.com/company/best-buy.

[24] See Best Buy (2017), Annual Report 2017, in: Best Buy, 2017-03-24, http://s2.q4cdn.com/785564492/files/doc_financials/2017/annual/BestBuy-2017-AnnualReport.pdf.

[25] See Best Buy (2023), Best Buy Reports Fourth Quarter Results, https://s2.q4cdn.com/785564492/files/doc_financials/2023/q4/Best-Buy-Reports-Fiscal-Fourth-Quarter-Results.pdf.

Waterstones[*]

Background and Objectives of the Case Study

When HMV sold Waterstones to Russian businessman and investor Alexander Mamut in 2011, the situation was dire for the UK's last pure-play bookstore chain [1]. The bricks-and-mortar book trade was increasingly suffering from the success of mail-order retailer Amazon, which was exerting immense price pressure. The e-book had also become a serious threat to the printed book during this time. The trend was to read books on electronic reading devices called e-book readers [2]. Around a quarter of all independent British booksellers went out of business between 2010 and 2015 as a result of developments in the book market [3]. Waterstones was also in a precarious position and was put up for sale by its owner HMV. The only alternative was to go out of business, as current managing director James Daunt admitted in an interview [4]. Daunt, a former investment banker and owner of a small chain of bookshops in London, took over after the change of ownership. He did the impossible. At the beginning of 2018, Waterstones increased its annual profit by 80% [5]. How was this achieved?

*The case study was developed in collaboration with Benjamin D. Klink (University of St. Gallen).

Value Proposition

In the 1990s, Waterstones was seen as a bookseller with an unrivaled range. Inviting customers to linger and browse, with exceptional books, was the hallmark of the company's success [6]. With the abolition of fixed book prices in the UK, the company gradually moved towards price leadership, competing with supermarkets and stationers for the casual reader. Soon, the maxim was to maximize sales. As the price-competitive threat of Amazon entered the market, the low-price strategy became even more important for Waterstones. But without a clear commitment to discount or even service leadership, the British bookseller found itself stuck in a diffuse middle ground. The strategy of competing with Amazon and the supermarkets on price was ultimately unsuccessful. The shopping experience[7] was characterized by mass-market merchandise of questionable literary value, three-for-the-price-of-two promotions, and a sterile store atmosphere, much to the annoyance of regular customers. Waterstones had lost both its identity and its appeal.

The turnaround began with a return to the company's roots. Under Daunt's leadership, Waterstones returned to the virtues that had made it great in the first place. The focus was now on the principles of classic specialty bookstores that make the hearts of discerning bibliophiles beat faster. Daunt's management team distilled this vision into

Table 4.12: Transformation of the Waterstones business model.

Value Proposition			
Your local bookstore: unique, personalized service and inspiration through customer intimacy.			
Service Delivery	**Service Offering**	**Cost Model**	**Earnings Model**
Flatter hierarchies and empowered employees by delegating core activities including evolution of the assortment and point-of-sale promotions	Focus on the cultivated book reader	Decentralized replenishment planning: reduced logistics costs and lower capital commitment	Elimination of listing fees and resulting acquisition of assortment control
Upgraded sales staff: Empowerment and people development measures	The 'high street book boutique': Customer intimacy and inspiration	Rationalized assortment to eliminate low-margin slow movers	Internalization of store-in-store offering, e.g. café
Ear-to-the-street: Information on trends is gathered directly in-store	Literary advice Literature-related events	Lower store rents to deduce fixed costs	Cross-selling: Expansion of complementary products relevant to customer segments
	Store ambiance that encourages reading, discovery and interaction		

Waterstones' new value proposition: "Your Local Bookshop" (see Table 4.12) [8]. The value proposition, which focused on differentiation from Amazon, quickly caught on. It marked a radical departure from Amazon's counter-concept— customer intimacy, unique service and inspiration instead of a mass outlet with dumping prices.

Service Offering

The value proposition was consistently implemented in the service offering. The business model was transformed in line with the new guiding star. From now on, the focus of efforts was on sophisticated, cultivated book readers. This customer group appreciates the ambience of a bookstore, enjoys spending time there to browse or work, and expands its literary horizons without focusing on price. From that point on the price-sensitive casual reader was no longer the focus [9].

As a result, Waterstones strengthened its services, customer advice and inspiration. Shop windows were no longer just stocked with popular literature paid for by publishers, but with titles chosen by the staff [10]. In some cases, there were again inspiring thematic installations on literary classics or literary statements on current social issues. The interiors of bookstores were also freed from the dictates of paid for product placement. The newfound autonomy meant that the product range could be streamlined, while at the same time allowing for a more welcoming store layout that reflected local tastes. Soon no two Waterstones were the same, giving the stores individuality and a local flavor [11].

Many stores were refurbished and their ambience improved, while a number of stores in poor locations were closed. Waterstones became the 'book boutique of the British high street'. It became a meeting place for literary enthusiasts, with—now again—its own cozy café, inviting people to linger. Inspiring shopping experiences, enriched by literature-related events such as author evenings with autograph sessions or themed events, delighted customers [12].

Service Delivery

All this was made possible by a completely new approach to service deliveryand— let's not hide it—an injection of cash from the new owner, Mamut, which enabled the company to persevere. Thus it was able to spend a little more time on implementing a successful business model transformation [13].

The core of the new strategy was the decentralization of the service delivery. This was to be seen as a turnaround from the efforts of previous years, which had led to uniformity and interchangeability. CEO Daunt reduced middle management by almost half and introduced flat hierarchies. From that point on store managers and staff were given much more responsibility, and the employees were given a great deal of freedom to shape the company [14].

Store staff became the focus of the service delivery. For example, they designed the store windows and developed sales promotions. Product assortment and sales floor design were now almost entirely in the hands of local management. This allowed them to respond to local characteristics and idiosyncrasies, adding authenticity to the proposition of customer intimacy. The advisory and technical skills of employees were strengthened through a significantly expanded and improved training system. In addition, local staff were able to contribute their valuable customer knowledge to service delivery. Popular books and genres, special customer requests—all this was taken into account and gave Waterstones an information advantage, especially over the centralized competition [15].

Cost Model

The consistent focus on local customer needs in the stores was also reflected in the cost model. It was common practice in the bookselling industry to centralize purchasing. Decisions about product placement, assortment and bulk orders were often based on how much a publisher was willing to pay a bookseller. Waterstones moved away from this practice. The move away from paid product placement initially cost the company around £27 million a year in revenue from publishers [16].

However, it freed up store and shelf space to be filled with popular and high-margin products, resulting in higher sales. It also eliminated the cost of returning unsold copies to publishers. In addition, the management streamlined product assortments. Inventory turns increased and capital employed decreased significantly. Store-specific replenishment planning reduced excess inventory and returns costs. As a result of these actions, the return rate to publishers dropped from approximately 20% to 2–3%[17].

Fixed costs were significantly reduced by renegotiating store rents. Personnel costs were also reduced through improved workforce planning. The sales staff were motivated by trust, a sense of purpose and individual support [18].

Earnings Model

The sales logic was largely maintained. The bookstore chain continues to make its money primarily from the sale of printed books. Only minor adjustments have been made. The decision to free itself from the external control of publishers has paid off. Instead of relying on publishers' royalties, Waterstones focused on customers and their willingness to buy. In line with this credo, the company has internalized earnings sources such as the in-store café. Elsewhere, the company has targeted cross-selling opportunities, as higher margins can be made on complementary products such as stationery, calendars and merchandising items [19].

Of course, Waterstones also has an online store, but it is closely aligned with the company's cross-channel philosophy and its brick-and-mortar stores. Accordingly, the company combines online shopping with inspiration and information. Customers can find information about local events, order books online via click & collect and pick them up in a local store, or purchase signed editions. In particular, the company's own integrated book blog, which presents and discusses new releases and literary classics, highlights the differences with Amazon's offering.

The Bottom Line

Waterstones has successfully transformed its business model by focusing on the market and differentiating itself from the competition. The management has reinforced the virtues of the specialty business without continuing to tolerate the cost structures associated with it. A multitude of measures have empowered staff and given a strong boost to the new service offering [20]. The financial strength of the new owner and the declining popularity of e-books undoubtedly helped [21, 22]. With the turnaround, bricks-and-mortar bookselling in the UK experienced a revival that was no longer thought possible [23]. According to its latest annual report, profits reached £60 million in 2021, by far the highest figure since the company returned to profitability in 2015, and sales reached £400 million [24].

References

[1]   See McCrum, R. (2010), Waterstone's has forgotten what bookselling is about, in: The Guardian, 2010-09-06, https://www.theguardian.com/books/booksblog/2010/sep/06/waterstones-bookselling.

[2]   See Sweney, M. (2017), 'Screen fatigue' sees UK ebook sales plunge 17% as readers return to print, in: The Guardian, 2017-04-27, https://www.theguardian.com/books/2017/apr/27/screen-fatigue-sees-uk-ebook-sales-plunge-17-as-readers-return-to-print.

[3]   See Heyman, S. (2015), Bix-Box Bookstores Don't Have to Die, in: Slate, 2015-12-15, http://www.slate.com/articles/business/moneybox/2015/12/barnes_noble_is_dying_waterstones_in_the_u_k_is_thriving.html.

[4]   See Top Drawer (2017), How I turned Waterstones' (mis)fortunes around, 2018-02-07, https://www.topdrawer.co.uk/academy-library/how-i-turned-waterstones-fortunes-around.

[5]   See Wood, Z. (2018), Waterstones' annual profits jump 80% as buyers loom, in: The Guardian, 2018-01-18, https://www.theguardian.com/books/2018/jan/18/waterstones-annual-profits-jump-80-percent-books-sale.

[6]   See Löhndorf, M. (2015), "Die Rückkehr eines Büchergiganten" (The Return of a Book Giant), in: Neue Züricher Zeitung, 2015-02-27, https://www.nzz.ch/feuilleton/die-rueckkehr-eines-buechergiganten-1.18491360 (in German only).

[7]   See Jeffries, S. (2009), How Waterstone's killed bookselling, in The Guardian, 2009-11-10, https://www.theguardian.com/books/2009/nov/10/waterstones-high-street-bookselling.

[8]   See Waterstones (2018), About us, 2018-02-15, https://www.waterstones.com/help/about-us/44.

[9]   See Campbell, L. (2013), Daunt: 'Two years' to transform Waterstones, in: The Bookseller, 2013-02-04, https://www.thebookseller.com/news/daunt-two-years-transform-waterstones.

[10]   See Hall, J. (2010), Waterstone's lets its stores choose the books again, in: The Telegraph, 2010-05-19, http://www.telegraph.co.uk/finance/newsbysector/retailandconsumer/7738346/Waterstones-lets-its-stores-choose-the-books-again.html.

[11]   See Heyman, S. (2015), Bix-Box Bookstores Don't Have to Die, in: Slate, 2015-12-15, http://www.slate.com/articles/business/moneybox/2015/12/barnes_noble_is_dying_waterstones_in_the_u_k_is_thriving.html.

[12]   See Armitstead, C. (2017), Balancing the books: how Waterstones came back from the dead, in: The Guardian, 2017-02-03, https://www.theguardian.com/books/2017/feb/03/balancing-the-books-how-waterstones-returned-to-profit.

[13]   See Fortado, L. (2018), Activist hedge fund Elliot in talks to buy Waterstones, in: Financial Times, 2018-01-30, https://www.ft.com/content/9781ac6a-051d-11e8-9650-9c0ad2d7c5b5.

[14]   See Dunn, W. (2017), How a new attitude to work saved Britain's bookshops, in: New Statesman, 2017-07-10, https://www.newstatesman.com/microsites/skills/2017/07/how-new-attitude-work-saved-britain-s-bookshops.

[15]   See Top Drawer (2017), How I turned Waterstones' (mis)fortunes around, 2018-02-07, https://www.topdrawer.co.uk/academy-library/how-i-turned-waterstones-fortunes-around.

[16]   See Dunn, W. (2017), How a new attitude to work saved Britain's bookshops, in: New Statesman, 2017-07-10, https://www.newstatesman.com/microsites/skills/2017/07/how-new-attitude-work-saved-britain-s-bookshops.

[17]   See Top Drawer (2017), How I turned Waterstones' (mis)fortunes around, 2018-02-07, https://www.topdrawer.co.uk/academy-library/how-i-turned-waterstones-fortunes-around.

[18]   See Armitstead, C. (2017), Balancing the books: how Waterstones came back from the dead, in: The Guardian, 2017-02-03, https://www.theguardian.com/books/2017/feb/03/balancing-the-books-how-waterstones-returned-to-profit.

[19]   See Wood, Z. (2018), Waterstones' annual profits jump 80% as buyers loom, in: The Guardian, 2018-01-18, https://www.theguardian.com/books/2018/jan/18/waterstones-annual-profits-jump-80-percent-books-sale.

[20]   See BBC (2017), Waterstones under fire for secret shops, in: BBC, 2017-02-27, http://www.bbc.com/news/business-39101186.

[21]   See Armitage, J. (2017), Business focus: A tale of troubles for Russian owner of Waterstones, in: Evening Standard, 2017-10-25, https://www.standard.co.uk/business/business-focus-a-tale-of-troubles-for-russian-owner-of-the-quintessentially-british-waterstones-a3667596.html.

[22]   See Pohlisch, O. (2015), "Kindle kommt nicht mehr gut" (Kindle Is No Longer Doing Well), in: taz, 2015-10-07, http://www.taz.de/E-Reader-Verkauf-gestoppt/!5240179/ (in German only).

[23]   See Wood, Z. (2018), Waterstones' annual profits jump 80% as buyers loom, in: The Guardian, 2018-01-18, https://www.theguardian.com/books/2018/jan/18/waterstones-annual-profits-jump-80-percent-books-sale.

[24]   See Craven, N. (2023), Waterstones' chief James Daunt: Covid was brilliant for us – it made people pick up books again, in: Thisismoney.co.uk, 2023-04-09, https://www.thisismoney.co.uk/money/markets/article-11952075/Waterstones-chief-James-Daunt-Covid-people-pick-books-again.html.

Washington Post*

"When you're writing, be riveting, be right, and ask people to pay." (Jeff Bezos)

Background and Objectives of the Case Study

The Washington Post (WP) has long been considered the flagship of the American media landscape. But between its glory days in the last century and its current heights, there has been a dizzying slide.

Founded in 1877 by Democrat Stilson Hutchins, the nation capital's newspaper went bankrupt in the chaos of the Great Depression [1]. Financier Eugene Meyer bought the paper at the time, and it would remain in the hands of the Graham family dynasty for eight decades [2]. The paper became famous for its coverage of the Watergate scandal, which eventually led to the resignation of then-President Nixon in 1974 [3]. Under the leadership of Donald Graham, the fourth scion of the dynasty, the paper became rich in Pulitzer Prizes and profits [4].

The WP's golden age came to an abrupt end with the triumph of the Internet in the late 1990s. Digitalization changed the distribution channels and earnings models of newspapers. The frequency with which news was published decreased, while competition for readers and advertisers increased.

The response was a stronger regional focus under the banner "For and about Washington". But the WP was not alone with this claim. POLITICO and the National Journal also competed for readers in the nation's capital, causing the WP to suffer a decline in sales and circulation [5]. Twenty years after its peak in 1993, daily print circulation had fallen by 40 percent. The former flagship of the American press had degenerated into a provincial paper. It had missed the digital turnaround, losing $53.7 US million in 2012 [6].

When Amazon founder Jeff Bezos took over the WP for $250 million US in August 2013, there were fears of capitulation and anxiety in the air. But soon after the acquisition, the tide turned for the newspaper. In October 2015, for the first time, Washingtonpost.com counted more unique visitors than the New York Times homepage (unique visitors are the total number of people who visit a website in a given period of time. Each visitor is counted only once). Page impressions that month were up 95% over the previous year [7].

The WP case illustrates that a constant willingness to change and a culture of experimentation require support and guidance. With his charisma and strong vision, Jeff Bezos not only inspired employees from the start, but also gave them the support they needed to experiment in new ways. At the heart of this was a clear, customer-centric value prop-

---

*The case study was developed in collaboration with Kathrin M. Neumüller (University of St. Gallen).

osition. Importantly, the value proposition not only orchestrated all value-creating activities, but also included profitable income sources. Bezos recognized that it was not enough to align services with customer needs. Rather, the goal was to inspire readers in an era of free mentality to be willing to pay for content. The goal was to create a pull effect.

Value Proposition

When Jeff Bezos bought the WP, he had no experience in the newspaper business. But as the founder of Amazon, a company worth more than $170 billion US, he had the credentials: a strong customer focus and a love of technology [8]. Bezos saw the WP not as a run-down metropolitan newspaper, but as a high-potential technology company that had lost sight of its customer focus.

In a letter, he asked the employees to reinvent the WP and focus on readers, not advertisers. Quality journalism and flexibility were now at the core of the value proposition. The WP promised its readers world-class journalism. They should enjoy a seamless customer experience and be able to enjoy journalistic content in different situations, regardless of their device (see Table 4.13). The high quality standards and

Table 4.13: Transformation of the Washington Post business model.

Value Proposition			
We are committed to providing our best-in-class journalism in a format that adapts to the needs of our readers.			
Service Delivery	**Service Offering**	**Cost Model**	**Earnings Model**
Development of all content management tools in-house	Relevant, quality investigative journalism with national and international coverage	Growth strategy	Paid digital subscriptions with a metered model (a certain amount of paid content can be is accessed for free)
Hiring of Internet-savvy journalists and IT professionals	Focus on young, digital readers as the main customer segment for the future	Cost savings by insourcing the IT department	Premium subscription model with supplementary services including free access to selected e-books
Fostering of a culture of experimentation	Faster loading website with an attractive design	Leveraging of synergies with Amazon	
Generation of journalistic content by analyzing big data	Posting of journalistic content on Facebook		

strong customer focus were reflected in the company's culture: Bezos moved the headquarters from a gray building on 15th Avenue in Washington to a futuristic-looking building on K Street [9].

Service Offering

The WP provides relevant, investigative, quality journalism under the motto "Journalism that matters". Its coverage is both international and domestic. For the future, the paper is focused mainly on growth. The WP is targeting a digital, younger readership as its main future customer segment—not an easy goal due to their lack of loyalty. To attract this younger readership, the WP has made several changes. It has increased the speed of the website, improved the layout for digital formats, introduced a personalized recommendation system, and linked the website to social media.

A wide range of apps is at the forefront of the digital strategy. Users can choose from four apps, depending on whether they are interested in local special reports, want to quickly skim text on their smartphone, watch videos on their Apple TV, or prefer the classic edition on their tablet at the breakfast table. The WP uses a multichannel strategy to reach a younger readership. Many social media users, for example, consume journalistic content directly on Facebook. Thanks to the free 'Instant Articles' service, they do not need to visit the WP website or pay for articles. Unlike other newspapers such as Bild or Spiegel Online, WP makes all of its articles available to social media users as 'Instant Articles'. This opens up its offering to a wider audience.

Service Delivery

The use of technology and a strong culture of experimentation play a key role along the entire value creation chain. At the heart of this experimentation is always the question: How can we make a story more exciting and interesting?

The approximately 1,000 journalists at WP are encouraged not only to create interesting and relevant content, but also to work in a data-driven way, supported by the analysis of big data and algorithms. To do this, news streams from washingtonpost.com and other newspapers (e.g., politico.com, nytimes.com, wsj.com) converge in a data center. Once there, they are categorized and analyzed by the software Clavis and then used as recommendations. Based on Amazon's recommendation mechanism, the Clavis program suggests stories to readers based on their website usage and Internet activity. Where is the reader right now? Are they at work or at home? Is the user coming from X (Twitter) or Google? What device are they using? What are their needs depending on the time of day? Clavis takes all of these factors into account and gives WP journalists clues about which stories are in demand. In the next step, a story is created in the in-house content tool. Before it is finally published, each editor has to choose from at least four different titles. The A/B testing program Darwin then checks which texts or videos the test readers prefer. The story with the most clicks is then published.

To facilitate this ideal integration between IT and content, WP is one of the few newspapers in the world to develop its IT in-house—be it apps, algorithms or editorial systems [10]. Bezos has hired 35 software engineers in addition to 140 journalists. In the newsroom, developers work hand in hand with analysts, product managers, video journalists, editors, and web designers to meet the needs of readers. This ensures that the tools are not only cutting edge from a technical perspective, but also provide a user-friendly front-end for editors. As a result, WP has evolved from a traditional newspaper to a high-tech journalism company.

Cost Model

Until the Bezos acquisition, cost-cutting was at the heart of the WP's strategy. Although this partially compensated for the decline in circulation in the late 1990s and early in the new millennium, journalistic quality and company culture suffered. There was a widespread feeling among journalists that they were working in a dying industry, where it was only a matter of time before they too suffered layoffs. Newsrooms were thinned out. Costs were cut. Although these measures met shareholders' profit expectations in the short term, they gradually drove WP into the financial abyss.

Bezos realized that cost savings could not come at the expense of quality. From now on, quality journalism would take center stage as the key differentiator. Bezos therefore spared no expense in his digital strategy, prioritizing the hiring of Internet-savvy journalists and IT specialists [11].

His primary focus: an aggressive 'Get Big Fast' phase of growth that prioritized acquiring as many readers as possible over profits at this phase of the strategy. Losses were considered acceptable growing pains. Today, employee compensation reflects not only the company's profits, but also employee initiative, experimentation, and dedication. While cost cutting remains a focus, Bezos is targeting other areas. The company's in-house IT department enables cost-effective, customized development of high-quality editorial tools and content management systems. Synergies are also leveraged, such as offering Amazon Prime members free access to the WP's digital subscription for six months before requiring a paid subscription, minimizing marketing and advertising costs.

Earnings Model

Bezos remains tight-lipped about the profitability of his private company. Much like at Amazon, his focus at the WP is on growth goals, prioritizing them over immediate profits. His earnings model emphasizes economies of scale by attracting as many paying digital subscribers as possible. Rather than generating high revenues from a select few readers, the strategy targets the mass market and generates revenues through growth.

The Internet's 'free media consumption' mentality is a challenge. Digital natives have grown up being able to read content without paying for it, resulting in less willingness to pay. To generate profits, the WP must rekindle readers' enthusiasm and convince them of the value it offers.

To boost growth in digital paid subscriptions the WP's metered model aims to attract readers with free articles and convert them into subscribers. All readers and app users start with free access to all WP editorial content, limited to a certain volume. Once that is exhausted, a pop-up encourages a four-week free trial. At a regular price of $40 US per year, the basic subscription is extremely affordable and reader-friendly. By comparison, The New York Times costs more than twice as much after a one-year trial subscription.

Besides the basic model, the premium subscription ups the ante with an additional month of access for a friend or family member, exclusive access to Pulitzer Prize-winning e-books by WP journalists, and the ability to share the account for one month, which encourages referrals. This strategy proved successful, as WP's subscriber base grew by 75 percent in 2016 over the previous year [12], and now stands at more than 2.5 million paid digital subscriptions.

The Bottom Line

Bezos transformed WP from a traditional newspaper into a high-tech publication focused on the customer experience. The value proposition revolves around the use of cutting-edge technology to meet customer needs. Rather than jeopardize quality journalism by cutting jobs, he invested in a growth strategy by integrating IT and hiring Internet-savvy journalists. The WP's unique earnings model sets it apart from its competitors. Instead of relying on high revenues from a small readership, it targets the mass market. The WP case demonstrates that solutions often transcend industry boundaries. For example, their technology-enabled referral marketing strategy wouldn't have been possible without looking beyond traditional newspaper practices.

References

[1]   See Barnes, R./Fahrenthold, D. (2013), The Grahams: A family synonymous with The Post and with Washington, in: The Washington Post, 2013-08-05, https://www.washingtonpost.com/politics/the-grahams-a-family-synonymous-with-the-post-and-with-washington/2013/08/05/94f26d04-fe1a-11e2-96a8-d3b921c0924a_story.html?utm_term=.fe375a7ab7c7.

[2]   See Fahri, P. (2013), Washington Post to be sold to Jeff Bezos, the founder of Amazon, in: The Washington Post, 2013-08-05, https://www.washingtonpost.com/apps/g/page/national/washington-post-co-timeline/374/.

[3] See Jentzsch, B. (2004), "Vor 30 Jahren trat Richard Nixon zurück" (Richard Nixon Resigned 30 Years Ago), in: Deutschlandfunk, 2014-08-08, http://www.deutschlandfunk.de/vor-30-jahren-trat-richard-nixon-zurueck.871.de.html?dram:article_id=124878 (in German only).

[4] See Fahri, P. (2013), Washington Post to be sold to Jeff Bezos, the founder of Amazon, in: The Washington Post, 2013-08-05, https://www.washingtonpost.com/apps/g/page/national/washington-post-co-timeline/374/.

[5] See PewResearch Center (2015), State of the News Media 2015, in: PewResearch Center, 2015-04-15, http://assets.pewresearch.org/wp-content/uploads/sites/13/2017/05/30142603/state-of-the-news-media-report-2015-final.pdf.

[6] See Kennedy. D. (August 8, 2016), The Bezos Effect, in: Harvard Kennedy School: Shorenstein Center, 2016-08-08, https://shorensteincenter.org/bezos-effect-washington-post/.

[7] See WashPostPR. (2017), The Post records 88.9 million unique visitors in October 2017, in: The Washington Post, 2017-11-17, https://www.washingtonpost.com/pr/wp/2017/11/17/the-post-records-more-than-86-million-unique-visitors-in-october-2017/?utm_term=.6aeac7787340.

[8] See Amazon. (2018), Amazon Global Sales From 1st Quarter 2007 to 4th Quarter 2017 (In Billions of Us Dollars), in: Statista, 2018-01-03, https://de.statista.com/statistik/daten/studie/197099/umfrage/nettoumsatz-von-amazoncom-quartalszahlen/ (in German only).

[9] See Kennedy. D. (August 8, 2016), The Bezos Effect, in: Harvard Kennedy School: Shorenstein Center, 2016-08-08, https://shorensteincenter.org/bezos-effect-washington-post/.

[10] See Aichinger, R. (2016), "Ein Blatt wendet sich" (The Tide Is Turning), in: brand eins, 2016-06-01, https://www.brandeins.de/magazine/brand-eins-wirtschaftsmagazin/2016/digitalisierung/ein-blatt-wendet-sich (in German only).

[11] See Seibert. T. (2017), "Politur am Profit" (Polish on the Profit) in: Der Tagesspiegel, 2017-09-03, https://www.tagesspiegel.de/medien/washington-post-unter-jeff-bezos-politur-am-profit/19496990.html (in German only).

[12] See Bond, S./Bond. D. (2017), Newspapers welcome more digital subscribers in time of fake news, in: Financial Times, 2017-02-15., https://www.ft.com/content/d97bef40-f19b-11e6-8758-6876151821a6.

Axel Springer SE[*]

Background and Objectives of the Case Study

Axel Springer SE, once a pure-play print publisher, has grown from its humble beginnings in a garage in Hamburg in 1946 to become the leading digital publisher in Europe [1]. What was unimaginable at the time became reality less than twenty years later: Axel Springer published 45% of all newspapers sold in Germany and 80% of all Sunday newspapers [2]. In the mid-1990s, however, the triumphant advance of the Internet impacted the newspaper industry in a major way. Readers increasingly migrated to digital formats or created their own blogs. Soon after, Internet users were posting their own videos on YouTube—faster than many reporters. The result: Between 1996 and 2017, the number of consumer magazines sold in Germany fell by

[*]The case study was developed in collaboration with Kathrin M. Neumüller (University of St. Gallen).

more than a third. Newspapers like the Financial Times Deutschland ceased publication for good. Axel Springer faced a similar fate in 2006. At the time, its digital lines of business accounted for just 1% of its total revenues [3]. Eleven years later, Dimension Data Deutschland and IDG Business GmbH awarded the company the 'Digital Leader Award – Special First Mover' prize. In 2017, the company generated 80% of its operating profit from digital lines of business [4]. But how did Axel Springer achieve this turnaround? The company responded to the threat to its existence by refocusing its value proposition. It recognized the impact of digitalization at an early stage and accurately assessed its speed. Building on this, the company increasingly supplemented its less growth-intensive print business with digital business fields.

Value Proposition

Axel Springer is an excellent example of a meaningful and consistently implemented value proposition. Under the leadership of Dr. Mathias Döpfner, who holds a doctorate in musicology, Axel Springer jumped on the digital bandwagon in 2002 [5]. With the focused value proposition "The successful establishment of independent journal-

Table 4.14: Transformation of the Axel Springer business model.

Value Proposition

To successfully establish independent journalism in the digital world. We want to become the leading digital publisher.

Service Delivery	Service Offering	Cost Model	Earnings Model
Hiring of start-up employees, IT specialists, social media editors, and data journalists	High-quality information and entertainment via digital channels and print media	Streamlining of work processes and central functions	Replacement of analog earnings sources with digital earnings sources
Establishment of a digital corporate culture	Readership-specific classified ads for those seeking information and interested in making purchases	Consolidation of group management and service functions at the headquarters in Berlin	Growth in circulation and advertising revenues through newspapers and portals in the WELT and BILD brand families
Creation of online and offline journalistic content for WELT in a newsroom		Merging of the WELT and BERLINER MORGENPOST editorial teams	Revenues from reach and performance-based marketing offerings for business customers
			Revenues from classified ads

ism in the digital world. We want to become the leading digital publisher", he anchored digitalization and excellence in the company's DNA (see Table 4.14).

The benefit of this clear message is that employees feel called to be entrepreneurial in digital businesses and focus on relevant projects that support the existing competitive advantage. The value proposition not only motivates employees, but also reflects the competitive advantage from the customer's perspective. Employees are given an important guideline. Axel Springer promises its readers to inform and entertain them independently and better than others.

Service Offering

Drivers from both the macro and micro environment were decisive for the adaptation of the service offering. In the macro environment, technological developments that enable ever faster data transfer have facilitated the rise of the digital book format. The micro environment is also in flux. Customers can access an almost infinite selection of digital books in a matter of seconds, without having to make the inconvenient trip to the nearest bookstore. If Axel Springer had stuck to print journalism at the beginning of the 21st century, the company would probably not exist today. Instead, Axel Springer redefined the relevant market at the beginning of the transformation. The focus is now on the promising information and entertainment market on the Internet [6].

The service portfolio is based on journalistic offerings and digital classifieds. In the former, Axel Springer appeals to readers with different levels of education and income. The offerings range from a live Bundesliga ticker on BILD.de to in-depth business reports in WELT or the business magazine *Bilanz*. Despite the newspaper crisis, BILD and WELT sold around 464,000 digital subscriptions at the end of 2017, and the trend is rising [7]. Axel Springer has long since stopped limiting its journalistic offerings to the domestic market and is now pursuing a consistent internationalization strategy. In Switzerland, for example, the joint venture Ringier Axel Springer Schweiz offers more than thirty titles with 880 issues per year. These include business media such as *Bilanz* or *Handelszeitung* as well as tabloid newspapers such as *Blick*.

The classifieds are aimed at Internet users with a specific interest in purchasing or information. They bring together those seeking and those offering. For example, job seekers can find their employer on StepStone, Germany's largest job exchange [8]. With 13.4 million page visits and 2.2 million app downloads, StepStone promises the company seeking employees three times more applications than other job boards [9]. The main added value lies in the fact that the information and purchasing process is simplified and the information asymmetry is reduced in favor of the searching company and the applicant.

Service Delivery

Axel Springer consistently aligns its core activities with its value proposition. The group has recognized that employees are the decisive factor in the successful implementation of a transformation. To respond to the disruptive changes in the media landscape, Döpfner focused on a digital corporate culture. Initially, he recruited people from digital start-ups, social media editors and data journalists. In early 2014, the company even set up a permanent office in Palo Alto, California, to identify new relevant technologies. In 2002, Axel Springer launched the 'Media Powerhouse' to promote the acquisition of digital knowledge and cross-departmental knowledge transfer. This two-day internal knowledge transfer workshop allows specialists to share their digital experience with colleagues from other departments.

In 2003, Axel Springer embarked on an internal consolidation process. As part of this process, the value creation chain was aligned across all media. All journalistic content now comes together in the newsroom and is prepared for online and print media across all titles. This includes all key process steps—from the creation of information and entertainment content to editing and production. This cross-media approach leverages the synergies, expertise and reach of each brand.

Cost Model

As part of the consolidation of the group, all management and service functions have been consolidated at the headquarters in Berlin. The merger of the editorial departments at WELT and BERLINER MORGENPOST led to a significant reduction in costs and a sustained improvement in the editorial quality of both newspapers. By making this move, Axel Springer demonstrates how internal structures can be streamlined without losing customer focus. The company continues to respond to the different needs of its readers with a high degree of regional differentiation. The BILD brand alone has 23 regional editions.

This internal streamlining also affected the workforce. Between 2001 and 2004, the number of employees fell by 18.7 % to 11,463. However, the most recent headcount of around 16,000 in 2022 also shows that the focus was not on cutting jobs per se, but on optimizing work processes and hiring people with digital expertise. Disruptive change means that established business models are displaced and that the skills built up within the company need to be realigned as a result. Axel Springer did not cut jobs primarily to reduce costs. Rather, existing print skills were supplemented with digital skills to intelligently streamline internal processes and align them with customers and the services of the future. These restructuring measures to make the Berlin site leaner and more customer-focused resulted in savings of €137 million in 2002 and an additional €74 million in 2003 [10].

Earnings Model

Rather than clinging to its successful past, Axel Springer recognized that it could no longer make money in the traditional publishing business. The company therefore replaced the less profitable publishing business with digital income sources.

Revenues come from three segments: classified ads, marketing offerings and paid offerings. Classified advertising is the main source of income (74% of EBITDA in 2019) [11]. The lion's share is generated by the 'Jobs' (StepStone Group) and 'Real Estate' (e.g. AVIV Group) segments. StepStone generates revenue by selling advertisements and job postings to job providers and by providing access to its online CV database. The AVIV Group also generates revenue by selling advertisements and advertising space to real estate agents, project developers, housing associations and private individuals.

Revenues in the Paid Models segment consist of circulation and advertising revenues. Circulation revenues are generated by paying readers, primarily in Germany, who purchase print and digital subscriptions. BILD.de and WELT.de, for example, rely on paid-content models. Both generate revenue through a freemium model in which some basic articles can be read for free. Premium services, however, are only available for an additional fee. In the case of BILD, this means that the reader can read a small number of articles within a basic offering. However, if they want to follow their favorite soccer team in real time and see the most important background articles and exclusive videos, they have to upgrade from the free basic service to the paid service BILDplus for €7.99 per month.

Advertising revenues are generated by marketing the reach of the online and print media of WELT and the BILD Group. Business customers have the opportunity to advertise in all newspapers and the associated online portals. BILD, for example, is Europe's largest daily newspaper with the greatest reach. In 2022, it maintained its market leadership in Germany with a 61% market share of newsstand newspapers. The paid offerings from the WELT and BILD Groups are the main revenue drivers, accounting for 45% of total revenues. They are in second place with 22% of EBITDA. The Media Impact joint venture, established with Funke Mediengruppe, handles cross-media marketing for advertisers across various channels, including banner ads, online videos, social media, and print. Billing is based on reach and performance [12].

The 'Marketing Offers' portfolio offers advertisers advertising space with compensation based on performance metrics (number of users and listeners) or generated interactions (e.g. clicks). Reach-based marketing allows advertisers to promote their products on platforms such as idealo.de and finanzen.net in exchange for a commission. Idealo.de is Germany's leading price comparison and product search portal with the highest reach. Topic-specific offerings and portals enable targeted advertising to specific customer segments.

The Bottom Line

Axel Springer's success in asserting itself against pure print publishers can be attributed to its strong focus on a digital, diversified business model. The company has demonstrated entrepreneurial courage and a calculated willingness to take risks to meet the challenges of disruptive change in the context of digitalization. Axel Springer views change as a continuous process, not an episodic event, which requires agility and flexibility. The value proposition of offering best-in-class journalism serves as a guiding principle for employees and with its strong focus on digital business areas, ensures not only a customer-focused but also profitable service portfolio. This includes the continuous replacement of analog income sources with digital income sources.

References

[1] See Axel Springer SE. (2017), Company portrait, in: Axel Springer, 2017-03-01, http://www.axel springer.de/artikel/Unternehmensportraet_40170.html (in German only).

[2] See Federal Association of Digital Publishers and Newspaper Publishers – BDZV (2018), "Entwicklung der verkauften Auflage der Tageszeitungen in Deutschland in ausgewählten Jahren von 1991 bis 2017 (in Millionen Exemplaren)" (Trends in the Paid Circulation of Daily Newspapers in Germany in Selected Years From 1991 to 2017 (In Millions of Copies),), in: Statista, 2018-01-01, https://de.statista.com/statistik/ daten/studie/72084/umfrage/verkaufte-auflage-von-tageszeitungen-in-deutschland/ (in German only).

[3] See The Economist. (2017-05-04), Axel Springer's digital transformation, in: The Economist, 2017-05-04, https://www.economist.com/news/business/21721688-heavyweight-newspapers-price-comparison-websites-axel-springers-digital-transformation.

[4] See Axel Springer SE (2017), 2017 Annual Report, in: Axel Springer SE, 2017-03-01, http://www.axel springer.de/dl/27565224/Geschaeftsbericht_2017.pdf (in German only).

[5] See "Institut für Medien- und Kommunikationspolitik" (Institute for Media and Communication Policy) (2016), Axel Springer SE, in: Mediendatenbank/mediadb.eu, 2016-06-01, https://www.me diadb.eu/datenbanken/deutsche-medienkonzerne/axel-springer-se.html (in German only).

[6] See Axel Springer SE (2017), Company Portrait, in: Axel Springer, 2017-01-02, http://www.axel springer.de/artikel/Unternehmensportraet_40170.html (in German only).

[7] See Axel Springer SE (2016), 2016 Annual Report, in: Axel Springer, 2017-04-05, http://www.axel springer.de/dl/27011919/Geschaeftsbericht_2016.pdf (in German only).

[8] See Axel Springer SE (2017), Company Portrait, in: Axel Springer, 2017-01-01, http://www.axel springer.de/artikel/Unternehmensportraet_40170.html (in German only).

[9] See Siebenhaar, H.-P. (2009), "Axel Springer poliert seine Bilanz auf" (Axel Springer Polishes up Its Balance Sheet), in: Handelsblatt, 2009-04-04, http://www.handelsblatt.com/unternehmen/it-medien /uebernahme-von-stepstone-axel-springer-poliert-seine-bilanz-auf/3252106.html.

[10] See Axel Springer SE (2003). 2003 Annual Report, in: Axel Springer SE, 2003-04-03, http://www.axel springer.de/dl/24751/gb_03_gesamt.pdf (in German only).

[11] See Axel Springer SE (2019), 2019 Annual Report, in: Axel Springer SE, 2023-01-18, https://www.axel springer.com/de/investor-relations/ir-publikationen (in German only).

[12] See Media Impact (2017), BILD Reach. "BILD ist Deutschlands größtes Tagesmedium" (Bild Is Germany's Largest Daily Newspaper), in: Bild, 2017-07-01, https://www.mediaimpact.de/artikel/BILD-Reichweite-BILD_736331.html (in German only).

De Beers[*]

Background and Objectives of the Case Study

De Beers, a South African company specializing in the mining and (B2B) wholesaling of rough diamonds, had spent decades building a monopolistic corporate structure. Since 1888, the company had secured between 80% and 90% of the global diamond market, making it the leading player in the rough diamond trade. De Beers achieved this position by controlling the majority of diamond mines, buying up the freely available supply of diamonds (acting as a buyer of last resort), and centralizing stockpiling and distribution. De Beers strategically exploited its dominant position by artificially restricting supply to keep prices high and stable. Traders who challenged De Beers' pricing power were punished and systematically squeezed out of the market [1]. After 1991, the situation in the rough diamond market changed slowly but steadily. Three developments could be observed:

- De Beers' monopoly position increasingly concerned competition regulators in Europe and the United States. Allegations of price-fixing and collusion led to De Beers being banned from operating in the United States in 1994 [2].
- Media reports described how African warlords and rebel leaders were profiting from the sale of what they referred to as conflict diamonds and used them to finance their soldiers [3]. The debate over conflict diamonds resonated with consumers and regulators.
- The opening up of Russia led to the dissolution of the exclusive trade agreements between the USSR and De Beers. Virtually overnight, the market was flooded with new rough diamonds from Russia. Mining rights in new mining areas such as Canada and Australia went to De Beers' competitors [4].
- The advent of the Internet increased price transparency in the diamond trade [5].

These four developments threatened De Beers' established business model, which was based on creating value through artificial scarcity. The two previous strategic pillars of the monopoly—buying up all available rough diamonds (acting as a buyer of last resort) and stockpiling all rough diamonds and centralizing their distribution—were no longer politically, legally or financially viable [6]. As a result, De Beers' share of the rough diamond market fell from 85% in 1987 to just under 65% in 1999 [7]. The markets recognized the problem as well, causing the share valuation to fall by 30%.

De Beers' management realized that only a change in the business model could stop the decline in sales and profits. A new business logic emerged: it was no longer the controlled supply of rough diamonds that determined the price, but the way the stones were mined, refined and distributed. The realignment of the company therefore had to

*The case study was developed in collaboration with Elias Barth (University of St. Gallen).

focus more on the refinement and distribution of diamonds. The purity of a diamond was no longer the only factor that determined its price. This realization made it necessary to pay more attention to verticalization. From then on, De Beers also sought to actively manage the interface to the end consumer, rather than leaving it to the wholesalers. Our case study describes a change in business model that represented a fundamental shift in direction for De Beers. Unlike most of the other cases studies provided in this book, De Beers went so far as to reformulate its value proposition.

Value Proposition

A central change concerned the role of De Beers in the market. Previously, De Beers had operated exclusively in the B2B market as a seller of rough diamonds. However, by offering cut and polished diamonds, the company now also focused on the end consumer. To do this, De Beers needed to articulate a new and compelling value proposition. For the first time, the marketing department was tasked with creating consumer desire for its own brand. Identifying potential starting points was not easy. In the end, they recalled the significance of diamonds as a symbol of eternal love. This concept was adopted and enriched with an additional benefit. The promise of eternal love was interchangeable and already a marketing focus for several competitors. Therefore, De Beers formulated its value proposition as follows: the customer receives an exclusive and rare quality, according to the motto, if it's to be a diamond, then make sure it's from De Beers. The legendary company has always been synonymous with diamonds, and the brand has long been highly desirable. Second, De Beers guaranteed conflict-free diamonds. For the first time, the company pledged to respect human rights, ensure humane working conditions, and adhere to strict ethical standards. This was a promise that was not, and still is not, taken for granted in the industry. These requirements led to a new value proposition: "Only De Beers diamonds are fairly sourced and can represent the eternal love of an engaged couple". (See Table 4.15)

The value proposition was derived from the purpose, mission and values that De Beers had reaffirmed in its annual report [8]. It triggered a profound change for the company. Financial resources and expertise that were previously lacking had to be made available to meet the new value proposition. The scope of the change is reflected in the following description.

Service Offering

De Beers diamonds promise exclusivity, high quality and that certain je ne sais quoi that all iconic brands have. In addition, the company expanded its product mix (e.g. handbags, scarves, etc.) to allow non-diamond customers to experience the De Beers brand. In addition, the exclusivity of the brand was to be increased through limited special editions (e.g. Millennium Diamond).

Table 4.15: Transformation of the De Beers business model.

Value Proposition			
Only De Beers Diamonds are fairly sourced and can represent the eternal love of an engaged couple.			
Service Delivery	**Service Offering**	**Cost Model**	**Earnings Model**
Certification requirements developed in accordance with the Kimberley Process[4]	Product portfolio expanded to include new product categories (handbags, silk scarves, etc.)	Increased marketing spend to position the brand in the B2C market (e.g. $170 million US in 1999)	Trade in rough diamonds retained and margins increased through certification
Introduction of best practice compliance requirements for partners	Limited editions such as the 'Millennium Diamond' relaunched	Marketing cost burden shared with retailers and partners	Flagship stores generate additional sales
Exclusive branding of the diamonds enhanced	Unique retail experience facilitated through partnership with LVMH	Unique cost model established through vertical integration of all finishing steps	Partner stores pay commissions
'Forevermark' introduced to signal quality and origin	Strategic retail presence created in markets with a high share of luxury customers (USA, Japan and UK)		De Beers online auctions generate commissions
	Reduced number of key accounts to focus on brand positioning		
	Online presence established as an additional channel		

Marketing had to adapt to these advantages and adjust the mix of instruments accordingly. Marketing campaigns, collaborations with celebrities and the targeted placement of diamonds in pop culture (movies, music, etc.) gave the brand the attention it needed. The management focused all marketing activities on positioning De Beers as a special diamond brand.

The high marketing spend in all advertising channels was supported by a new distribution strategy designed to appeal to the target consumer segment [9]. De Beers entered the B2C luxury retail segment directly through a partnership with LVMH. This involved the targeted selection of locations with a high proportion of luxury consumers (USA, Japan and UK). The company drastically reduced the number of retail partners from 120

---

4 Kimberley Process (KP): KP certification ensures that certified diamonds are not mined to finance war or conflict (conflict diamonds).

to 80 to emphasize the exclusive nature of De Beers. De Beers also decided early on to use the online sales channel to promote and later distribute selected products.

Service Delivery

In order to deliver on the value proposition, and in particular the goal of seamless traceability, De Beers needed to better control its supply chain. The linchpin of this effort was to document the origin of diamonds. The first steps included the introduction of mandatory best practice and compliance standards. These had to be adhered to by the company's own mines and suppliers in order to fully prove the origin of the diamonds [10]. In 2002, De Beers became an active participant in the development of the Kimberley Process. This is an internationally recognized and complex process for determining the origin of diamonds and ensuring that they have not been used to finance conflict [11]. Today, only diamonds that meet the requirements of this process can be imported into most Western countries. De Beers has actively participated in the certification process. The new requirements have contributed to the successful implementation of the self-declared value proposition. Each supplier, distributor and De Beers itself have to strictly adhere to the requirements of this certification process [12].

At the same time, the certification process has raised the barriers to entry for competitors. Implementing a similar process would have significantly increased their costs. Many also lacked the expertise to undertake such a process. Controlling the value creation chain, from extraction to refinement and sale, created additional value for De Beers. The consulting firm Bain & Co. estimates the potential increase in value associated with certification, which affects 'willingness to pay' at more than 58% [13].

Earnings Model

De Beers has lost its monopoly position as a result of the market changes described above. It could no longer control the supply of diamonds. Rough diamond prices were correspondingly volatile. Revenues from the sector fell by 17% in 2012 as a result of the increased supply of diamonds, forcing De Beers to rethink its approach [14]. De Beers could no longer generate sufficient profits from mining and trading rough diamonds alone. A new earnings model had to be developed.

A milestone in the company's history was its entry into the B2C market. De Beers wanted to benefit from retail margins and no longer be satisfied with the role and margin of a wholesaler. This move opened up other important income sources for the company. In addition to trading rough diamonds, which was an existing income source with diminishing returns, the company also entered the retail sector in 2000 with 'De Beers Diamond Jewellers Limited'. De Beers now has stores around the world, from store-in-store solutions such as Galeries Lafayette to more than 30 independent stores in major cities. Online sales have become another significant income source in recent years, with DeBeers.com offering a wide range of diamond-encrusted jewelry aimed at affluent consumers. The site's attractive presentation even includes directions to nearby stores and online appointment booking. This omnichannel concept leverages multiple income sources, including sales from its own stores, commissions from third-party retailers, and its online stores. Since 2008, De Beers Auction Sales has provided an additional platform for buying and selling diamonds online through auctions. In 2017, these new income sources generated almost 30% of the Group's EBITDA [15].

Cost Model

Expansion comes with increased costs. Building and managing a store network (rent, staff, etc.) and marketing are key areas of expenditure. De Beers, like many luxury brands, has invested heavily in advertising to build brand awareness. While marketing costs have long remained at 1% of sales, the change in business model caused them to rise to 10%. The change in business model increased these costs to 10% [16]. In 2000 alone, De Beers spent approximately $170 million US on marketing. To ease the pressure on their budget, they involved retailers in brand development costs. Retailers who wanted to sell De Beers diamonds exclusively had to contribute financially to the marketing costs.

This verticalization helped the company to optimize its B2B costs. De Beers' deeper understanding of the trials and tribulations of both mine operators and retailers fostered trust and long-term relationships between De Beers and its partners. About 95% of De Beers' B2B contracts were long-term, compared with their key competitor Alrosa that only managed 55% [17]. De Beers appears to have successfully spread its incremental costs across producer, wholesaler, and retailer activities.

The company's cost model efforts are reflected in its impressive return on capital employed[5] (ROCE). Since the business model change in 1999, De Beers has improved this metric from just under 2% to over 7% in 2021, demonstrating a faster return on capital than ever before [18].

The Bottom Line

Faced with turbulent times in 1999, De Beers embarked on a five- to six-year journey to transform its business model. In the space of five to six years, the company suc-

---

5 Return on capital employed (ROCE) is a financial ratio used to measure the profitability of a company. It is a measure of how efficiently a company's capital is being used. ROCE is the ratio of earnings before interest and taxes (EBIT) to capital employed.

ceeded in initiating a substantial and successful self-disruption. The sudden decline of their long-standing diamond monopoly prompted them to rethink their value proposition, service offering, service delivery, cost model, and earnings model. Their strong capitalization likely facilitated this comprehensive transformation, and De Beers acted from a position of strength and with foresight. Had the company waited a few more years, the decline in its results would likely have been much greater. Sixteen years later, De Beers is thriving. Between 2010 and 2016, they achieved an average EBITDA margin of 23%, with a stable 37% rough diamond market share in 2016 [19]. In addition, more than 700 million De Beers diamonds were sold directly to consumers through more than 2,000 stores [20], solidifying its presence in the B2C market alongside luxury jewelers such as Tiffany & Co, Bulgari, and Van Cleef & Arpels.

References

[1]   See Reilly, S. (2004), De Beers SA – A Diamond is Forever, in: Stern University, 2004-12-01, http://pages.stern.nyu.edu/~rwiner/De%20Beers%20case.pdf.

[2]   See McAdams, D./Reavis, C. (2008), DeBeers's Diamond Dilemma, in: MITSloan, 2008-01-01, https://mitsloan.mit.edu/LearningEdge/strategy/DeBeersDilemma/Pages/DeBeers-Diamond-Dilemma.aspx.

[3]   See Rudnicka, E./Mamros, L./DeRiggi, B./Munshower, B. (2010), The Diamond Supply Chain, in: Eighth LACCEI Latin American and Caribbean Conference for Engineering and Technology (LACCEI'2010) "Innovation and Development for the Americas", in: laccei, 2010-06-04, http://www.laccei.org/LACCEI2010-Peru/published/ACC115_Rudnicka.pdf.

[4]   See Kretschmer, T (1998), De Beers and Beyond: The History of the International Diamond Cartel, in: Stern University, 1998-01-01, http://pages.stern.nyu.edu/~lcabral/teaching/debeers3.pdf.

[5]   See Mamonov, S./Triantoro, T. (2017), Subjectivity of Diamond Prices in Online Retail: Insights from a Data Mining Study, in: Journal of Theoretical and Applied Electronic Commerce Research, Vol 13 (2), pp. 15-28.

[6]   See The Economist (2004), The diamond cartel, in: The Economist, 2004-07-15, www.economist.com/node/2921462.

[7]   See Stein, N. (2001), The De Beers Story, in: Fortune, 2001-02-19, http://archive.fortune.com/magazines/fortune/fortune_archive/2001/02/19/296863/index.htm.

[8]   See De Beers (2007), Living up to diamonds – operating and financial review, in: De Beers Group, 2008-03-01, https://www.debeersgroup.com/content/dam/debeers/corporate/documents/Archive%20Reports/Operating_and_Financial_Review_2007_March_2008.PDF.downloadasset.PDF, p. 2.

[9]   See Bream, R. (2004), Rough Diamond Prices Poised to Continue Rising, in: Financial Times, 2004-01-12, http://courses.aplia.com/problemsetassets/micro/palmer_diamonds/article.html.

[10] See Conklin, D./Cadieux, D. (2005), De Beers and the global diamond industry, Ivey Business School Case Study 905M40.

[11] See Kimberley Process (2018), What Is The KP, in: Kimberley Process, 2018-01-01, https://www.kimberleyprocess.com/en/what-kp.

[12] See Spar, D. (2006), Markets: Continuity and Change in the International Diamond Market, in: The Journal of Economic Perspective, Vol. 20(3), pp. 195–208.

[13] See Bain & Company, (2013), The Global Diamond Report 2013: Journey through the Value Chain, in: Bain & Company, 2013-08-27, http://www.bain.com/publications/articles/global-diamond-report-2013.aspx.

[14] See ibid.

[15] See Anglo American, (2017), Key Financial Information, in: Anglo American, 2018-04-25, http://www.angloamerican.com/investors/financial-results-centre/key-financial-information.

[16] See Conklin, D./Cadieux, D. (2005), De Beers and the global diamond industry, Ivey Business School Case Study 905M40.

[17] See Vettori, G. (2015). The Financial Revolution of the De Beers, in: LUISSThesis, 2016-03-07, http://tesi.eprints.luiss.it/15699/1/179151.pdf.

[18] See De Beers. (2017), Preliminary Financial Results For 2016, in: De Beers Group, 2017-02-21, https://www.debeersgroup.com/en/news/company-news/company-news/preliminary-financial-results-for-2016.html.

[19] See De Beers. (2017), The Diamond Insight Report 2017, in: De Beers Group, 2017-01-01, https://www.debeersgroup.com/content/dam/de-beers/corporate/documents/Reports/Insight/InsightReport2017/Diamond-Insight-Report-2017_ONLINE.pdf.downloadasset.pdf.

[20] See Sheahan, P. (2016), Matter, BenBellaBooks, Dallas, pp. 153-158.

John Deere[*]

Background and Objectives of the Case Study

Smart refrigerators that automatically order food on demand. Smart door locks that unlock when your connected smartphone approaches. Smart thermostats that control the temperature in your home. Billions of connected devices now make up the Internet of Things (IoT), helping to make many aspects of consumers' lives easier. But consumers are not the only ones benefiting from IoT developments, but also businesses. By deploying IoT solutions, businesses can also reduce their operating costs, increase productivity, enter new markets, or even expand their service offering. John Deere, the venerable US agricultural equipment company, has embraced this digital transformation, creating new earnings sources and successfully transforming its business model. In this case study, we explain how John Deere achieved this.

Value Proposition

Since the company's founding in 1837, John Deere's mission has been to "help landowners get the most out of their land." While agriculture has changed dramatically since then, the value proposition has not needed to— quite the contrary, in fact. John Deere's promise to its customers is not product-specific, but timeless. The company's

*The case study was developed in collaboration with Gianluca Scheidegger (University of St. Gallen).

focus is not on improving an existing product by, for example, adding better engines to its tractors, but on the customer's problem itself. John Deere focuses on the common challenge of farmers: how to get the most out of their land. This leads the company to constantly question the status quo and consider new (technological) possibilities: "Is this really the best way to farm? Can't we do it better?" (see Table 4.16). John Deere not only creates a functional benefit for the customer (best possible quality) with this value proposition, but is also committed to the efficient use of limited resources (social benefit). It is a value proposition that has won over many customers around the world.

It is the only reason why John Deere, as a long-established company, has managed to remain relevant in the increasingly digitalized agricultural equipment market and to identify emerging trends such as IoT. Today, other large agricultural equipment manufacturers like Caterpillar are not the only competitors. Hundreds of smaller ag-tech start-ups are making life even more difficult for John Deere and increasing the pressure to innovate. One example of a successful ag-tech start-up is the Israeli company CropX. It sells cloud-based software that allows users to increase crop yields by saving water and energy. Using sensors in the field, the system automatically delivers the right amount of water to each plant, rather than watering an entire field at once.

Table 4.16: Transformation of the John Deere business model.

Value Proposition

To help farmers better manage their land.

Service Delivery	Service Offering	Cost Model	Earnings Model
Investment in technology solutions and acquisition of several agricultural technology companies	Products are fitted with sensors to 'talk' to other John Deere products	Increase in R&D spending	New earnings sources from other lines of business (e.g. forestry or financial services)
Regular employee surveys facilitate early identification of dissatisfaction and fresh needs	2012: Development of the 'MyJohnDeere' data analysis platform	Development of a more flexible cost structure	Constant income streams from the sale of services
		JD CROP as a systematic process to reduce costs	Customer lock-in due to incompatibility with competing products
Move to a more flexible manufacturing process	Expansion of offerings in non-agricultural business	Supply chain restructured to reduce inventory and freight costs	Transformation from a pure agricultural equipment manufacturer to a data and services company
	(e.g. forestry or financial services)		

Service Offering

By connecting products like soil sensors to the irrigation system, John Deere benefits from an entire ecosystem of smart products and services. Since 2012, the company's MyJohnDeere platform has connected farm equipment, weather data and irrigation systems through the Internet of Things (IoT). The platform helps farmers optimize their operations and manage their land more efficiently. A real added value for farmers who, according to an interview with an ag-tech CEO in Forbes magazine, have little time to innovate on their own: "You only get 40 attempts [as a farmer] to farm a field. If a 20-year-old farmer works until he's 60, there are only 40 crops in between. In the technology industry, you usually get 40 attempts in a week." [1]

As mentioned above, John Deere wanted to reduce its exposure to the American agricultural economy, so it increasingly focused on other lines of business. In 2017, only 68% of its total revenue came from the agricultural sector [2]. The construction and forestry sectors combined accounted for 19% of total sales in 2017 [3]. John Deere's financial services are becoming increasingly popular with customers. Expensive equipment can be leased, rented, insured or paid off in installments directly from the manufacturer. The company wants to make its equipment affordable for as many people as possible. John Deere has evolved from a simple product supplier to a problem solver with a wide range of services, consulting services and the latest technology. This allows farmers to choose from an attractive range of high quality products tailored to their needs.

Service Delivery

Land management is a very complex process. There are many factors to consider, such as weather, soil conditions and different types of seed. John Deere is committed to helping its customers optimize their farming operations. The company's engineers are constantly innovating to help farmers do just that. The way land is farmed has been revolutionized over the millennia, including the introduction of precision agriculture in the 1980s. In precision farming, each piece of land is managed according to soil and climate conditions [4]. Even small sections within a single field are taken into account. Analysts predict that the global precision farming market will grow by 89% from 2022 to 2027, reaching $14.4 billion US by 2027 [5].

To not only follow this trend in precision farming, but to help shape it, John Deere has packed a lot of technology into its equipment. The goal is to help farmers better manage their land. To make this possible, John Deere has acquired some of the necessary technological know-how: an important step was the acquisition of a GPS tracking software company (NavCom Technology) in 1999 [6]. Years before GPS technology was ready for the masses with navigation devices from TomTom or Google Maps, farmers were using location data to optimize routes or avoid overlapping fertilization [7]. While self-driving vehicles are immediately associated with technology companies like Tesla,

Apple or Google, John Deere tractors have been driving autonomously for more than twenty years [8]. In most cases, farmers are still behind the wheel, but they have a supervisory role in the planting or harvesting process. This makes it easier to cultivate fields at night or by workers who are less familiar with the area. It is estimated that about two-thirds of all US farmers now use self-driving agricultural vehicles [9].

The sensors in John Deere's equipment and vehicles generated a growing volume of data that needed to be processed. John Deere therefore made a pivotal move in 2008 by acquiring T-Systems International, a technology company with expertise in big data, cloud computing and systems security for an undisclosed sum [10]. John Deere's $350 million US acquisition of Blue River Technology in 2017 underscores the company's commitment to expanding its technology expertise [11]. Blue River Technology is a leading agricultural technology company focused on developing smart solutions for precision agriculture. The company has already won various awards for its innovative products [12].

However, John Deere does not only want to secure its innovative strength through acquisitions, but also by hiring specialists. This is the only way the company can remain competitive in delivering its services. There is a massive global shortage of experts in artificial intelligence, data analytics, and robotics [13, 14]. Without skilled people, change cannot succeed. This makes it all the more important to be perceived as an attractive employer by skilled workers. For this reason, John Deere conducts employee surveys every two weeks to identify dissatisfaction early and take action before employees leave for competitors or productivity declines [15]. Most companies conduct such surveys at most once a year [16]. John Deere also ensures a steady supply of internal talent by offering attractive development programs for university graduates. John Deere can only meet the increasing complexity of service delivery in the digital age if it has the necessary specialists.

The dynamic business environment requires not only the right resources, including highly skilled people, but also adapted processes. John Deere wanted to respond more quickly to market changes without increasing inventory. In 2001, the company's management therefore began to adapt its supply chain strategy. They realized that operating an efficient supply chain with significantly lower inventory levels required faster production and distribution processes. A robust planning process based on monthly adjusted sales forecasts was implemented. At the same time, the company shifted from batch production to a more flexible manufacturing process: each product could be manufactured flexibly on a daily basis. This change required more flexible assembly lines with rapid replenishment of all components for all products. Daily production of each model allowed John Deere to make production changes faster than would have been possible with monthly batch production. It was no longer necessary to wait until the next batch to increase production of a particular model [17].

Cost Model

John Deere's transformation from a pure hardware manufacturer to a data and services company didn't come cheap. Research and development alone increased from $550 million in 2000 to $1.4 billion US in 2013 [18]. To maintain profitability, cost optimization in other areas became imperative.

In 2001, under the leadership of then CEO Robert W. Lane, the company embarked on a re-evaluation of its existing supply chain strategy. Inventory levels needed to be reduced to free up fixed capital. At the time, finished goods inventory for retail and consumer products was estimated at a staggering $1.4 billion US. The company had projected inventory levels of $2 billion US to support projected sales growth [19].

Through careful analysis of individual product demand, a plan was developed to reduce the value of the machinery inventory to $1 billion US. For example, instead of maintaining roughly the same level of mower inventory throughout the year, inventory was kept high during peak sales months (March through July) and reduced for the remainder of the year [20].

Beyond supply chain adjustments, another critical cost reduction measure was implemented. Today, the company refers to its continuous cost optimization process as 'JD CROP' (John Deere Cost-Reduction Opportunities Process). Suppliers are encouraged to submit 3% annual cost reduction proposals through a dedicated platform. John Deere covers part of the cost of implementing these suggestions, and the savings are shared with the suppliers themselves. Suppliers with the most valuable suggestions receive additional recognition through awards from John Deere [21].

Earnings Model

John Deere's original business model was to sell high-quality agricultural equipment such as tractors, balers, and combines directly to farmers, with revenue generated solely from equipment sales. Today, agricultural equipment sales are steadily declining in key markets such as Europe and the United States [22, 23]. In John Deere's early years, nearly half of the US workforce was employed in agriculture; today, it is only 2% [24].

As a result, John Deere sought ways to adapt its earnings model and expand its product and service offerings. Selling only tractors and other farm equipment did not promise success in a shrinking market. In addition, John Deere's sales were heavily dependent on the economic well-being of its predominantly American farmer base. In an interview, Loren Troyer, director of order fulfillment, underscored the potential dangers of such dependence. For decades, John Deere has been steadily building lines of business independent of agriculture [25]. For example, a significant new source of income comes from the financial services mentioned in the service offering section. Farm equipment can be leased or purchased in installments, revolving credit is offered, and crop insurance is available. By 2021, financial services accounted for 8.5% of total sales [26].

Generating regular, recurring revenue from customers was a critical goal for John Deere. Their value proposition required innovation to improve land management, and with the rise of digitalization and its opportunities, this goal was achieved. High-margin services, such as consulting and repair, were added to the traditional farm equipment portfolio alongside a platform solution. For example, a farmer ordering a cotton harvester can now purchase a five-year subscription to the online machine configurator for Internet and platform connectivity for their machine for $1,600 US [27]. These subscriptions have effectively increased farmer loyalty to John Deere in the long term. While their products and services are well coordinated and provide value to customers through interconnectivity, they lack compatibility with competitors' offerings. This phenomenon, known as the lock-in effect, means that once certain product and service components are sourced from a particular manufacturer, switching to competitors would involve significant costs (requiring the replacement of all previous products).

The Bottom Line

In summary, John Deere's high level of innovation strength has enabled the 180-year-old company to remain relevant in a rapidly evolving market. They adapted their earnings model early on to focus on new products and markets. At the same time, they optimized costs to devote more resources to research. To strengthen its value proposition, John Deere actively participated in the development of precision agriculture and acquired ag-tech companies to gain the necessary expertise. The continuous and long-term transformation process has proven successful. From 2001 to 2021, net sales increased by 266% to $44 billion US [28].

References

[1] See McGrath, M./Sorvino, C. (2017), The 25 Most Innovative Ag-Tech Startups, in: Forbes, 2017-06-28, https://www.forbes.com/sites/maggiemcgrath/2017/06/28/the-25-most-innovative-ag-tech-start-ups/#290606ad4883.

[2] See John Deere. (2017), John Deere's Net Sales and Revenue Streams in FY 2017, by Major Segment (In Millions US Dollars), in:Statista – The Statistics Portal, 2018-02-14, https://www.statista.com/statistics/466524/net-sales-and-revenues-streams-of-john-deere-by-segment/.

[3] See ibid.

[4] See Gebbers, R./Adamchuk, V. (2016), Precision Agriculture and Food Security, in: Science, Vol. 327, pp. 828-830.

[5] See Statista. (2022), Forecast market value of precision agriculture worldwide from 2021 to 2027, 2022-08-16, https://www.statista.com/statistics/721921/forecasted-market-value-of-precision-farming-worldwide/.

[6] See Crunchbase, (2018), John Deere Acquisitions, 2018-02-09, https://www.crunchbase.com/organization/john-deere/acquisitions/acquisitions_list.

[7] See Tibken, S. (2016), How today's farmers got a head-start on tomorrow's tech, in: c|net, 2016-07-05, https://www.cnet.com/news/how-todays-farmers-got-a-head-start-on-tomorrows-tech-self-driving-vehicles-gps-mapping-apps/.

[8] See ibid.

[9] See ibid.

[10] See Crunchbase, (2018), John Deere Acquisitions, 2018-02-09, https://www.crunchbase.com/organiza tion/john-deere/acquisitions/acquisitions_list.

[11] See ibid.

[12] Blue River Technology, (2018), Home, 2018-02-12. http://www.bluerivertechnology.com/.

[13] See Columbus, L. (2017), IBM Predicts For Data Scientists Will Soar 28% By 2020, in: Forbes, 2017-05-13, https://www.forbes.com/sites/louiscolumbus/2017/05/13/ibm-predicts-demand-for-data-scientists-will-soar-28-by-2020/#56ccd4607e3b.

[14] See The Economist, (2016), Million-dollar babies, in: The Economist, 2016-04-02, https://www.econo mist.com/news/business/21695908-silicon-valley-fights-talent-universities-struggle-hold-their.

[15] See Power, B. (2016), Why John Deere Measures Employee Morale Every Two Weeks, in: Harvard Business Review, 2016-05-24, https://hbr.org/2016/05/why-john-deere-measures-employee-morale-every-two-weeks.

[16] See ibid.

[17] See Cooke, J. (2007), Running inventory like a Deere, in: Supply Chain Quarterly, Vol 4, http://www.supplychainquarterly.com/topics/Logistics/scq200704deere/.

[18] See John Deere, (2014), John Deere Committed to Those Linked to the Land: Investor Presentation, 2013-12/2014-01, http://www.deere.com/en_US/docs/Corporate/investor_relations/pdf/presenta tionswebcasts/2013/2013decjan_presentation.pdf.

[19] See Cooke, J. (2007), Running inventory like a Deere, in: Supply Chain Quarterly, Vol 4, http://www.supplychainquarterly.com/topics/Logistics/scq200704deere/.

[20] See ibid.

[21] See John Deere, (2018), Options for CP690 Self-Propelled Cotton Picker, 2018-03-22, https://configure.deere.com/cbyo/#/en_us/configure/40878073/options.

[22] See CEMA, (2016), Market Outlook FFA, http://cema-agri.org/sites/default/files/publications/Market %20Outlook%20FFA%20-%202016%20FINAL.pdf.

[23] See FCA. (2016). Update on U.S. Farm Equipment Trends, 2016-04-22, https://www.fca.gov/Down load/EconomicReports/7%20UpdateOnFarmEquipmentTrends.pdf.

[24] See McGrath, M./Sorvino, C. (2017), The 25 Most Innovative Ag-Tech Startups, in: Forbes, 2017-06-28, https://www.forbes.com/sites/maggiemcgrath/2017/06/28/the-25-most-innovative-ag-tech-start-ups /#290606ad4883.

[25] See Cooke, J. (2007), Running inventory like a Deere, in: Supply Chain Quarterly, Vol 4, http://www.supplychainquarterly.com/topics/Logistics/scq200704deere/.

[26] See John Deere, (2022), John Deere's (Deere & Company's) Net Sales in FY 2021, by Major Segment (In Millions US Dollars), in:Statista – The Statistics Portal, 2022-12-15, https://www.statista.com/statis tics/466524/net-sales-and-revenues-streams-of-john-deere-by-segment/.

[27] See John Deere, (2018), Options for CP690 Self-Propelled Cotton Picker, 2018-03-22, https://configure.deere.com/cbyo/#/en_us/configure/40878073/options.

[28] See Deere & Company, (2022), Annual Report 2022, https://s22.q4cdn.com/253594569/files/doc_fi nancials/2022/ar/2022-John-Deere-Annual-Report.pdf.

Nintendo*

Background and Objectives of the Case Study

Nintendo was once the global leader in game consoles, with a market share of over 90% [1]. But those days are over. By 2015, Nintendo was struggling to maintain its 10% market share. Its revenue that year ($4.6 billion US), however, was similar to its revenue in 2002 [2]. There have been several instances in the company's 134-year history where it has evolved and become the leader in a new market segment. The gaming segment had changed in many ways since the 1980s and 1990s, with mobile gaming being the most recent and important trend. Nevertheless, the traditional gaming segment still existed as a potential niche, although it was probably set for a long period of slow decline. As a traditional video game manufacturer, Nintendo embraced these trends. It faced many questions as it tried to develop a new strategy in this new environment. Nintendo competed with Sony and Microsoft in the traditional console segment, but its competitive advantage was increasingly threatened by the mobile gaming trend. Should Nintendo compete in hardware, software, or both? This case study illustrates how Nintendo did just that.

Value Proposition

Nintendo's mission is to put a smile on the faces of everyone we touch. We do this by creating new surprises that people around the world can enjoy together. [3]

At Nintendo, the customer's gaming experience in all its dimensions is paramount. The company strives to achieve an optimal balance between hardware and software that emphasizes the strengths of both. It is also committed to constantly challenging the way games are played. By focusing on the gaming experience, Nintendo differentiates itself from the competition and appeals to entirely new customer segments. The company promises to be different. The fact that Nintendo consistently delivers on this promise makes the brand iconic. For Nintendo, complete control over the design of the gaming experience is therefore a key differentiator and a central aspect of its value proposition to customers (see Table 4.17). Similar to Apple, Nintendo insists on developing both hardware and software in-house. It is this independence that allows the company to bring products like the Nintendo Wii to market.

---

*The case study was developed in collaboration with Christopher Schraml (University of St. Gallen).

Table 4.17: Transformation of the Nintendo business model.

Value Proposition			
"Creating smiles for generations"			

Service Delivery	Service Offering	Cost Model	Earnings Model
Nintendo owns a wealth of intellectual property (e.g. Mario, Zelda, Luigi, Pokémon, Donkey Kong and many more).	Games consoles (3 Nintendo Switch models)	Small number of hybrid console variants (Nintendo Switch) leads to lower development and production costs	Focus on selling game consoles (Nintendo Switch)
	Video games for Nintendo Switch		Focus on selling subscriptions to Nintendo Switch
Talented game console and video game developers	Mobile games for smartphones, tablets	Offering digital games online (App Store or Nintendo Switch Online) instead of physical games results in significantly lower storage, transportation and distribution costs.	games (Nintendo Switch Online)
Healthy competition among development teams leads to innovative products			Sale of mobile freemium games
	Subscription to online video games (Nintendo Switch Online)		
Collaboration with software houses to develop games (e.g. Pokémon Go)		Direct sale of games to end consumers avoids high costs for distributors and retailers	Sale of merchandise
	Character merchandise		Revenue from licensing the IP rights to its characters
	Super Nintendo World theme parks in Osaka, Japan and Los Angeles, USA		Sale of game cards
			Revenue from Nintendo theme parks in Osaka and Los Angeles

Service Offering

Nintendo has been striving to fulfill its value proposition ("Creating smiles for generations") since 1889, when it began manufacturing Hanafuda playing cards in Kyoto, Japan. Just over one hundred years and a string of successful product launches (including the *Nintendo Entertainment System*™ (NES™), Game Boy) later, Satoru Iwata (the creator of Pokémon and Super Smash Bros.) was appointed CEO in 2002. This heralded a change of vision at Nintendo, as Iwata realized that game console development was focusing too much on technology, such as more realistic graphics and high-definition sound. This made video games more and more expensive to produce, raising their prices and making them less attractive to the mass market. That went against the value proposition. So two years later, Nintendo introduced a completely redesigned portable gaming system—the *Nintendo DS*. The Nintendo DS was clearly aimed at the majority of consumers who were passionate about the fun and variety of games, but not the technical features. The Nintendo DS was a huge success, with more than 154 million units sold [4]. This strategic move to create an entirely new type of game system was aptly summed up by then VP of Marketing and Corporate Affairs, Perrin Kaplan:

> *At Nintendo, we call our strategy 'Blue Ocean'. [...] A Blue Ocean thrives on the idea of creating a market where none originally existed— going where no one has gone before. [...] We make games that expand our customer base in Japan and America. Yes, those who have always played games are still playing, but with titles like Nintendogs, Animal Crossing and Brain Games, we've also made people who've never played games love them. These games are 'Blue Ocean' in action.* [5]

On January 9, 2007, Steve Jobs made an announcement about the launch of Apple's latest product—the iPhone. This seemingly unrelated event had a significant impact on Nintendo's business model and service offerings. In 2008, Apple's App Store opened its doors to software developers, bringing casual games to the forefront of popular smartphone applications.

While Nintendo lacked a mobile game offering at the time, analysts urged the company to shift its focus to software development and create games specifically for mobile phones and tablets. In response, Nintendo entered the mobile gaming arena, leveraging its intellectual property, particularly popular franchises like Mario Brothers and Pokémon, to maintain relevance. The spectacular 2016 launch of Pokémon Go, developed by Niantic, and the success of Super Mario Run on iOS marked significant milestones. Despite these ventures into mobile games, Nintendo's core strategy remained focused on another console launch: the Nintendo Switch.

Once again embracing the 'Blue Ocean' strategy, Nintendo released the Switch in March 2017, designed for a seamless transition between the living room and mobile gaming. The Nintendo Switch is especially designed for a wide range of gamers, offering both local multiplayer and online gaming experiences. Nintendo describes the Switch's core value proposition as a 'anytime, anywhere, with anyone' gaming concept [6]. Today, the Switch is Nintendo's only console[6], and with over 75 million units sold, it is on track to become one of the most successful consoles of all time. This success is no accident. The Switch embodies the key elements of Nintendo's value proposition and seamlessly blends them into a unique offering [7]. To further solidify its commitment to value, Nintendo launched the online subscription service Nintendo Switch Online at a competitive price ($19.99 US per year) that is significantly lower than its competitors offerings in the form of Xbox Gold und Playstation Plus. This service enables seamless integration with mobile phones and unlocks exciting cross-platform gaming possibilities. Nintendo Switch Online subscribers have access to an unparalleled library of exclusive Nintendo games [8]. One analyst summed it up nicely: "With the release of the

---

6 Three versions of this console are available (Nintendo Switch, Nintendo Switch Lite, Nintendo Switch OLED model)

Switch and the online cloud membership (Nintendo Switch Online/Nintendo Account), the company is shifting its business model from releasing hardware-centric consoles to building an online software platform with regular, iterative hardware releases." [9]

Service Delivery

Nintendo's achievements are built on a foundation of intellectual property, including iconic characters like Mario, Zelda, Luigi, Pokémon and Donkey Kong. Since 1984, healthy competition among Nintendo's development teams has fostered innovation and creativity, strengthening this foundation. In 2011, then CEO Satoru Iwata realized that conducting traditional focus groups (like Sony and Microsoft did) with passionate gamers was not enough to deliver on Nintendo's value proposition. Instead, the company shifted its focus to studying non-gamers. This shift revealed that popular casual games didn't require high-end graphics or sound. As a result, Nintendo strategically reduced these elements to a 'good enough' level. In addition, the lower graphics quality significantly reduced development costs compared to PlayStation or Xbox games, allowing Nintendo to create a vast library of affordable video games [10].

Recognizing the need for specific skills and knowledge not readily available internally, Nintendo has partnered with software companies for game development. One notable example is the popular mobile game *Pokémon Go*, where Nintendo collaborated closely with Niantic, Google and its Google Earth and Google Maps teams.

In summary, it can be said that all of Nintendo's core service delivery activities are aimed at developing new growth markets. Rather than poaching existing customers from its competitors, the company always prefers to target new customer segments. To do this, Nintendo tries to find out why certain people are not (yet) playing video games. This approach of 'democratizing' the video game market can be directly derived from Nintendo's value proposition and is also reflected in the company's service offering [11].

In order to launch products such as the Nintendo Wii or the Nintendo Switch, Nintendo relies on two main resources. First, highly creative game console and video game developers, and second, sufficient financial resources. There have been many talented developers in Nintendo's history, with Shigeru Miyamoto probably being the most important. The financial resources have also allowed the company to take risks. Even after the unsuccessful Wii U, Nintendo had enough capital to start over. Creativity and risk-taking are part of Nintendo's DNA and deeply ingrained in its culture. Nintendo is not intimidated by failure and always strives to find new ways forward [12].

Cost Model

Traditionally, Nintendo has always had two consoles on the market at the same time. But because the Nintendo Switch is a combination of home console and handheld, the company was suddenly able to concentrate the costs of hardware and software development, marketing, and support into a single product. Together with research and development, the individual console components account for the majority of production costs. The various console components are sourced from specialized suppliers and vary widely in price depending on the desired performance requirements. Nintendo's conscious decision not to compete on console performance therefore allowed for lower purchase prices, which ultimately led to lower selling prices and the positioning of the Switch as a 'secondary' console [13].

Compared to the production of physical games, the cost of providing a digital version is many times lower. This is in addition to the storage and transportation costs that can be saved with digital games. In addition, the fact that Nintendo can now sell a significant portion of its games directly to the end user with its online subscription service means at least partial disintermediation of the retail channel and thus an additional improvement in margins.

Earnings Model

According to the annual report, the Switch platform, which includes hardware and software sales, accounted for a good 95% of Nintendo's total revenue ($13.25 billion US) in the 2022 financial year [14]. Since Nintendo traditionally earns very little from licensing fees (combined with mobile game sales, about 3% of total revenue, or $440 million US), the company has always relied on sales of its own games. However, with the advent of free-to-play mobile games, it became increasingly difficult for Nintendo to justify its high margins to customers. For this reason, just a few months after the launch of Nintendo Switch, Nintendo launched the online subscription service Nintendo Switch Online. An annual membership costs $19.99 US per year and offers players a number of benefits. Nintendo Switch Online is a paid service that allows users to play compatible Nintendo Switch games online, access a selection of classic NES games with online functionality, backup stored data for most games and access additional features for the Nintendo Switch Online smartphone app. In addition, Nintendo Switch Online members can take advantage of exclusive special offers from Nintendo. The *Nintendo Switch Online + Expansion Pack* for $49.99 US per year gives users access to more exclusive games. Nintendo benefits from lower revenue volatility thanks to subscription revenue. In an otherwise highly cyclical market, the introduction of the subscription model has led to more stable sales and made the company less dependent on regular new releases or major holidays [15].

Nintendo monetizes mobile games through a 'freemium' business model.. This model allows users to download Nintendo's game applications for free and play them up to a certain level, but if they want additional features and functions, they have to pay for them (with 'in-game purchases'). To generate revenue, Nintendo uses the popularity of its characters in the form of theme parks. The first *Super Nintendo World* opened in March 2021 in Osaka, Japan. For the equivalent of about $70 US, visitors can experience the world of Mario and his friends with life-size attractions [16]. The concept seems to have been well received, as the first Super Nintendo World outside of Japan opened in February 2023 as part of Universal Studios in Los Angeles [17]. In the future, Nintendo plans to spend up to $2.7 billion US on Nintendo infrastructure such as theme parks and new stores [18].

The Bottom Line

Contrary to the expectations of many analysts, Nintendo successfully transformed its business model and once again proved its raison d'être. An operating profit of $4.9 billion US on revenues of $14 billion US in 2022 clearly demonstrates the success of Nintendo's business model transformation [19]. The company has constantly remained true to its value proposition through all of its adjustments. It is this drive to be different that makes Nintendo so unique in an industry that sometimes seems very homogeneous. The fact that Nintendo opened its first theme park in Osaka in March 2021 is further proof of this. No other company in the video game industry would be able to make such a move.

References

[1]   See Kotaku UK (2014), How Sonic Helped Sega Win the Early 90s Console Wars, in: Kotaku, 2014-10-31, https://kotaku.com/how-sonic-helped-sega-win-the-early-90s-console-wars-1653185046.
[2]   See Nintendo (2002, 2015), Annual Reports 2002, 2015.
[3]   See Nintendo (2023), About Nintendo, 2023-05-11, https://www.nintendo.com/about/.
[4]   See Nintendo (2023), IR Information: Dedicated Video Game Sales Units, 2023-05-11, https://www.nintendo.co.jp/ir/en/finance/hard_soft/index.html.
[5]   See Forbes (2006), Nintendo's New Look, 2006-02-07, https://www.forbes.com/2006/02/07/xbox-ps3-revolution-cx_rr_0207nintendo.html?sh=6c2d1d316781.
[6]   Nintendo (2018), Six Months Financial Results Briefing for Fiscal Year Ending March 2018, 2018-03-30, https://www.nintendo.co.jp/ir/pdf/2017/171031_2e.pdf.
[7]   See VGChartz. (2020), Lifetime unit sales of the Nintendo Switch console worldwide from March 2017 to January 2021 (in millions) [Graph], In Statista, 2022-08-11, https://www.statista.com/statistics/687059/nintendo-switch-unit-sales-worldwide/.
[8]   See Evangelho, J. (2018), Why Is Nintendo's Switch So Successful? It's All About The Marketing, 2018-06-20, https://www.forbes.com/sites/jasonevangelho/2018/06/20/why-is-nintendos-switch-so-successful-its-all-about-the-marketing/?sh=7dada78636c9.
[9]   See New Company Deep Dive (2020), Nintendo – Switching the business model, in: Asymmetric Skew, 2020-11-18, https://asymmetricskew.substack.com/p/nintendo-switching-the-business-model.
[10] See INSEAD (2019), Case Sturdy IN1575: Nintendo Switch: Shifting from Market-Competing to Market-Creating Strategy.
[11] See Pinker, A. (2019), What we can learn from the innovation culture at Nintendo, 2019-05-03, https://medialist.info/en/2019/05/03/what-we-can-learn-from-the-innovation-culture-at-nintendo/.
[12] See ibid.
[13] See Aurégan & Tellier (2019). Nintendo in the Pursuit of the Blue Ocean.

[14] See Nintendo (2022), Annual Report 2022.

[15] See Culpan, T. (2018), Nintendo Flicks the Switch on a Lucrative New Revenue Stream, 2018-05-08, https://www.bloombergquint.com/opinion/nintendo-flicks-theswitch-on-a-lucrative-new-revenue-stream.

[16] See Klook (2022), Everything You Need to Know About Super Nintendo World at Universal Studios Japan, 2022-12-29, https://www.klook.com/blog/universal-studios-japan-super-nintendo-world-guide/.

[17] See Biron, B. (2023), Super Nintendo World opens in Los Angeles next month with a Mario Kart-themed ride, gigantic Bowser statue, and Princess Peach cupcakes—take a look inside, 2023-01-22, https://www.businessinsider.com/photos-super-nintendo-world-theme-park-opening-la-mario-brothers-2023-1?r=US&IR=T#super-nintendo-world-is-opening-its-much-anticipated-first-theme-park-outside-of-japan-next-month-in-los-angeles-1.

[18] See Klook (2022), Everything You Need to Know About Super Nintendo World at Universal Studios Japan, 2022-12-29, https://www.klook.com/blog/universal-studios-japan-super-nintendo-world-guide/.

[19] See Nintendo (2022), Annual Report 2022.

OTTO[*]

Background and Objectives of the Case Study

73 years after its founding and two business model transformations later, Werner Otto Versandhandel, founded in Hamburg and now known as Otto within the Otto Group, is one of Europe's most successful traditional mail order businesses with sales of more than €6.3 billion in 2022[7] and approximately 6,000 employees [1, 2]. The company's success story began with the iconic 'Otto Catalog,' which was first published in 1950 [3]. The growing popularity of the catalog eventually led to Otto becoming the world's largest mail order company in the mid-1980s [4]. As the millennium approached, however, the importance of the Internet grew. Despite the novelty and niche nature of the technology at the time, Otto responded quickly and made its first foray into e-commerce in 1995 with the launch of the Otto.de website and shopping deals on CD-ROM. By 1997, Internet orders already accounted for 7% of the Otto Group's total sales. Despite initial fears of cannibalization of the two sales channels, Otto continued to push e-commerce [5]. Thanks to this early focus on online business, Otto was able to successfully master the digital transformation of the market and establish itself as an online retailer. With a

7 OTTO reports sales as Gross Merchandise Value (GMV), i.e. the combined sales from retail and marketplace business. According to the IRFS, OTTO generated external sales of around €4.52 billion in the 2022/23 financial year.

*The case study was developed in collaboration with Christopher Schraml (University of St. Gallen) and Lisa Gerner.

total of 97% of its customers switching to e-commerce, Otto decided to finally discontinue catalog mailings in 2018 [6].

Back in the 2014/15 financial year, when the company posted its first annual loss in its history, it became clear that simply offering an online store was no longer enough to remain competitive [7]. At the same time, Otto's biggest competitor, Amazon, was shaping the market as an open digital trading platform for third-party sellers and their goods [8]. So in 2017, the decision was made to expand Otto.de into an open platform, ushering in the second business model transformation in the company's history.

Value Proposition

With its customer-centric focus, Otto was able to achieve great success right from the start. In the early years, adapting the business model to meet the needs of baby boomers drove the expansion of the former catalog retailer. An early focus on online business also helped the company respond in time to the changing needs of its customers [9].

Table 4.18: Transformation of the OTTO business model.

Value Proposition

OTTO's recipe for success to this day: To fulfill the wishes of our customers and take care of them in the future. Technologies are the key for this.

Service Delivery	Service Offering	Cost Model	Earnings Model
Efficient business processes thanks to largely in-house processing (e.g. deliveries by Hermes, the in-house delivery service)	Very wide range of products and brands thanks to the integration of marketplace merchants on the platform	Reduction in fixed costs by transferring the storage of new product ranges to marketplace merchants	Additional revenue from a monthly fee from each marketplace merchant for using the online marketplace
A technologically superior IT infrastructure facilitates the efficient onboarding of marketplace merchants to offer their products on the online marketplace.	Opening up the platform means that customers can access a wide range of services from marketplace merchants		Additional revenue from commissions for each product sold through the online marketplace
Superior data management allows marketplace merchants to advertise effectively	Staging of primary data for advertising purposes allows marketplace merchants to advertise effectively		Revenue from the sale of Otto's primary data to marketplace merchants for advertising purposes

Today, Otto knows that it is no longer enough to simply sell products as an online retailer. Rather, in addition to a wide range of products, the company needs to offer the right services to make the customer experience something special. The success of the transformation in value proposition can be explained in part by its meaningfulness [10]. The functional benefit of the online retailer's value proposition emphasizes the advantages of the wide range of products and the increase in value through the associated services (cf. Table 4.18). An emotional benefit can also be created through the company's history, which is reflected in the brand awareness and authenticity of the founding family [11]. A social benefit can also be identified as well, however, with the platform positioning itself under the values of fair, personal and inspiring [12]. In addition, the company has been committed to sustainable business practices for more than 30 years as a corporate goal firmly anchored in its culture [13].

Service Offering

The transformation from an online retailer to an open platform in a so-called 'two-sided market' entails a number of changes for Otto's service offering [14]. On the one hand, the development also requires the inclusion of new customer segments, namely those partners who can sell their own products over the platform [15]. Otto wants to become a problem solver and sees the platform's business model as particularly suitable, as it allows customers to be offered services in the form of comprehensive solutions in addition to products [16]. In addition to augmented reality (AR) solutions, these include services such as 'OTTO NOW' or the intelligent ordering option 'OTTO ready', which are designed to make everyday life easier for customers [17]. With more than 2.9 million daily visits to the website and more than 4,000 marketplace partners, this results in strong network effects, which are reflected in an even more comprehensive product range, new product lines and a significantly wider choice of brands for customers [18]. In figures, this means that customers have access to more than 14.5 million products from over 19,000 brands and 5,000 marketplace partners, as well as a total of 103 different services [19].

Service Delivery

As a pure trading company, Otto imported products from suppliers all over the world in addition to offering its own brands [20]. The evolution of the business model to an open online platform (online marketplace) has changed the way services are delivered. On an open online platform, not only products that Otto itself purchases are sold, but also products that are offered by third parties over Otto's online platform. As a result, the core of Otto's service offering has expanded to include the provision of millions of products from thousands of marketplace partners and the provision of various services. In order to deliver on this scale, Otto needed to build extensive IT capabilities to modernize its technology infrastructure and create automated on-boarding systems for its partners [21].

In order to continuously drive this transformation forward and anchor the developments in the company, the internal organization and processes were adapted to the new business model by 2023 as part of the 'NEW' project launched in 2020 [22].

Another success factor in Otto's delivery of services is its employees. The fact that they are at the heart of the company's transformation was already evident in 2015 with the Otto Group's 'Culture Change 4.0' project, which aimed at actively involving employees in the innovation process using digital platforms, among other things [23]. As of 2021, Otto had around 6,200 employees, including 2,400 in service and customer support, who play a key role in the company's successful transformation and performance [24]. The central position of the platform provider's employees and the focus on technological progress are also reflected in the guiding principle of the new employer branding: "A company for people. Driven by technology." [25]

To ensure continuous development and improvement of processes, the majority of processes are handled in-house. For example, products are delivered using the Hermes delivery service, which also belongs to the Otto Group, with continuous investment in the expansion of logistics capacities to enable new next-day deliveries [26]. In addition, Otto also handles all payment processing on the online marketplace to ensure that customers enjoy a smooth experience [27].

Cost Model

The transformation from an online retailer to a platform with a marketplace function also has an impact on Otto's cost model. On the one hand, investments in new technologies and a modern IT landscape as well as the development of on-boarding systems for partners are essential for the development of the platform. Since 2017, around €100 million have been invested annually [28].

Additional costs are also incurred through the targeted recruitment of new talent in IT. In addition, additional resources and skills are required for the creation of digital services such as 'Otto READY', which represent another important pillar of the new business model. Then again, more efficient and scalable processes and structures have already been established as part of the 'NEW' strategy project, which has led to initial cost savings. For example, the resulting automation and standardization led to staffing adjustments in certain organizational areas. However, the evolution into a marketplace enables Otto to expand its product portfolio by placing additional deals from around 5,000 marketplace partners [29]. This leads to an increase in customer value without additional logistics costs, since the logistics is handled directly by the partners. As a result, Otto benefits from the commissions the company receives from the marketplace partners for each product sold over the marketplace, but has lower fixed costs and less capital tied-up because it does not have to stock new product ranges.

Earnings Model

As part of the restructuring, Otto's earnings model was also adjusted by adding addi-tional income sources to the former transaction-based mail order business. Today, similar to its competitor Amazon, products from marketplace partners are sold along-side the company's own range, for which Otto charges a basic monthly fee per retailer and a commission for each product sold [30]. While the monthly fee is €39.90 per mer-chant, regardless of the number of articles, the commission varies between 7% and 18% depending on the product category [31]. In addition to transaction-based income sources, Otto generates revenue by offering services. While certain services are charged for (e.g. installation service for built-in electrical appliances, assembly service for furniture), others are offered free of charge (e.g. return of old appliances, free fabric, wood and up-holstery samples) [32]. In the longer term, free services can also generate indirect reve-nue as they aim at increasing customer satisfaction [33]. In addition, the new 'Retail Media' pillar, which was established in 2020, enables Otto to generate revenues outside its core business. For example, Otto's marketplace partners can book advertising for their products not only directly in the Otto online store, but also on websites outside the Otto online store (e.g. cookery portals, online weather services) in order to increase the brand's visibility among customers [34]. On January 1, 2023, Otto started offering its pri-mary data for advertising customers exclusively through Otto Advertising, in order to provide them not only with data packages for advertising purposes, but also to be able to repeatedly derive and implement adjustments to campaigns from the primary data [35].

The Bottom Line

With the transformation of its business model from a pure online retailer to a plat-form company, Otto has demonstrated its agility and customer focus for the second time in its history. Otto was quick to seize the opportunity presented by changes in the market and decided to transform the company into a marketplace and service provider. This decision demonstrates the central role the value proposition ("Fulfilling the wishes of our customers and taking care of them in the future. Technologies are the key for this.") has to play in a business model transformation. Changing the cost model also made it possible for the company to reduce its fixed costs, make new in-vestments, and align the delivery of its services with new technologies and needs. This was the only way to expand the existing retail offering to include the new mar-ketplace partners' products and services, and ultimately meet new customer needs and create new income sources.

References

[1]   See OTTO (2023), OTTO generates around €6.3 billion in revenue in 2022, 2023-03-31, https://www.otto.de/unternehmen/de/presse/otto-erwirtschaftet-2022-rund-6-3-milliarden-euro-umsatz (in German only)

[2]   See Brindöpke, M. (2021), "Plattformen: Otto: Das Ende der Multishop-Strategie?" (Platforms: Otto: The End of the Multishop Strategy) Etailment.de, 2021-10-26, https://etailment.de/news/stories/Platt formen-Otto-Das-Ende-der-Multishop-Strategie-23646 (in German only).

[3]   See Linz, C., Müller-Stewens, G. & Zimmermann, A. (2021), Radical Business Model Transformation: How leading organizations have successfully adapted to disruption (second edition). London: Kogan Page.

[4]   See Grosse Bley, M. (2019), "Vom Stiefkind zum Liebling – Die Entwicklung von E-Commerce am Beispiel OTTO", (From Poor Relation to Darling – The Development of E-commerce at Otto), Management-circle.de, 2019-11-27, https://www.management-circle.de/blog/entwicklung-e-commerce-beispiel-otto/ (in German only).

[5]   See ibid.

[6]   See Linz, C., Müller-Stewens, G. & Zimmermann, A. (2021), Radical Business Model Transformation: How leading organizations have successfully adapted to disruption (second edition). London: Kogan Page.

[7]   See Klein, L. (2019), "Nur verkaufen reicht nicht mehr" (Just Selling Is No Longer Enough), Otto.de, 2019-06-11, https://www.otto.de/newsroom/de/kundenfokus/otto-wird-plattform (in German only).

[8]   See Petry, T. (2019), "Digital Leadership: Erfolgreiches Führen in Zeiten der Digital Economy" (Digital Leadership: Leading Successfully in the Digital Economy) (2nd Edition), Freiburg: Haufe Lexware.

[9]   See Grosse Bley, M. (2019), "Vom Stiefkind zum Liebling – Die Entwicklung von E-Commerce am Beispiel OTTO", (From Poor Relation to Darling – The Development of E-commerce at Otto), Management-circle.de, 2019-11-27, https://www.management-circle.de/blog/entwicklung-e-commerce-beispiel-otto/ (in German only).

[10] See Rudolph, T. & Schweizer M. (2019), "High 5: erfolgreiche Geschäftsmodelltransformation in disruptiven Zeiten" (High 5: Successful Business Model Transformation in Disruptive Times), St. Gallen: Research Center for Retail Management at the University of St. Gallen (2nd Edition).

[11] See Erle, C. (2016-08-18), André Müller on OTTO's success factors in e-commerce. Management-circle.de. Retrieved from: https://www.management-circle.de/blog/interview-andre-mueller-otto-erfolg-e-commerce/ (in German only).

[12] See Gondorf, L. (2019), "Die Transformation zur Plattform" (The Transformation to the Platform): "Wir wollen niemanden kopieren" (We Don't Want to Copy Anyone), Otto.de, 2019-06-13, https://www.otto.de/newsroom/de/technologie/die-transformation-zur-plattform.

[13] See Otto (n.d.), "Was uns bewegt: Nachhaltigkeit" (What Moves Us: Sustainability), Otto.de, 2023-05-11, https://www.otto.de/unternehmen/de/was-uns-bewegt/nachhaltigkeit (in German only).

[14] See Baums, A. (n.d.). "Digitale Plattformen – DNA der Industrie 4.0" (Digital Platforms – The DNA of Industry 4.0). Plattform-maerkte.de. Retrieved from: http://plattform-maerkte.de/dna/ (in German only).

[15] See Fuchs, J. (2017), "Analyse: Otto-Gruppe baut radikal um: Die neue Plattformstrategie im Überblick", (Analysis: Otto Group Undergoes Radical Restructuring: The New Platform Strategy at a Glance), T3n.de, 2017-05-15, https://t3n.de/news/otto-marktplatz-plattform-strategie-bilanz-2017-823962/ (in German only).

[16] See Klein, L. (2019), "Nur verkaufen reicht nicht mehr" (Just Selling Is No Longer Enough), Otto.de, 2019-06-11, https://www.otto.de/newsroom/de/kundenfokus/otto-wird-plattform (in German only).

[17] See Remy, A. (2019), "Kaufoption, Kurzmiete, Kindermöbel: Das ist neu bei OTTO NOW", (Option to Buy, Short-Term Rental, Children's Furniture: This Is New at Otto Now), Otto.de, 2019-05-27,

https://www.otto.de/newsroom/de/kundenfokus/kaufoption-kurzmiete-kindermöbel-das-ist-neu-bei
-otto-now (in German only).

[18]	See Remy, A. (2022), "Händler, Marktplatz, Plattform – was heisst das eigentlich?" (Retailer,
Marketplace, Platform – What Does It All Mean?) Otto.de, 2022-01-28, https://www.otto.de/news
room/de/kundenfokus/haendler-marktplatz-plattform-was-heißt-das-eigentlich (in German only).

[19]	See OTTO (2023), OTTO generates around €6.3 billion in revenue in 2022, 2023-03-31, https://www.
otto.de/unternehmen/de/presse/otto-erwirtschaftet-2022-rund-6-3-milliarden-euro-umsatz (in
German only).

[20]	See footnote 18.

[21]	See Frommhold, M. (2019), "Wie steuert man den größten Umbruch der Unternehmensgeschichte?"
(How to Manage the Greatest Upheaval in the Company's History), Otto.de, 2023-02-25,
https://www.otto.de/newsroom/de/kundenfokus/der-größte-umbruch (in German only).

[22]	See Frommhold, M. (2021), "Was wird neu durch 'NEW' bei OTTO?" (What's New With 'New' at
Otto?), Otto.de, 2021-04-12, https://www.otto.de/newsroom/de/kultur/was-wird-neu-durch-new-bei-
otto (in German only).

[23]	See Linz, C., Müller-Stewens, G. & Zimmermann, A. (2021), Radical Business Model Transformation:
How leading organizations have successfully adapted to disruption (second edition). London:
Kogan Page.

[24]	See Otto (n.d.), "Wer wir sind: Auf einen Blick", (Who We Are: At a Glance) Otto.de, 2023-05-11,
https://www.otto.de/unternehmen/de/wer-wir-sind/auf-einen-blick (in German only).

[25]	See Di Bari, F. (2022), "Neues Jahr, neue Arbeitgeberbotschaft: 'Wir setzen auf Techtimonials'", (New
Year, New Message for the Workforce: 'We Rely on Tech Testimonials') Otto.de, 2022-01-05,
https://www.otto.de/newsroom/de/kultur/hr-marketing-wir-setzen-auf-techtimonials (in
German only).

[26]	See Gondorf, L. (2019), "Es geht nicht darum, viele Services zu haben, sondern die richtigen" (It's
Not About Having Lots of Services, but the Right Ones), Otto.de, 2019-07-15, https://www.otto.de/
newsroom/de/kundenfokus/es-geht-nicht-darum-viele-services-zu-haben-sondern-die-richtigen (in
German only).

[27]	See Klein, L. (2020), "Als Payment-Dienstleister übernehmen wir die komplette
Zahlungsabwicklung", (As a Payment Service Provider, We Take over the Complete Payment
Processing) Otto.de, 2020-09-01, https://www.otto.de/newsroom/de/technologie/otto-baut-eigene-
payment-gesellschaft-auf (in German only).

[28]	See Frommhold, M. (2021), "Was wird neu durch 'NEW' bei OTTO?" (What's New With 'New' at
Otto?), Otto.de, 2021-04-12, https://www.otto.de/newsroom/de/kultur/was-wird-neu-durch-new-bei-
otto (in German only).

[29]	See Otto (n.d.). "Wer wir sind: Auf einen Blick", (Who We Are: At a Glance) Otto.de, 2023-05-11,
https://www.otto.de/unternehmen/de/wer-wir-sind/auf-einen-blick (in German only).

[30]	See Otto Market (n.d.), "Gemeinsam handeln!" (Acting Together!), Otto.market, 2023-05-11,
https://www.otto.market/.html (in German only).

[31]	See Otto Market (n.d.), "Sortiment im Überblick!" (Assortment at a Glance), Otto.market, 2023-05-11,
https://www.otto.market/de/sofunktionierts/sortimente-uebersicht.html (in German only).

[32]	See Surholt, F. (2019), "Die zehn besten OTTO-Services und wie ihr sie bestellt" (The Ten Best Otto
Services and How to Order Them), Otto.de, 2019-07-23, https://www.otto.de/newsroom/de/kunden
fokus/beste-otto-services (in German only).

[33]	See Gondorf, L. (2019), "Es geht nicht darum, viele Services zu haben, sondern die richtigen" (It's
Not About Having Lots of Services, but the Right Ones), Otto.de, 2019-07-15, https://www.otto.de/
newsroom/de/kundenfokus/es-geht-nicht-darum-viele-services-zu-haben-sondern-die-richtigen (in
German only).

[34] See Remberg, A. (2021), "Was ist Retail Media?" (What Is Retail Media?), Otto.de, 2021-04-12, https://www.otto.de/newsroom/de/technologie/was-ist-retail-media (in German only).
[35] See ibid.

4.3 Failed Business Model Transformations

Financial Times Deutschland*

Background and Objectives of the Case Study

Even as it bid farewell to the media world on December 7, 2012, the Financial Times Deutschland (FTD) did not lose its sense of humor. Only two words adorned the pitch-black front page on that gloomy Friday: "Finally black".

At first, the FTD's future looked quite bright. As a weekday national business newspaper on salmon pink paper, it was supposed to bring color to the gray German media landscape. It was founded in 2000 by Hamburg-based Gruner + Jahr and Pearson, the British publisher of the Financial Times (FT) in London. After a failed transformation, which Gruner + Jahr initiated in 2008, the paper closed its doors. It never once operated in the black in its entire history. The loss is estimated at more than €250 million [1].

Unlike many of its competitors, the FTD did not fall victim to the banking and financial crisis of 2007/2008. In fact, interest in financial topics grew and more newspapers were sold. So why was the FTD unable to establish itself in the German market? This case study shows how important it is to consistently implement a meaningful and focused value proposition and to align the service offering with a specific customer segment.

Value Proposition

Fronted by the value proposition "Knowing what will be important", the FTD promised its readers a head start in knowledge through relevant, opinionated articles on economic and financial topics that are outside mainstream economic policy (see Table 4.19) [2]. It positioned itself as a provider of ideas and an initiator. The goal was to appear more exclusive, newsworthy, and international than its competitors. Although this is a perfectly sensible and focused value proposition, it was not consistently implemented. The reasons for this were a lack of thematic focus and the dilution of the corporate culture in the course of the transformation.

---

*The case study was developed in collaboration with Kathrin M. Neumüller (University of St. Gallen).

Table 4.19: Transformation of the FT Deutschland business model.

Value Proposition			
"Knowing what will be important" promises readers a head start in knowledge and relevance.			
Service Delivery	**Service Offering**	**Cost Model**	**Earnings Model**
Journalist team consisted of experienced journalists and career changers	High-quality coverage of business and financial affairs	Merger of Gruner + Jahr's business media led to significant cost savings	Advertising revenues lagged far behind those of competitors
As of 2008, secondary activities were delivered by the publisher (e.g. controlling, IT, marketing).	Limited thematic focus Incorrect assessment of the size of the target audience interested in economics	Cost savings increased the climate of fear among journalists, jeopardizing quality journalism	Declining print circulation as main source of earnings Unconvincing distribution strategy (high number of free copies; inconsistency between high quality and low price)
This led to increased complexity and dilution of the brand	Uncoordinated cross-channel approach (e.g. ftd.de, "FTD zum Hören" podcast) prevented the development of a core readership		
Shared newsroom increased lack of profile (loss of journalistic diversity, brand dilution)			

Service Offering

In the newspaper industry, print had long been a proven medium. The FTD also stuck with this proven approach. After all, it was exposed to disruptive technologies and offerings that emerged in the course of digitalization. In the case of the FTD, it was primarily a change in social behavior that drove the disruption process. Readers were increasingly tending to access information in a variety of formats—be it blogs, news portals or podcasts. Traditional media, such as TV or print newspapers, came under intense pressure.

Although the FTD was valued as a neutral reporter on financial issues, its unconvincing digitization strategy left it far behind its competitors [3, 4]. As late as 2007, managing director Christoph Rüth (active 2000–2009) predicted that sales of the printed newspaper would continue to grow, but not as fast as sales of digital formats. At that time, the news portal FTD.de was only designed as a supplement to the print version, although readers were looking for the advantages of real-time reporting [5, 6]. After all, in the age of robo-advisors, who wants to wait for yesterday's stock prices in print? A look at the social media reach of German print media (by number of readers reached, as of January 2011) reinforces this impression: Der Spiegel reached 19 times more readers than the FTD [7].

In addition to the unrecognized opportunity presented by digitalization, the failure was also due to a poorly coordinated omnichannel concept. People interested in business could obtain information from a wide range of offerings: the 'Wirtschaftswunder' blog, specially created web videos, radio reports, the FTD podcast 'FTD zum Hören,' the news program 'Business Telex,' and the financial information portal 'markets.de' [8, 9]. As a result, the product portfolio looked more like a hodgepodge of offerings than a well-coordinated omnichannel concept that seamlessly linked online and print channels.

Not only were the channels not coordinated enough, but the thematic focus was also too broad. Unlike its parent brand, the FTD even covered sports, cars, and lifestyle, as well as giving financial advice. This meant that it was more diversified in terms of content than the FT, even though the latter was in a much better financial position. The problem was that business-minded readers could hardly be inspired by quizzes, weather forecasts for German and international cities, or the Olympic Games in Beijing, let alone be retained in the long term. Despite the good reputation of the London-based parent brand, the FTD had failed to attract a sufficiently large and loyal readership since its launch.

Service Delivery

The FTD had an excellent starting point in terms of content. The editorial team consisted of respected German journalists, career changers and editors from the London FT. Financially, however, the FTD was on shaky ground from the start. In 2008, Gruner + Jahr initiated restructuring measures along the entire value creation chain. First, the FTD was fully integrated into Gruner + Jahr. Second, the company merged the editorial teams from all its business media. From then on, FTD, Börse Online, Impulse and Capital shared a newsroom in Hamburg [10]. In the course of this consolidation, the parent company provided the downstream services in the value creation chain, including controlling, IT, accounting, marketing and point-of-sale activities.

The full integration of the FTD into Gruner + Jahr had a negative impact on the availability of human capital and thus on the newspaper's ability to innovate. First, the umbilical cord to the London parent brand, whose synergies FTD had benefited from for years, was severed. From then on, it could no longer rely on the world's largest network of correspondents. The exchange with the colleagues from London, who initiated innovations at the FTD with their ideas and brought British corporate culture with them, also ceased. At the same time, Gruner + Jahr could only support the FTD to a limited extent. For one thing, the publisher did not have the human capital to coordinate the FTD's reporting across all channels. Second, the publisher lacked experience with the medium of a daily newspaper, as its media portfolio consisted primarily of weekly newspapers.

Cost Model

The editorial offices in Munich and Cologne were closed in 2008 as part of a tough round of cost-cutting [11]. The focus on one editorial location led to 110 editors being laid off. Initially, all the editors from the four previously independent business newspapers were laid off. They were then asked to reapply for positions in the central newsroom.

These structural changes created uncertainty and led to an increased workload. From this point on, editors worked under worse conditions than before the restructuring, as they found themselves in different, often lower-paid, non-tariff employment relationships [12]. First and foremost, quality journalism suffered as a result. Second, the lack of security had a paralyzing effect on the innovation process. Disruption itself is characterized by a high degree of uncertainty and risk. If a company fails to build structures and tools to manage and even profit from this uncertainty, a potentially innovative culture atrophies into a culture of fear. In the case of the FTD, this means that the journalists felt overwhelmed by the disruptive aggressors due to a lack of resources and little internal support. They fell into a kind of 'shock paralysis' where the only thing that mattered was survival. A focused and exemplary value proposition is imperative because it empowers people in times of disruptive change and gives them a clear direction.

Overall, these cost savings were not enough to offset the losses from declining revenues. In 2009, Gruner + Jahr's consolidated revenues totaled €2.5 billion, a 9.4 percent drop on the previous year [13]. Between 2006 and 2012, Gruner + Jahr recorded a 22% decline in revenues, to which the FTD contributed significantly [14].

Earnings Model

The FTD's revenues were largely based on the advertising market, which was highly dependent on the general economic situation. In 2006, the newspaper grew faster than any other national newspaper, with an increase of 24.6% in the advertising market. However, its gross advertising revenue was only half that of its competitor Handelsblatt [15]. The fewer readers the paper reached, the less attractive it became for advertisers. The FTD was caught in a vicious cycle of insufficient reach and insufficient advertising revenues.

At the same time, the increasing use of the Internet led to a serious structural change. With the triumphant advance of the Internet in the mid-1990s, it was not only media consumption that changed. Advertisers also recognized that more and more readers were migrating to the Internet and shifting their activities from print to online. As a result, the FTD's previous earnings model came under pressure because online revenues were not growing fast enough to compensate for the decline in the newspaper market [16].

The earnings model also relied on revenues from the declining print business. The publisher was relying on an unconvincing sales strategy. In the third quarter of 2012, shortly before it was shut down, FTD still sold an average of 102,000 newspapers a day—not bad for a German specialist medium at first glance. However, the number of free copies distributed on planes and trains exceeded the number of paid subscriptions: 46,000 issues were distributed daily as in-flight copies, with only about 3,000 sold at newsstands and 42,000 to subscribers [17]. However, most of the latter were not billed as full subscriptions. Trial and student subscriptions further reduced profits. The value proposition of providing relevant, quality journalism was not being consistently delivered. The contradiction lay in the fact that the value proposition, including the variety of channels and offerings, could not be refinanced with the chosen earnings model. The earnings model was based mainly on print editions, which were either given away for free or sold for a modest €2.20 [18]. This case illustrates that it is not enough to focus the value proposition and service offering on the customer and try to inspire them. Rather, a meaningful value proposition goes hand in hand with a profitable earnings model. This focuses the attention of employees on future, profitable business activities and segments.

The Bottom Line

The FTD's failed transformation can be traced back to a number of causes. The newspaper's focus was too broad, both in terms of content and in its choice of distribution channels. This 'fragmentation' meant that the FTD was unable to build a loyal readership willing to pay for its high-quality content. The service offering and the variety of channels were more like a shotgun approach rather than a well-coordinated omnichannel concept aimed at creating added value by linking online and print. A second reason is the lack of a digital strategy. Instead of looking for opportunities in digitalization and adapting to changing customer needs such as convenience and speed, FTD focused on a high print circulation.

As part of the transformation, Gruner + Jahr merged the editorial teams of all business publications into a single newsroom to reduce costs. This resulted in poorer working conditions, which had a negative impact on the quality of journalism. On the other hand, the cultural identity of the FTD suffered from the merging of the editorial teams, so that the value proposition was no longer consistently exemplified. The FTD case illustrates that an atmosphere of uncertainty can have a paralyzing effect on the innovation process. If employees lack internal support, the company runs the risk of falling into 'shock paralysis' and falling victim to disruptive aggressors.

References

[1]   See Pohlmann, S. (2012), "Aus für 'Financial Times Deutschland' bestätigt" (End of Financial Times Deutschland Confirmed), in: Der Tagesspiegel, 2017-11-23, https://www.tagesspiegel.de/medien/zei tungssterben-aus-fuer-financial-times-deutschland-bestaetigt/7425886.html (in German only).

[2]   See Geissler, C. (2009), "Kompetenzbasiertes Markenmanagement in Verlagsunternehmen"
      (Competency-based Brand Management in Publishing), Gabler Verlag/GWV Fachverlage GmbH,
      Wiesbaden, pp. 180-187.

[3]   See Uken, M. (2012), "Warum wir die Financial Times Deutschland vermissen werden" (Why We Are
      Going to Miss the Financial Times Deutschland), in: Zeit Online, 2012-12-07, http://www.zeit.de/wirt
      schaft/2012-12/financial-times-deutschland-wuerdigung/komplettansicht (in German only).

[4]   See Keese, C. (2012),"Wir waren Wilde und Revolutionäre" (We Were Savages and Revolutionaries),
      in: Die Welt, 2012-11-22, https://www.welt.de/wirtschaft/article111428417/Wir-waren-Wilde-und-
      Revolutionaere.html (in German only).

[5]   See Stöcker, C. (2012), "Das Internet ist nicht an allem schuld" (The Internet Is Not to Blame for
      Everything), in: Spiegel Online, 2012-11-22, http://www.spiegel.de/netzwelt/web/financial-times-
      deutschland-der-einfluss-des-internets-a-868576.html (in German only).

[6]   See Horizont 2007), "Lachsrosa Futter für die Wirtschaftswelt" (Salmon Pink Fodder for the Business
      World), in: Wiso, 2007-04-12, https://www.wiso-net.de/document/HOR__040712141%7CAHOR__
      040712141 (in German only).

[7]   See MEEDIA (2011), Social Media Reach of German Print Media by Number of Users Reached (as
      of January 2011), in: Statista, 2011-01-01, https://de.statista.com/statistik/daten/studie/172491/um
      frage/social-media-reichweite-deutscher-printmedien/ (in German only).

[8]   See Horizont 2007), "Lachsrosa Futter für die Wirtschaftswelt" (Salmon Pink Fodder for the Business
      World), In: "Report Wirtschafts- und Entscheidermedien" (Business and Media Decision-Maker
      Report), 2007-04-12, https://www.wiso-net.de/document/HOR__040712141%7CAHOR__040712141 (in
      German only).

[9]   See Geissler, C. (2009), "Kompetenzbasiertes Markenmanagement in Verlagsunternehmen"
      (Competency-based Brand Management in Publishing), Gabler Verlag/GWV Fachverlage GmbH,
      Wiesbaden, pp. 180-187.

[10] See Steinkirchner, P. (2012), "FTD – Ich habe dich gern gelesen" (FTD – I Read You Avidly), in:
      WirtschaftsWoche, 2012-11-23, https://www.wiwo.de/unternehmen/dienstleister/aus-fuer-
      wirtschaftszeitung-ftd-ich-habe-dich-gern-gelesen/7429414.html (in German only).

[11] See Bertelsmann (2009), Annual Report 2008, in: Bertelsmann, .2009-03-01, https://www.bertels
      mann.de/media/investor-relations/geschaeftsberichte/geschaeftsbericht-2008.pdf (in German only).

[12] See Koniezcny, O. (2013), "Arbeiten im Newsroom: Vor- und Nachteile der Neuorganisation von
      Zeitungsredaktionen" (Working in the Newsroom: The Pros and Cons of Newspaper Newsroom
      Restructuring), Diplomica Verlag, Hamburg, pp. 64-66.

[13] See Gruner + Jahr (2010), Gruner + Jahr Masters Economic Crisis and Maintains Operating Profit
      Despite Slump in Advertising Markets, in: Gruner + Jahr, 2010-03-24, https://www.guj.de/news/neuig
      keiten/gruner-jahr-meistert-wirtschaftskrise-und-kann-trotz-einbruchs-der-werbemaerkte-das-
      operative-ergebnis-gut-behaupten/ (in German only).

[14] See Bertelsmann, (2018), Turnover of Gruner + Jahr Between 2005 and 2016 (In Millions of Euro), in:
      Statista, 2018-03-26, https://de.statista.com/statistik/daten/studie/74659/umfrage/umsatz-von-
      gruner-und-jahr-seit-2005/ (in German only).

[15] See Horizont (2018), Gross Advertising Revenue of National Newspapers in Germany in 2011 and
      2012 (In Millions of Euro), in: Statista, 2018-03-18, https://de.statista.com/statistik/daten/studie/
      75109/umfrage/bruttowerbeumsatz-der-ueberregionalen-zeitungen-in-deutschland/ (in
      German only).

[16] See Lagetar, M./Mühlbauer, C. (2012), "Unter Druck" (Under Pressure), in: Gadringer, S./Kweton, S./
      Trappel, J./Vieth, T. (ed.), "Journalismus und Werbung" (Journalism and Advertising). "Kommerzielle
      Grenzen der redaktionellen Autonomie" (Commercial Limits to Editorial Autonomy), Springer
      Fachmedien, Wiesbaden, pp. 123-144.

[17] See Steinkirchner, P. (2012), "FTD – Ich habe dich gern gelesen" (FTD – I Was an Avid Reader), in WirtschaftsWoche, 23.11.2012, https://www.wiwo.de/unternehmen/dienstleister/aus-fuer-wirtschaftszeitung-ftd-ich-habe-dich-gern-gelesen/7429414.html (in German only).

[18] See Stöcker, C. (2012), "Das Internet ist nicht an allem schuld" (The Internet Can't Be Blamed for Everything), in: Spiegel Online, 2012-11-22, http://www.spiegel.de/netzwelt/web/financial-times-deutschland-der-einfluss-des-internets-a-868576.html (in German only).

TomTom[*]

Background and Objectives of the Case Study

When US President Bill Clinton opened up the Global Positioning System (GPS) to the private sector in May 2000, an Amsterdam-based company saw an opportunity: Tom-Tom [1]. As child of the early 1990s the Dutch company originally started out as a developer of B2B solutions, including barcode scanners and software for reading sensor data. Soon after, the company entered the consumer market with additional applications for the popular PDA handhelds of the time—including the first mapping software. When GPS became available for the first time, TomTom's developers combined it with mapping software. And so the 'TomTom Navigator' was born, the forefather of all future navigation systems. The company began its triumphant march with the world's first fully portable navigation device, the 'TomTom Go'. Soon, navigation systems were to become part of everyday life in many cars [2]. But the Ikarus flight did not last long: After posting record figures in 2007, the company was forced to report losses in the first quarter of 2009 [3]. Sales were only a third of what they had been two years earlier. Once again, there seems to have been a fundamental change in the field of navigation solutions. In 2016, the number of navigation systems sold in Germany was below the level of ten years prior [4]. As we will see, this was due to changes in customer behavior and preferences, a development triggered by the breakthrough of smartphones and new disruptive competitors.

Value Proposition

There were many reasons for TomTom's decline, but most of them can be traced back to a fundamental lack of direction. TomTom's diffuse value proposition was the main culprit here. It promised customers that it would "improve their lives" by "combining the expertise of its people in navigation, digital content and guidance services" (see Table 4.20) [5]. The company described itself as 'device-agnostic,' meaning that it would be guided by user preferences.

---

[*]The case study was developed in collaboration with Benjamin D. Klink (University of St. Gallen).

Based on the requirements for a convincing value proposition, it can be seen that TomTom was unable to meet these requirements in several dimensions. For example, the value proposition's lack of uniqueness is evident when compared to competitors such as Garmin, for whom the proposition could be just as valid. The proposition was also too general to fulfill its lighthouse function both internally and externally. It did not define how TomTom would differentiate itself from the competition. It also failed to explain why consumers should prefer the Dutch company.

The vague value proposition ultimately led to a wrong definition of the market. For example, the company focused on in-car navigation, where a physical navigation system certainly have made sense. However, it was the more holistic market definition of its competitors that proved to be TomTom's undoing. There is no doubt that a broader understanding of the market would have been an important basis for a successful defense strategy. Perhaps the company would have acted very differently if it had understood the market in broader terms. A definition of the value proposition as "navigation in all situations" would have made it easier for the Dutch company to swap the bundling of map material, software and device for more flexible product constellations much earlier.

Table 4.20: Transformation of the TomTom business model.

Value Proposition			
To improve the lives of customers through TomTom's combined expertise in navigation, digital content and guidance services across all relevant platforms.			
Service Delivery	**Service Offering**	**Cost Model**	**Earnings Model**
The development of navigation devices was seen as a core business	Dogmatic focus on the (motorized private) transport sector	Higher costs by bundling mapping software with the device	Adherence to the proprietary paradigm of physical navigation devices
Crowd sourcing opportunities in free map creation and improvement remained unrecognized and untapped	Underestimation of the importance of the growth in smartphones in combination with services and applications such as Google Maps	High cost base due to map licensing and subsequent acquisition of map provider Tele Atlas	Expensive pricing structure compared to market entrants
Map data were licensed instead	Failure to link to additional benefits for the user resulting in an increasingly unattractive service offering	Failure to realize potential cost savings through automated optimization with transaction data or free map optimization by users	Blindness to innovative, alternative earnings models
User data remained unused, e.g. to provide up-to-date traffic information quickly and cheaply			Map updates as a income source

Service Offering

More and more users were abandoning dedicated navigation devices in favor of smartphones. But instead of taking the changing needs of the customer segment seriously, the company clung to its own device for too long [6]. However, that is not to say that TomTom did not see the writing on the wall. TomTom had its own navigation app in the app stores from the major mobile operators early on [7]. But the fear of cannibalization was the company's undoing. Since the launch of the TomTom Go device, the core of the service offering had been the sale of physical navigation systems. The device, including maps and navigation guidance, was seen as an inseparable product bundle. Not so with Google.. The search engine monopolist saw its Google Maps service as a kind of 'Maps as a Service' concept. It was not a device that combined maps and navigation at the core of the offering. Instead, it was a set of information services that were at least partially monetized through advertising. To be attractive to advertising partners, Google needed the largest possible user base. In keeping with the search engine's formula for success, the service was free from the start [8]. TomTom, whose maps for the smartphone app still cost up to €100, could not compete [9].

In addition to Google's free navigation offering, user habits were gradually changing. For TomTom, navigation on the road was the relevant market, so drivers were the core customer segment. The competition thought more broadly. The Internet user who looked up the opening hours of a store online then wanted to know the quickest way to get there by public transport or by bike. On the way, she used her smartphone for mobile navigation. She then applied this behavior to other situations. For example, when she was driving— after all, Google's service was free. This development was made possible by the breakthrough of the smartphone with the introduction of the iPhone in 2007. Instead of buying an expensive new device costing hundreds of dollars, people increasingly used their existing smartphone with free maps [10]..

Users were increasingly able to enjoy unique additional services. Early on, Google made it possible to view detailed information about a destination. This included business hours, business profiles, points of interest in the area, and reviews from other users. Years before TomTom, Google was also able to integrate the current traffic situation into the navigation system. At the same time, Google did not charge for this additional service [11]. TomTom introduced this service with some delay and only for its luxury models [12]. Google's disruption was therefore facilitated by three factors: the open flank in the entry-level price segment, the incumbent's fear of cannibalization, and changing user habits. Once it gained momentum, the search engine giant was able to consistently make its offering more attractive by offering additional services.

Service Delivery

As discussed in the previous section, TomTom's management focused heavily on concepts that had been successful and proven in the past. The car navigation system, known internally as a PND (Personal Navigation Device), directed the categories in which thinking took place [13]. The core activity of service delivery was therefore the development and production of navigation devices—at least in the eyes of those in charge. The bundle made up of device, software and map material was seen as an inseparable unit. This was underscored by the high prices charged for map updates.

In addition, the company relied exclusively on the expertise of its own developers for product development. After all, they had already developed similar software for the Palm handheld. The maps were licensed from Tele Atlas, the same company that provides the maps for Google. The decision to acquire Tele Atlas was a late one [14]. By that time, Google already had its own map data and had ended its relationship with Tele Atlas [15].

Google's focus has always been on intelligent and, above all, cost-effective solutions for creating maps. Early on, the company encouraged its users to mark interesting and relevant locations on the maps and add (up-to-date) information. This means that individuals can not only add new attractions for all to see, but they can also leave photos of the area or reviews. Google offers an option for businesses to add themselves. They can add relevant details such as business hours, phone numbers, contact addresses, prices and more. In this way, Google gets users work for them. Google has also made very effective use of user data. By using anonymized movement data, Google was able to cost-effectively optimize its maps and identify traffic disruptions early [16].

Yet TomTom has also used crowdsourcing approaches. As early as in 2007, the company allowed users to report map errors and share them with other users via a map share feature. However, users had to enter the changes into the device and then connect it to a computer for synchronization [17]. These systemic barriers suggest a half-hearted approach. As a result, the benefits to the business were limited, since the success of such concepts depended largely on their ease of use.

Cost Model

Due to the more labor-intensive nature of service delivery, TomTom's cost structure was completely different from that of its challenger, Google. Google relied on cloud-based and therefore highly scalable delivery of maps and navigation. The cost base was therefore highly variable. In contrast, TomTom focused on stand-alone physical navigation systems. In addition to the development of the routing software, there were also development and production costs for the associated devices and accessories. These fixed costs were reflected in the higher prices of the PNDs.

The lower proportion of intelligent and low-cost data-driven map optimization and creation mentioned above also resulted in higher fixed costs. For example, due to the need for personnel to perform map optimization and correction. In addition, Google's success led to high one-time costs associated with the acquisition of map provider Tele Atlas. In retrospect, this move came far too late. Google had already established itself in the market.

Earnings Model

TomTom clung to the paradigm of proprietary physical navigation devices (PNDs) for too long. Innovative and alternative revenue strategies were not pursued because the company feared cannibalization by app solutions. Existing income sources had to be defended. As a result, TomTom relied for too long on the transaction-based earnings model of the retail world, and thus on the sale of high-priced navigation systems and map updates. This left the entry-level price segment wide open.

Because Google was for free, users were willing to forgive its initial lack of voice-based guidance. This was finally added in 2010. Once established, the competition was able to win over users with its unbeatable combination of navigation and useful information (see Service Offering). By adding voice guidance, Google was effectively offering the same service for free. From a consumer perspective, the high upfront cost of a navigation device was replaced by the low monthly cost of a mobile data plan. This was made possible in part by Google's earnings model, which relied on advertising rather than unit sales.

However, it should be noted that the success of the US competitor was probably also due to the enormous financial strength of its parent company. Nevertheless, it is worth asking whether TomTom would have been in the same predicament had it embraced its smartphone app as a model for the future at an early stage. In that case, the Dutch company would probably have consistently designed its offering as an affordable subscription from the outset and adopted a truly 'device-agnostic' approach.

The Bottom Line

Disruptors fundamentally change the business logic of an industry. TomTom itself created such a disruption in the field of navigation solutions with the invention of the navigation device and benefited greatly from it, especially until the second half of the 2000s [18]. Road maps soon became a thing of the past with the introduction of the TomTom Go device. But even highly innovative and successful disruptors are not immune to decline. This can happen if they fail to recognize the signs of renewed disruption in the market.

The case illustrates the importance of a good value proposition because it defined the market too narrowly. As a result, the other four dimensions bypassed the market. TomTom fell behind in terms of service delivery. In retrospect, underestimating the importance of mobile devices was fatal. TomTom was overtaken by the search engine giant Google and staggered into a serious crisis [19]. The passive shock paralysis of the company's management and the rigidity of its thinking caused the business model transformation to fail. As a result, TomTom reported an operating loss of €11 million in the key end-customer segment in the 2017 financial year. This was catastrophic, as it was responsible for a good 46% of the company's revenue [20].

References

[1] See National Coordination Office for Space-Based Positioning, Navigation, and Timing (2018), Selective Availability, 2018-02-09, https://www.gps.gov/systems/gps/modernization/sa/.
[2] See TomTom NV (2018), History, 2018-02-07, http://corporate.tomtom.com/history.cfm.
[3] See TomTom NV (2009), Annual Reports and Accounts 2009, pp. 16-18.
[4] See Statista (2018), Sales of Navigation Devices in Germany From 2005 to 1st Half 2017 (In 1,000 of Units), 2018-02-09, https://de.statista.com/statistik/daten/studie/3902/umfrage/entwicklung-der-verkaufszahlen-von-navigationsgeraeten-seit-2005/ (in German only).
[5] See TomTom NV (2009), Annual Reports and Accounts 2009, pp. 16-18.
[6] See Taub, E. A. (2015), What Stand-Alone GPS Devices Do That Smartphones Can't, The New York Times, 2015-07-15, https://www.nytimes.com/2015/07/16/technology/personaltech/what-stand-alone-gps-devices-do-that-smartphones-cant.html.
[7] See Wortham, J./Helft, M. (2009), Hurting Rivals, Google Unveils Free Phone GPS, in: The New York Times, 2009-10-29, http://www.nytimes.com/2009/10/29/technology/companies/29gps.html.
[8] See Hauk, M. (2014), "Daten für Milliarden" (Data for Billions), in: Süddeutsche, 2014-10-18, http://www.sueddeutsche.de/digital/geschaeftsmodelle-von-google-und-facebook-daten-fuer-milliarden-1.2270247 (in German only).
[9] See Wortham, J./Helft, M. (2009), Hurting Rivals, Google Unveils Free Phone GPS, in: The New York Times, 2009-10-29, http://www.nytimes.com/2009/10/29/technology/companies/29gps.html.
[10] See Hofer, J. (2015), "Die Untoten der Windschutzscheibe" (The Zombies on the Windshield), in: Handelsblatt, 2015-05-25, http://www.handelsblatt.com/unternehmen/it-medien/tragbare-navigationsgeraete-die-untoten-der-windschutzscheibe/v_detail_tab_print/1180805 (in German only).
[11] See Wang, D. (2007), Stuck in Traffic?, 2007-02-28, https://googleblog.blogspot.ch/2007/02/stuck-in-traffic.html.
[12] See Taub, E. A. (2011), Live Traffic Comes to TomTom, 2011-01-05, https://gadgetwise.blogs.nytimes.com/2011/01/05/live-traffic-comes-to-tomtom/.
[13] See Financial Times (2016), TomTom: lost and found, in: Financial Times, 2016-04-19, https://www.ft.com/content/246b42ba-0621-11e6-a70d-4e39ac32c284.
[14] See Financial Times (2008), TomTom troubles, in: Financial Times, 2008-04-08, https://www.ft.com/content/b765e14e-056f-11dd-a9e0-0000779fd2ac.
[15] See Wortham, J./Helft, M. (2009), Hurting Rivals, Google Unveils Free Phone GPS, in: The New York Times, 2009-10-29, http://www.nytimes.com/2009/10/29/technology/companies/29gps.html.
[16] See Wang, D. (2007), Stuck in Traffic?, 2007-02-28, https://googleblog.blogspot.ch/2007/02/stuck-in-traffic.html.

[17]   See Biersdorfer, J. D. (2007), Updating Maps on the Spot and Sharing the Fixes, in: The New York Times, 2007-06-14, http://www.nytimes.com/2007/06/14/technology/14gps.html.

[18]   See Arthur, C. (2015), Navigating decline: what happened to TomTom?, in: The Guardian, 2015-07-21, https://www.theguardian.com/business/2015/jul/21/navigating-decline-what-happened-to-tomtom-satnav.

[19]   See NASDAQ (2018), Stock Prices of TomTom NV 2008-2018, 2018-02-12, https://www.nasdaq.com/symbol/tmoaf/stock-chart?intraday=off&timeframe=10y&splits=off&earnings=off&movingaverage=None&lowerstudy=volume&comparison=off&index=&drilldown=off.

[20]   See TomTom NV (2017), Annual Report 2017, p. 6.

Praktiker*

Background and Objectives of the Case Study

"20% off Everything – Except Pet Food": When the German readers among you think of the Praktiker DIY chain today, this advertising slogan will inevitably come to mind. But to attribute Praktiker's insolvency in 2013 solely to margin-draining discount campaigns would be to ignore the bigger picture.

The devastating end was preceded by a long success story. The company was founded in 1978 in Kirkel, Germany, and later acquired by Metro AG. From the very beginning, Praktiker focused strategically on the discount principle and since 1982 under the claim "The low-cost DIY store" [1]. The 1980s saw a gold rush in the DIY sector. Praktiker also grew strongly by expanding its store network in Germany and abroad. New stores included those from BayWa, Real-Kauf, Bauspar, extra BAU+HOBBY and Top-Bau [2]. With the acquisition of Max Bahr in 2007, Praktiker became the second largest DIY chain in Germany after Obi. In the same year, sales amounted to more than €3.9 billion with an operating result (EBITA) of €116 million [3]. At the peak of its expansion in 2009, the store network comprised nearly 440 stores in nine European countries and almost 24,000 full-time employees [4–6]. These appeared to be not bad prospects.

But appearances were deceptive, as Praktiker had been in crisis since the mid-1990s. To meet the challenges of increasingly fierce competition, the company launched a business model transformation in 2002 [7]. But this ended in bankruptcy eleven years later. This case study shows that only a consistent and focused business model transformation can be successful. The desired success cannot be achieved by optimizing each of the five key drivers in isolation. Rather, it requires a holistically orchestrated business model transformation that is consistently pursued to completion.

---

*The case study was developed in collaboration with Kathrin M. Neumüller (University of St. Gallen).

Value Proposition

The original value proposition, "The Cheap DIY Store," contributed significantly to the unfavorable assessment of overall performance because of the negative connotation of the word 'cheap'. The proposition was replaced in 1999 by "Can't Be Done, Doesn't Exist" (see Table 4.21). Praktiker targeted do-it-yourselfers and hobbyists with this proposition. Originally intended as an expression of the self-image of DIY enthusiasts, the claim raised hopes for a pronounced service focus and thus placed high demands on employees. DIY store customers usually want to know not only where to find certain tools in the store, but also how to use them [8]. Praktiker was perceived as the price leader from the very beginning. However, the company was unable to meet its high customer service standards. Recognizing this problem, Praktiker adjusted its value proposition as part of its transformation strategy. The new claim was: "This Price Speaks for Itself". The goal of the repositioning was to combine the low price image with service that was perceived as at least average [9, 10]. But until that happened, the group continued to operate without a clear value proposition. The temporary lack of a value proposition reflected the group's lack of direction and created internal uncertainty. It did not meet the requirement of aligning all value-creating ac-

Table 4.21: Transformation of the Praktiker business model.

Value Proposition			
Adaptation from "Can't Be Done, Doesn't Exist" to "The Price Speaks for Itself". The partial lack of a value proposition led to disorientation among the workforce.			
Service Delivery	**Service Offering**	**Cost Model**	**Earnings Model**
Phase 1 (cost reduction) and Phase 2 (price campaign to increase liquidity) of the three-phase transformation strategy were successful.	Quality leadership targeted with sister brand Max Bahr Cost leadership by Praktiker	As part of the transformation, cost-cutting measures were initiated and successfully implemented	Earnings model designed for growth rather than investing in existing DIY stores to increase return on sales
Phase 3 (closure or upgrade of stores in need of restructuring) not consistently implemented	Praktiker was perceived as price leader, but was weak in terms of service	Streamlining the assortment had a positive effect on logistics costs and capital employed Expansion of store network massively increased costs (different concept, long leases, stores acquired in poor condition)	Revenues generated by high sales

tivities with the company's strategic direction. Rather, it slowed down the jointly borne change processes during the transformation.

Service Offering

Praktiker pursued two strategies. One was quality leadership with the premium brand Max Bahr [11]. It offered a wide range of products and expert advice at a good price-performance ratio. In addition to hobby do-it-yourselfers, it also catered to professionals. The second involved Praktiker pushing for price leadership. Here, the focus was on price-conscious do-it-yourselfers. The group presented itself as a full-range supplier with a broad assortment of products for renovation, construction, workshop, home, garden and leisure. This included own brands and products from well-known suppliers. Although Praktiker was the price leader, customers were already complaining about the advice they received in the 1980s. Often dilapidated stores and B-locations also had a negative impact on the perception of employees' abilities.

Service Delivery

Poor customer service and often dilapidated stores had a significant impact on service delivery. The dark blue logo with neon yellow lettering, flashy marketing claims and chaotic, warehouse-like stores did not make for a relaxed shopping experience. The unsightly retail space hardly inspired customers to improve their homes, let alone invite them to linger.

The price-sensitive customer accepted this poor shopping experience as long as there were few alternatives. When the entire home improvement industry opened new stores in the 1980s, cutthroat competition erupted. In addition to these macro-level driving forces, micro-level driving forces also contributed to the change process. Customers began using apps to find the best deals. As a result, Bauhaus, Hornbach and Obi established themselves as premium providers for professional tradespeople. Praktiker was under pressure to adapt its business model and thus also its internal structures and processes.

The transformation of the business model affected all five key drivers.. The overall goal was to reposition the brand with a stronger focus on customer service. To achieve this, organizational structures and processes had to be adapted. The transformation was carried out in three phases. In the first phase, some less profitable markets were closed in order to streamline the organizational structure and reduce costs. In the second phase, the "20% off Everything – Except Pet Food" campaign, which was designed as a flash in the pan, provided liquidity. It had an immediate impact, as customer frequency increased and EBITA improved from €23 million in 2003 to €59.3 million in 2004 [12]. In the third phase, the organizational structure was to be revised with these financial re-sources. Underperforming stores were to be closed or restructured.

However, the third phase was not implemented. The positive development from the price offensive—like-for-like sales grew by 10.8% in 2003—prompted Metro to take its DIY chain public [13]. Praktiker generated proceeds of €108 million from the successful IPO [14]. However, contrary to initial plans, only part of the money was in-vested in the German stores in need of restructuring. Instead, the capital was used for expansion in Eastern Europe. In 2009, the international business fell into a deep reces-sion with a decline in sales of 15.7% [15]. Instead of becoming a long-term driving force of growth, the Eastern European business turned out to be a chronic drag.

All that remained of the original restructuring efforts was the Easy-to-Shop con-cept. The aim was to make Praktiker stores more customer-friendly with a clearer lay-out. Weak locations were to be revitalized and the product range geared more to customers who wanted to save time as well as money when shopping. This concept was well received by customers and resulted in increased sales in the remodeled stores. However, these increases were not sufficient to prevail in the internal competi-tion for limited investment funds [16, 17].

The constant focus on expanding the store network had a negative impact on ser-vice delivery processes. First, there was a lack of financial resources to improve the cus-tomer service skills of the staff. Second, the physical resources—in this case, the DIY stores—were not being upgraded. These play a central role in service delivery as they contribute significantly to the shopping experience. Third, the large store network in-creased the complexity of sourcing goods due to an ever-increasing number of suppliers.

Cost Model

In a stable business environment, it is sufficient to optimize the cost model. Based on the goal of cost leadership, the transformation strategy initiated measures to reduce costs. These included the closure and restructuring of stores alongside the optimiza-tion of the logistics network and the product range. In 2000, Praktiker invested €100 million in streamlining its product range and remodeling 16 DIY stores [18]. In the 2001 financial year alone, Praktiker invested a further €39 million in opening new stores in Germany and abroad, closing smaller stores in Germany and streamlining the assortment concept [19]. The streamlining of the assortment resulted in a 23% re-duction. This in turn had a positive impact on logistics costs and capital employed. In total, CEO Werner closed 45 DIY markets between 2001 and 2010. 2,000 jobs were cut, mostly in the stores [20].

These cost-cutting measures were very successful, but they did not solve the real problem. The main problem was that the branch network was far too large. Almost half of Praktiker's stores were acquired from smaller competitors and differed in for-mat and concept. Long and unfavorable leases and the poor condition of the stores added to the costs. The constant growth resulted in disproportionately high costs that were not offset by the additional sales generated. The Easy-to-Shop concept was a (failed) attempt to realign the service offering and thus simplify the cost model.

Earnings Model

In line with the discounter principle, Praktiker tried to generate revenues primarily through high sales volumes. The "20% off Everything – Except Pet Food" campaign and the expansion into foreign markets were designed to generate rapid growth. To counteract the decline in sales in the 1990s, increasingly aggressive growth strategies were necessary.

A look at the life cycle phases of industries— emergence, growth, maturity and saturation—offers an explanation for the group's development. During the DIY industry's heyday in the 1980s, the industry's strategy was mainly based on growth through expansion of the distribution network. The density of DIY stores in 1982 was less than half that of 2012 [21]. During this growth phase, value creation was mainly generated by additional sales and not by increasing profits through improved stores or an adapted product assortment.

As the industry moved from the growth phase to the maturity phase and the market became saturated, Praktiker missed the moment to transform its earnings model and focus on earnings growth. In contrast to Praktiker, Hornbach was able to increase productivity: While Hornbach generated sales of €2,230 per square meter in 2012, Praktiker's figure was only €1,253 [22]. A sustainable strategy contrary to the short-term expectations of the capital market would have led to operational improvements in the existing stores [23]. The Easy-to-Shop concept was a first step towards improving profitability. It removed slow-selling and low-margin products from the assortment and improved the in-store shopping experience.

The Bottom Line

The main reason for the insolvency was an inconsistently implemented business model transformation . Praktiker clung to a poorly managed store network and pursued a strategy that was not geared to sustainable growth. The company missed the moment to switch from a 'high growth' to a 'low growth' strategy. This case study shows that while high sales and turnover can generate liquidity, a business model transformation requires an adapted, sustainable earnings model. It also highlights the importance of a focused value proposition that orchestrates actions and internal activities.

References

[1]   See Maucher, C. (2014), "Praktiker ist pleite '20 Prozent auf alles – außer Tiernahrung'" (Praktiker Is Broke '20 Percent off Everything – Except Pet Food'), in: Focus, 2014-03-17, https://www.focus.de/finanzen/news/unternehmen/praktiker-ist-pleite-20-prozent-auf-alles-ausser-tiernahrung_id_3700777.html (in German only).

[2]   See Praktiker (2006), Praktiker 2005 Annual Report, in: Equity Story, 2006-05-01, http://www.equitystory.com/download/companies/praktiker/Annual%20Reports/DE000A0F6MD5-JA-2005-EQ-D-00.pdf (in German only).

[3]   See Praktiker (2009), Praktiker 2008 Annual Report, in: Moreir, 2009-04-01, http://moreir.de/download/companies/praktiker/Annual%20Reports/DE000A0F6MD5-JA-2008-EQ-D-00.pdf (in German only).

[4]   See ibid.

[5]   See Praktiker (2006), Praktiker 2005 Annual Report, in: Equity Story, 2006-05-01, http://www.equitystory.com/download/companies/praktiker/Annual%20Reports/DE000A0F6MD5-JA-2005-EQ-D-00.pdf (in German only).

[6]   See ibid.

[7]   See ibid.

[8]   See Kernstock, J. (2007), "Behavioral Branding als Führungsansatz" (Behavioral Branding as a Leadership Approach), in: T. Tomczak, F. Esch, J. Kernstock, A. Herrmann (eds.), Behavioral Branding. "Wie Mitarbeiterverhalten Die Marke Stärkt" (How Employee Behavior Strengthens the Brand), Gabler Verlag, Wiesbaden, pp. 3-34.

[9]   See Praktiker (2006), Praktiker 2005 Annual Report, in: Equity Story, 2006-05-01, http://www.equitystory.com/download/companies/praktiker/Annual%20Reports/DE000A0F6MD5-JA-2005-EQ-D-00.pdf (in German only).

[10] See MetroGroup (2001), METRO AG 2000 Annual Report, in: MetroGroup, 2001-04-01, https://archiv.metrogroup.de/publikationen (in German only).

[11] See Praktiker (2009), Praktiker 2008 Annual Report, in: Moreir, 2009-04-01, http://moreir.de/download/companies/praktiker/Annual%20Reports/DE000A0F6MD5-JA-2008-EQ-D-00.pdf (in German only).

[12] See MetroGroup (2005), METRO AG 2004 Annual Report, in: MetroGroup, 2005-1-4, https://archiv.metrogroup.de/publikationen (in German only).

[13] See MetroGroup (2004), METRO AG 2003 Annual Report, in: MetroGroup, 2004-04-01, https://archiv.metrogroup.de/publikationen (in German only).

[14] See Praktiker (2006), Praktiker 2005 Annual Report, in: Equity Story, 2006-05-01, http://www.equitystory.com/download/companies/praktiker/Annual%20Reports/DE000A0F6MD5-JA-2005-EQ-D-00.pdf (in German only).

[15] See Praktiker (2010), Praktiker 2009 Annual Report, in: Equity Story, 2010-04-01, http://www.equitystory.com/download/companies/praktiker/Annual%20Reports/DE000A0F6MD5-JA-2009-EQ-D-00.pdf (in German only).

[16] See Praktiker (2009), Praktiker 2008 Annual Report, in: Moreir, 2009-04-01, http://moreir.de/download/companies/praktiker/Annual%20Reports/DE000A0F6MD5-JA-2008-EQ-D-00.pdf (in German only).

[17] See Schröder, H. (2012), "Handelsmarketing – Strategien und Instrumente für den stationären Einzelhandel und für Online-Shops Mit Praxisbeispielen" (Retail Marketing – Strategies and Instruments for Over-The-Counter Retail and Online Stores With Practical Examples), Gabler Verlag, Wiesbaden, pp. 81-118.

[18] See Praktiker (2006), Praktiker 2005 Annual Report, in: Equity Story, 2006-05-01, http://www.equitystory.com/download/companies/praktiker/Annual%20Reports/DE000A0F6MD5-JA-2005-EQ-D-00.pdf (in German only).

[19] See MetroGroup (2002), METRO AG 2001 Annual Report, in: MetroGroup, 2002-04-01, https://archiv.metrogroup.de/publikationen (in German only).

[20] See Schlautmann, C. (2006), "Der Mann mit der Kreissäge" (The Man With the Buzzsaw), in: Handelsblatt, 2006-08-18, http://www.handelsblatt.com/unternehmen/management/praktiker-chef-wolfgang-werner-der-mann-mit-der-kreissaege/2694380.html (in German only).

[21] See gemaba Gesellschaft für Markt- und Betriebsanalyse GmbH (2012), "Baumarkt-Strukturuntersuchung 2012" (2012 DIY Market Structure Survey), in: EHI handelsdaten.de, 2012-12-12, https://www.handelsdaten.de/bau-und-heimwerkermaerkte/kennzahlen-der-baumaerkte-deutschland-jahresvergleich (in German only).

[22] See Dähne Verlag. (2018). Space Productivity of German DIY Companies Internationally Between 2012 and 2016 (In Euros per Square Meter), in: Statista, 2018-04-11, https://de.statista.com/statistik/daten/studie/206136/umfrage/deutsche-baumaerkte-nach-flaechenproduktivitaet/ (in German only).

[23] See Fisher, M./Gaur, V./Kleinberger, H. (2017), Curing The Addiction To Growth, in: Harvard Business Review, Vol. 95(1), 66-74.

Air Berlin*

Background and Objectives of the Case Study

After US pilot Kim Lundgren lost his job with Pan American Airlines in the 1970s, he decided to start his own charter airline. Thus Air Berlin Incorporated was born. The first flight from Berlin-Tegel to Palma de Mallorca followed on April 28, 1979—one of Air Berlin's main destinations until its bankruptcy. When Lundgren lost the special flight rights over Berlin after the fall of the Berlin Wall, Joachim Hunold took over 82.5% of Air Berlin Inc. in 1991 and founded Air Berlin GmbH & Co. Luftverkehrs KG.

With a clear value proposition, Hunold positioned Air Berlin as a low-cost charter airline transporting German vacationers from regional airports to attractive Mediterranean destinations. The strategy worked, and the airline became very popular with German package tourists. As more low-cost carriers entered the German market in the early 2000s, Air Berlin gradually adapted its business model. In this case study, we show how the original value proposition was increasingly diluted— with devastating consequences.

Value Proposition

Management failures, poor investments, damaging strategic partnerships, etc: There is no shortage of explanations for Air Berlin's bankruptcy. However, these failures are not the core causes of the airline's failure, but rather the symptoms of a much more serious problem: a fuzzy value proposition. The coordinating role of a focused value proposition is especially important in a turbulent market like the airline business. Not only does it allow you to clearly differentiate yourself from the competition, it also gives your employees the direction they need.

---

*The case study was developed in collaboration with Gianluca Scheidegger (University of St. Gallen).

Due to takeovers and the price war with Ryanair, EasyJet and others, the well-known value proposition of the 1990s has become increasingly diluted. Once known for its value for money, the airline tried to push prices down even lower at the expense of service and service quality. As a result, Air Berlin increasingly began to resemble its low-cost competitors—except that it lacked the cost structure to sustain low prices. In addition, the route network was expanded to include more destinations, diluting the focus on Mediterranean vacation destinations. At the same time, Air Berlin was gradually trying to establish itself among business travelers, further muddying its product mix and positioning.

Air Berlin was heading for turbulent times, caught between price and quality leadership and lacking a unifying value proposition (see Table 4.22). To make matters worse, oil prices rebounded to high levels between 2009 and 2014 after a slump at the end of 2008. Additionally, competition from the Middle East intensified and more low-cost carriers entered the market.

Air Berlin's unclear value proposition meant that customers could not see clear benefits. Prior to its bankruptcy, Air Berlin was unable to convince customers, particularly in terms of functional benefits. It offered neither the best price, nor the best quality, nor an excellent service.

Table 4.22: Transformation of the Air Berlin business model.

Value Proposition

In the 90s: Low-cost charter airline that flies German air travelers from regional airports to attractive Mediterranean destinations.

From around 2005: Good service at reasonable prices. Both for business and leisure travelers. Frequent switch of focus between business and leisure travelers over the years.

Service Delivery	Service Offering	Cost Model	Earnings Model
Acquisition of and shareholdings in various airlines	Reduced ticket prices	'Shape & Size' savings program	Direct sales of individual seats
	Route network expansion through strategic partnerships	Increased operating costs due to acquisitions	Introduction of new 'Your Fare' fare structure
Strategic partnership with Etihad			
		Sale and leaseback of aircraft	

Service Offering

Under pressure from emerging low-cost airlines, Air Berlin decided in early 2000 to focus more on its profitable core business of Mediterranean flights and to expand its service offering. In September 2002, the airline began offering low-cost flights to major European cities. Hunold entered the price war with the low-cost carriers and also lowered prices for traditional Spanish destinations. The subsequent strategic partnership with Etihad further expanded the service offering for long-haul flights. However, customers had to accept a stopover in Abu Dhabi.

The expansion of the service offering and the partnership with Etihad led Air Berlin's strategic direction to move further away from its original customers. Instead of focusing on one profitable customer segment, the company wanted to satisfy everyone with its new offering: price-sensitive business and leisure travelers with short, medium and long-haul destinations. This strategy did not work well: Air Berlin was now competing with all the airlines at once, but was unable to set itself apart in any area. EasyJet and Ryanair were cheaper; Lufthansa, British Airways and SWISS were superior in terms of quality.

Service Delivery

By 2003, Air Berlin had become Germany's second-largest airline in terms of passengers, thanks to the expansion of its flight capacity and low ticket prices. Just one year later, the company continued its course of expansion rigorously. Hunold decided not only to grow organically, but also to invest in and acquire various airlines in the DACH region. As a first step, Air Berlin acquired 24% of the Austrian airline Niki. An IPO in 2006 brought fresh capital into Air Berlin's coffers. This was used to acquire the German airline dba and the leisure airline LTU. The company also acquired a stake in Swiss airline Belair.

In January 2012, Air Berlin entered into a strategic partnership with the Gulf airline Etihad in order to offer its customers a comprehensive service offering and to avoid liquidity problems despite red figures and a cost-cutting program. Etihad took a 29.9% stake in Air Berlin and combined parts of its network with Air Berlin in a codeshare partnership. However, the partnership with Etihad hardly helped Air Berlin—in 2013 Air Berlin already recorded further heavy losses of €315.5 million [1]. Etihad had its own goals: to divert passenger flows from Germany via the Gulf region. As a result of the cooperation with Etihad, Air Berlin had to almost completely outsource its profitable long-haul business to its partner.

Cost Model

The acquisitions and the goal of serving several different customer groups (leisure and business travelers) not only complicated the service delivery process, but also drove up costs. The newly acquired airlines were difficult to integrate into the group. Instead of realizing economies of scale from the acquisitions, the group's operating costs increased with the diversity. While low-cost competitors kept costs down by maintaining a uniform fleet—Ryanair flies only Boeing 737-800s and EasyJet only Airbus A320s and A319s— Air Berlin now operated seven different aircraft types from three different manufacturers. This resulted in higher maintenance costs as well as more complex flight capacity planning and increased pilot training costs. Take Ryanair, for example. If an aircraft has a technical problem and needs to be replaced, another air-craft of the same type can be easily substituted. Seats, pilots and capacities are trans-ferred 1:1 to the replacement aircraft. However, when an airline operates multiple aircraft types, this process becomes much more complicated. If an identical aircraft is not available, the pilot had to be replaced because each type of aircraft requires specific training; passenger seats must be reassigned; and the new, possibly smaller, aircraft may not be able to accommodate all the passengers, requiring further adjustments.

Facing financial difficulties, Air Berlin began to restructure its cost model. Long-time CEO Hunold stepped down and Hartmut Mehdorn took the helm. He imple-mented a strict cost-cutting program called 'Shape & Size' for the struggling airline. The cost model was overhauled. The fleet was downsized, and unprofitable destina-tions acquired during Hunold's expansion phase were removed from the route net-work. Air Berlin sold and leased back a significant portion of its aircraft. This leaseback strategy generated tax benefits and freed up financial resources, but also increased ongoing costs through lease payments.

By partnering with Etihad and implementing a cost-cutting program, Mehdorn was able to double Air Berlin's net profit in the third quarter of 2012. After a record after-tax loss of €420.4 million in 2011, the airline reported an operating profit of €70.2 million in its 2012 annual report [2].

Earnings Model

Initially, Air Berlin only generated revenue from ticket sales through package tour op-erators. From 1998, this was supplemented by the sale of 10% of seats directly to end customers. The elimination of travel agency fees generated additional revenue of ap-proximately DM35 million in 1998 [3]. At the same time, the company entered the scheduled airline business: Starting in 1998, Air Berlin's 'Mallorca Shuttle' connected German regional airports with the Spanish vacation island of Mallorca. This new earnings model, based on the sale of individual seats, proved successful in the follow-ing years. By 2001, approximately 25% of seats were sold individually.

Ideally, strategic decisions about the earnings model are aligned with the com-pany's value proposition. However, Air Berlin's unclear positioning led to a number of critical mistakes in adapting its earnings model. Around the turn of the millennium, when low-cost carriers entered the market, the earnings model remained largely un-changed. For example, in contrast to the low-cost competition, non-alcoholic beverages and snacks were still offered free of charge. Only later, when the model of offering cheap tickets, good service and free refreshments seemed unsustainable, was the earnings model gradually shifted to ancillary revenues. Because Air Berlin had entered the price war with low-cost carriers, revenues from ticket sales declined. Additional sales should now compensate for this. In 2012, Air Berlin introduced a new fare structure called 'YourFare'. The cheapest fare, 'JustFly', now charged separately for services previously included in the ticket price: in-flight beverages and meals, seat reservations, fee-based rebooking, baggage, and even pre-evening check-in now cost extra.

Ultimately, neither the expanded service offering nor the revenue and cost model measures were able to save Air Berlin. After a brief respite due to positive results in 2012, Air Berlin's losses increased steadily from 2013, culminating in a record loss of €781.9 million in 2016, with an operating margin of -17.6% [4]. In 2017, Etihad ended its financial support for Air Berlin, forcing the airline to file for bankruptcy.

The Bottom Line

One of the main reasons for Air Berlin's demise was undoubtedly its unclear strategic positioning, resulting from numerous acquisitions, changes in management and strategy, and the lack of an overarching value proposition. As the German business magazine Wirtschaftswoche aptly put it in 2017, "The airline has simply become superfluous over the years."[5] Air Berlin was not superior to its competitors in any dimension. As a hybrid airline that sought to serve both leisure and business travelers on short, medium, and long-haul routes, it was overtaken by the competition in each of these segments. In its core leisure business, it had to cede market share to the low-cost competition, which did not differ significantly from Air Berlin in terms of service offering, but had a much more favorable cost structure. In the less price-sensitive market for business travelers, Air Berlin was never really able to establish itself, as business customers tended to rely on more comfortable and reliable airlines such as Lufthansa, British Airways or SWISS. In summary, the Air Berlin case illustrates how important it is to have a clear and overarching value proposition to successfully orchestrate all the dimensions of a business model.

References

[1]   See Air Berlin, (2013), Air Berlin 2013 Annual Report.
[2]   See Air Berlin, (2012), Air Berlin 2012 Annual Report.
[3]   See Tagesspiegel, (1998), "Air Berlin im Steigflug" (Air Berlin Is Taking Off), in: Der Tagesspiegel, 1998-03-06, https://www.tagesspiegel.de/wirtschaft/air-berlin-im-steigflug/32540.html (in German only).
[4]   See Air Berlin, (2016), Air Berlin 2016 Annual Report.
[5]   Schaal, S. (2017), "Eine Flugline, die sich überflüssig gemacht hat" (An Airline That Made Itself Redundant), in: WirtschaftsWoche, 2017-08-10, http://www.wiwo.de/unternehmen/dienstleister/air-berlin-pleite-eine-fluglinie-die-sich-ueberfluessig-gemacht-hat/20194228.html (in German only).

5 Challenges and Guiding Principles for Corporate Governance

In the previous chapters we learned a great deal lot about the 'what' of self-disruption and which key drivers need to be taken into account for self-disruption. However, companies also have to answer the question of 'how' to achieve a successful transformation: What are the structures and processes that will ensure a successful transformation of the business model? This chapter serves to shed light on the framework and the soft factors for change.

For existential reasons, people and organizations have always had to adapt to the world around them and constantly change. The forces of change are not a new phenomenon, but today they are more diverse, deeper and more dynamic, driven primarily by the digitalization of business models. First, the focus of change management here is on the ability to anticipate change as a core competency. This includes identifying trends and patterns in new (technological) changes and anticipating the resulting needs, requirements and consumer desires. Second, the ability to adapt and develop one's own business model at an early stage is becoming increasingly important for successful management. Companies in stable to slightly dynamic environments follow a **mechanistic system of organization and management** (see Figure 5.1). These organizations are divided into clearly defined areas and have a strong hierarchical structure. The flow of decisions and information is top-down and highly formalized. There are committees that progressively define and implement strategies and policies at different levels of the hierarchy. These processes tend to be very well defined, and routinizing them makes things more stable, ordered, and predictable. This has the advantage that many fads never get implemented, because they get lost somewhere in the committee mill.

To make the complexity of the environment as manageable as possible, the mechanistic system relies heavily on rules. This has led to the view that dynamic market changes need to be met by analyzing the environment and the business more closely than ever. This implies that future market developments can be easily predicted and anticipated in the long term. This leads to increasingly complex programs for trend management, benchmarking analyses, big data management and market research projects. The results are typically fed into a broad, in-depth strategy development process once a year, which in turn leads to a wide range of initiatives in the form of projects that are developed and implemented on an annual basis. These processes are characterized by objectives, milestones, standardized procedures, routines, and habits.

Major changes are considered exceptional and are the subject of change programs, some of which may be far-reaching in nature. The programs are designed to streamline the organization and prepare it for the future, and usually have a (hidden)

Note: The corresponding references can be found at the end of the chapter.

https://doi.org/10.1515/9783110772111-005

	Widespread Management Style in a Stable to Dynamic Environment	Management Style Required in a Disruptive Environment
Leadership	Mechanistic management system	Organic management system
Style	Authoritarian	Participative
Interpersonal relationships	Ordering	Cooperative
Formalization	Strong	Weak
Discussion	Formal, down the line communication	Informal, network-like communication structures
Motivation	Conformity, loyalty and obedience	Initiative, creativity, dedication to the job at hand
Instructions	Specified in detail	General, recommending
Decision-making responsibility	Centralized decision-making authority	Multiple decision-making points

Figure 5.1: Distinction between managing stable and turbulent environments (source: Burns & Stalker [1994]).

efficiency character. Such multi-project plans occur once or twice a decade and keep organizations busy for months with the objective of adapting structures and processes to the new circumstances.

For organizations in both stable and dynamic environments, this mechanistic management system can work successfully. Environmental changes can be successfully addressed in a timely manner through the annual strategy cycle, and recurring change programs in three-, five-, or seven-year cycles ensure that organic inefficiencies are eliminated. Change is therefore primarily a recurring, episodic event.

5.1 Challenges

However, mechanistically designed management systems reach their limits in unstable markets where disruptive forces are unleashed. Although the changes are often detected by sophisticated early warning systems and reported to top management for strategic discussion, a variety of challenges arise that ultimately impair the ability of organizations to act.

Challenge 1: Disorientation

The changing environment and particularly disruptive developments rarely follow a yearly plan. As a result, the mechanical processing of annual objectives usually becomes a farce, as project goals are torpedoed by new developments in the marketplace. This leads to frustration, especially among project team members, because either the work is not in line with reality (if the original project objectives are adhered to), or the project task has to be constantly adapted to new circumstances. What counts today will be obsolete tomorrow. As a result, a lack of direction creeps in and a lack of awareness of the impact that project work can have. This lack of impact translates into a lack of appreciation for the work.

As a result, the day-to-day running of the business becomes increasingly important. As strategic work seems less impactful and more exhausting, many employees and managers retreat to the factor over which they still have direct influence—immediate day-to-day operations.

Challenge 2: Reluctance to Change

The willingness to make fundamental changes diminishes with the retreat into day-to-day operations. People cling to old success factors because they provide stability, especially when the environment is changing disruptively. Any attempt to change is seen as threatening this stability and is therefore passively or even actively resisted.

This reluctance to change is one of the reasons why, in recent years, companies have created more and more staff units that try to anticipate change in individual areas or the company as a whole, outside of day-to-day operations. However, this organizational solution is usually only a stopgap, because the department is often treated as a foreign body in the organization (and has no influence).

Challenge 3: Dwindling Credibility of the Leadership

The mechanistic management system operates with a clearly regulated top-down approach. Although this has been increasingly supplemented by dialogical elements in recent years, the hierarchy still largely determines the course of the company, and employees are managed accordingly with legitimized formal power. However, the dynamic nature of objectives makes this almost impossible to manage, as constantly changing strategic and operational objectives undermine management credibility. This gradually leads to resistance or, in the worst case, internal resignation. Since many managers are only familiar with leadership in mechanistic systems, this leads to insecurity, an insistence on the formal position of power, or even excessive demands that lead to burnout.

Challenge 4: Dysfunctional Incentives

This insecurity in the system leads to grasping at straws that yield either non-monetary or monetary rewards and recognition. This recognition can have a stabilizing effect or secure and promote one's own function and career in the company, especially in phases of disorientation. In retail, this grasping at straws is usually to be found in sales. Anything and everything is done to achieve sales targets. The customer is often forgotten in all this. To increase sales, the pressure on inventory is increased with more product lines, more displays, or more promotions. However, this ignores the fact that this push effect drastically reduces the customer's enjoyment of the shopping experience [1]. This also explains the distrust of many consumers and why they feel they are being manipulated by retailers. Unless incentives are tied to customer value (and this does not mean simply tying them to customer satisfaction surveys), the push effect will continue.

Challenge 5: Lack of Tools for Change

At the strategic level, the precursors of disruption are often the subject of internal documentation and discussion in strategy committees. This usually results in statements of intent and visions that can be found in a company's brochure or its annual report. For example, they describe the possibilities that digitalization offers and outline a new direction for the company. However, the actual changes tend to be very modest. This is due in part to a lack of tools to effectively manage change. The usual assumption is that the situation can be managed with the usual form of initiatives. For example, digitalization initiatives or an omnichannel offensive. In this parallel world, however, deep change is limited. There is a lot of talk about fluid organizations, but an open-plan office à la Google is still a long way from a fluid hierarchy. The tools for turning the vision of the future into reality are lacking.

Challenge 6: Fear of Cannibalization

Besides lacking the tools to change, fear of cannibalization also represents a major obstacle. Because disruption has the potential to challenge the present business model in its entirety, change in anticipation of disruption always has an existential cannibalization effect. For example, if the online channel is pushed, sales will flow away from existing brick-and-mortar stores, threatening their existence, or at least their cost structure. For management teams, implementing an omnichannel strategy can be hindered by this effect. While building on past successes is natural in dynamic times, disruptive change requires a different approach. In such dynamic environments, the challenge is to gradually unwind the current business model and transition to a new earnings model. This requires a calculated willingness to take risks and the courage to make decisive decisions.

This shift requires moving away from a mechanistic management system to an **organic management principle**, which we believe is the foundation for successful transformation in disruptive phases. An organic system prioritizes agility over the bureaucratic formalism of its mechanistic counterpart. This management principle ensures that, in the face of uncertainty and a lack of transparency, changes are not only quickly identified, but that it is also possible to react to them in a faster and more flexible manner. Within this organic approach, the interplay of strategy, structure, and competencies becomes increasingly critical. This requires a network-like organizational structure that is closely aligned with the customer-centric value creation chain. Functional silos are no longer the employees' home turf, but the service chain on the entire customer journey. As a result, hierarchies become less relevant and new leadership skills are required. Decisions are made based on expertise, always with a holistic view of the organization. The top-down principle becomes less important and gives way to participation and leadership as key drivers of success. The 'episodic process of change' is replaced by the maxim of 'change as a continuous process'.

5.2 Guiding Principles

While there are indeterminable variants of the two generic management approaches portrayed and polarized here (see Figure 5.1), we focus on these two archetypes to provide clearer and more actionable guiding principles for transforming an organization from a mechanistic to an organic management system in the following because it is more accentuated and therefore more descriptive. These principles provide the reader with starting points for change, but they have to be adapted to the specific context of each organization.

Guiding Principle 1: Visualizing the Future

Constant willingness for change requires stability and direction or the system can become overwhelmed. The hurdles described in Challenge 1 arise from the lack of stability in small-scale day-to-day operations and the loss of an individual sense of purpose due to dynamic objectives. This dynamic environment requires a calm counterpoint in the form of a clear vision and strong core values regarding a well defined strategic direction. Charismatic leaders, especially in family-owned businesses, often excel at providing this guiding light. In management-driven companies, a strong vision is typically needed that is easy to understand, inspiring, and easily embraced by everyone. By visualizing the vision, social mission, and economic performance or customer proposition, the company creates a sense of direction for the employees and— from within—for the customers.

While a vision based on a guiding principle is nothing new, its effective and consistent implementation is the key challenge as shown in a similar way in the next guiding principle below. A flashy video outlining next year's strategy may be refreshing and create identification, but if the day-to-day work looks completely different or the video is not followed by new impulses, any effort to convey meaning is in vain. In this book, we recommend focusing on developing a value proposition to visualize the company's path to the future.

Guiding Principle 2: Leadership

Leadership is no longer about simply 'delegating goals and tasks downward'. Instead, it is about effectively communicating the vision and its realization to employees in a way that inspires and motivates them [2]. It means identifying and leveraging the unique skills of each employee and placing them in the right roles within the organization. Leaders must establish strategic guardrails while encouraging the highest degree of flexibility within those boundaries. Clearly defined processes cover routine tasks while the room left for new ideas should be as generously dimensioned as possible. Trust, inspiration, and enjoyment form the foundation for this approach. Collaboration within the organization now transcends functional silos and occurs along the value creation chain.

Guiding Principle 3: Fluidity

Networked collaboration across departmental boundaries is critical to success. This fluidity breaks down siloed thinking and focuses on the value creation chain with the goal of increasing customer value. Decisions are made with an eye to the system as a whole in a large number of semi-autonomous specialist committees. This is why it is so important to visualize the future. In the absence of a shared vision or a consensual self-image, there is a risk that decentralized bodies will make conflicting decisions and pursue divergent goals. Although people still have their home base in the department, they are deployed where their expertise is needed. The organization is moving from a static structure to a permanent project organization where the skills of different departments are brought together depending on the issue at hand. This has the advantage of increasing agility because there is a constant flow of knowledge.

Guiding Principle 4: Agility and Ambidexterity

Organizational agility is based on the ability to identify change and to quickly derive and implement appropriate actions. This agility is often associated with a classic innovation process, although this process is usually highly regulated, formalized, and goal-oriented. Agility, on the other hand, sees innovation as an intrinsic part of the day-to-day work. Innovation is not something that happens on top of daily operations, but is lived every day. This gives renewal from within a different meaning, and change is no longer the exception, but the norm. It starts with monitoring the market and identifying new opportunities and continues with developing concepts and implementing them. As part of this, we believe that lowering the barriers to implementation is an important factor. In mechanistic management systems, it is often the case that the success of a new concept must be quantitatively proven before it can be implemented. This ensures that many good ideas are implemented too late or not at all due to lack of proof. An agile organization is characterized by the ability to quickly and easily test new ideas and make informed decisions about whether to implement or drop them. This requires a strong culture of error that allows for failure.

Organizational ambidexterity is when a company simultaneously pursues agility in innovation and efficiency in its core business. Ambidexterity means being able to do both. This approach encourages companies to do one without sacrificing the other. Accordingly, companies should be agile in responding to change and future opportunities while striving to improve efficiency in day-to-day operations [3]. Changing the entire organization from a culture of marginal product improvement and operational efficiency to one of innovative agility is very risky. Research on organizational ambidexterity recommends using the efficient organization of the core business to create the freedom for agile teams to pursue new ideas and innovations [4]. Several studies have shown that companies that strive for organizational ambidexterity perform better as a business [5].

Guiding Principle 5: Empathy

Drawing the right conclusions in the search for new business models and in day-to-day decision making requires the systematic collection of market and customer insights. With the new methods made possible by digitalization, algorithms and artificial intelligence can be used to gain more and more insight into (future) customer behavior. Big data is bringing us closer to the long-awaited transparent customer. But what good is this data without enriching it with empathy and evidence? Algorithms are not yet at the point where they can be the catalyst for a flash of inspiration or a piece of evidence to reinterpret the solution to a customer need. Empathy is about reconnecting action with thought, message with understanding, and service with customer value. It requires the willingness and ability to recognize and understand the feelings, motives, and needs of other people. This is why a combination of the analytical world and empathy is effective. However, because empathy is an intrinsic part of a company's culture, successful profiling also requires a fundamental transformation—an investment that will pay dividends not only in the short term, but also in the future.

Guiding Principle 6: Holism

In the realm of management system transformation, a holistic approach is paramount. Tinkering with isolated elements is usually counterproductive. Increased investments in market research won't deliver the desired results without a simultaneous focus on building empathetic capabilities or the willingness to challenge existing processes. Appeals from C level executives to leave the departmental silos and act like a network will not bear fruit unless structural adjustments and incentive systems are also adapted. We referred to the fit of the individual activities in Chapter 3.4. An efficient and effective basis for a successful transformation can only be created if all key drivers in the company are subordinated to a value proposition and the thoughts and actions of employees are aligned with it.

References

[1] See Schweizer, M. /Rudolph, T. (2004), "Wenn Käufer streiken" (When Consumers Go On Strike), Gabler Verlag.

[2] See Ohnemüller, B. M. (2017), "Die Dekade der Menschlichkeit" (The Decade of Humanity), In: "CSR und Digitalisierung" (CSR and Digitalization), pp. 809–821, Springer Gabler, Berlin, Heidelberg.

[3] See Raisch, S./Birkinshaw, J. (2008), Organizational Ambidexterity: Antecedents, Outcomes, and Moderators, in: Journal of Management, 34(3), pp. 375–409.

[4] See Raisch, S./Birkinshaw, J. (2008), Organizational Ambidexterity: Antecedents, Outcomes, and Moderators, in: Journal of Management, 34(3), pp. 375–409.

[5] See Lubatkin, M. H./Simsek, Z./Ling, Y./Veiga, J. F. (2006), Ambidexterity and performance in small-to medium-sized firms: The pivotal role of top management team behavioral integration, in: Journal of Management, 32(5), pp. 646–672.

Index

https://doi.org/10.1515/9783110772111-006

www.ingramcontent.com/pod-product-compliance
Lightning Source LLC
Chambersburg PA
CBHW061813210326
41599CB00034B/6981